ERNST TROELTSCH
Systematic Theologian of Radical Historicality

American Academy of Religion Academy Series

edited by
Carl A. Raschke

Number 55
ERNST TROELTSCH
Systematic Theologian of
Radical Historicality
by
Toshimasa Yasukata

Toshimasa Yasukata

ERNST TROELTSCH
Systematic Theologian of
Radical Historicality

Scholars Press
Atlanta, Georgia

ERNST TROELTSCH
Systematic Theologian of Radical Historicality

by
Toshimasa Yasukata

© 1986
American Academy of Religion

Library of Congress Cataloging-in-Publication Data

Yasukata, Toshimasa, 1952–
Ernst Troeltsch : systematic theologian of
radical historicality.

(AAR Academy series ; 55)
Bibliography: p.
1. Troeltsch, Ernst, 1865–1923. I. Title.
II. Series: American Academy of Religion academy
series ; no. 55.
BX4827.T7Y37 1986   230'.044'0924   86-20412
ISBN 1-55540-069-8 (alk. paper)
ISBN 1-55540-070-1 (pbk. : alk. paper)

Printed in the United States of America
on acid-free paper

To My Parents

ACKNOWLEDGEMENTS

This study has its origin in my doctoral research at Kyoto University, Japan, under Professor Kazuo Muto and Professor Wataru Mizugaki. Its central theme arose out of the perplexity in which I found myself when I started research on the thought of Ernst Troeltsch. I was entirely overwhelmed by the immense variety of concerns and the broad scope of investigation in the lifework of this towering figure in the world of theology at the turn of the century. How is it possible to comprehend the full spectrum of his diversified thought in a systematically unified way? This is the major question which occupied me from the very beginning of my research.

After three years of basic research on Troeltsch at Kyoto, I came to the U.S.A. and continued my research in the Ph.D. program at Vanderbilt University from the 1980/81 academic year onward. I soon found that the understanding of Troeltsch among American scholars and students is limited and often distorted. The main reason for this is, I should say, that Americans no longer wish to study German thought in the German original, while the bulk of Troeltsch's writings, not to mention a large number of recent studies of his works by German scholars, has not been translated. Faced with this unhappy situation, I keenly felt a need to attempt to offer a more complete and well-balanced picture of Troeltsch to the American reader. This is, briefly, the story behind this study.

I would like to express my thanks to all who directly or indirectly contributed to the writing of this dissertation. Thanks are offered, first of all, to three institutions which facilitated my research: Department of Christian Studies at Kyoto University, Japan, the Graduate School of Vanderbilt University, U.S.A., and the Faculty of Evangelical Theology at the Georg-August-Universität, Göttingen, West Germany. I am especially grateful to the Graduate School of Vanderbilt University for providing a University Graduate Fellowship during the 1981–1983 academic years. Furthermore, I am indebted to the Rotary Foundations of The Rotary International, Evanston, Illinois, and Kyoto Rakuhoku Rotary Club, Kyoto, Japan, for honoring me as a 1980–1981 Graduate Fellow. I am deeply indebted to my former teachers, Dr. Kazuo Muto, now professor emeritus at Kyoto University, who first directed my attention to Troeltsch, and Professor Wataru Mizugaki of Kyoto University, who was my chief adviser at Kyoto and has constantly encouraged my study of Troeltsch. My first reader, Professor Peter C. Hodgson has been extremely helpful to me during the process of completing this dissertation. I thank him for many suggestions leading to substantial improvements. My second and third readers, Dean H. Jackson Forstman and Professor Eugene TeSelle, have repeatedly shown their kindness and have offered valuable advice. Thanks are also due to the rest of my committee: Professors Dale A. Johnson and Robert Williams. Professor Johnson was most considerate towards me during my first year at Vanderbilt, when I had not yet adjusted to the university life of a foreign country.

My special thanks are due to Professor Gerd Lüdemann of the Georg-August-Universität, Göttingen, without whose kind invitation to Göttingen and without whose deep empathy and many other extraordinary generosities this dissertation would have been long in being completed. Thanks are also due to his assistant, Jürgen Wehnert, who offered his office for my use.

Several of my fellow students at Vanderbilt University and the Universität Göttingen assisted me in many ways; among them, Bruce Wagner, Thomas Walsh, F. Stanley Jones, and Ann Millin deserve special mention. In particular, F. Stanley Jones read the entire type-written draft and made innumerable stylistic suggestions. If this dissertation is at all readable, that is largely owing to him. No words are adequate to express my appreciation of his friendship and my gratitude for his labor.

Finally, I would like to thank my wife, Etsuko, for her help in typing, proofreading, and similar chores, not to mention the many personal sacrifices she made along the way.

TABLE OF CONTENTS

LIST OF ABBREVIATIONS

CW   *Die Christliche Welt*
G.S.   Troeltsch, Ernst. *Gesammelte Schriften*
RGG *Die Religion in Geschichte und Gegenwart*
ThLZ *Theologische Literaturzeitung*
ZThK *Zeitschrift für Theologie und Kirche*

NOTE ON TRANSLATIONS:

    This study is based on the bulk of Troeltsch's German original writings as well as the immense secondary literature on Troeltsch written in German. The translations from German are my own, except in cases where existing standard translations can be made use of without any modifications. Because the German texts include various words that have no exact English equivalent, I have added the original German in parentheses whenever appropriate, hoping that the flavor of Troeltsch's thinking would be therewith better conveyed to the reader.

INTRODUCTION
THE TROELTSCH PROBLEM

Ernst Troeltsch had been forgotten in the professional theological discussion in his homeland, Germany. The situation in which his theology found itself in other countries was almost the same. He suffered an eclipse created by the masters of dialectical theology. During the period of the "Barthian captivity"/1/ of Protestant theology his thought was viewed as "*vorbei* (passé)" and was "practically *verboten*."/2/ However, as early as 1960 H. R. Niebuhr prophesied a Troeltsch revival. He wrote: "There are signs, however, that the eclipse is passing and that in theology as well as in the sociology of religion and in history Troeltsch's methods and convictions will again become effective."/3/ Niebuhr's prophecy has come true. New interest in Troeltsch's work actually began to emerge in Germany during the early sixties when theologians awakened from their "kerygmatic dreaming"/4/ caused by the Barth-Bultmann domination of the theological scene. The large number of the Troeltsch studies which have appeared since 1960 presents a sharp contrast to the grand neglect into which Troeltsch had fallen until then. Thus, the work of Troeltsch has now attained new relevance *(neue Aktualität)*/5/ in the contemporary theological discussion. The founding of the *Ernst-Troeltsch-Gesellschaft* in Germany in 1981 witnesses well to this new interest in Troeltsch.

James Luther Adams holds the Troeltsch revival to be "largely due to the fact that some of the major insights and questions associated with his [Troeltsch's] name are now seen to require further reflection."/6/ According to the judgment of Wolfhart Pannenberg, Troeltsch has "formulated the truly fundamental questions and tasks for theology in the twentieth century."/7/ Be that as it may, I endorse Trutz Rendtorff's opinion that "the breadth, the bold and sober radicalism, and the Christian passion with which Troeltsch has opened up new horizons for theology can be for us today a power of orientation in the task imposed upon us."/8/ In any case, one thing is

sure, namely, as Robert J. Rubanowice states, that "the grand neglect into which Troeltsch had fallen . . . is no longer permissible in
the pluralistic context of contemporary theology."/9/

The new relevance of Troeltsch, however, does not mean that
such clarity has been attained on the whole range of his thought that
a consensus about its theological significance could be found among
Troeltsch scholars. Quite the contrary. The significance of Troeltsch
as a theologian is yet to be examined. Here the fundamental difficulty which, from the outset, confronts every Troeltsch scholar is the
immense variety of perspectives and dimensions in his thought.
Troeltsch "was a complex man and lived in a complex time."/10/ His
work covers a wide spectrum of fields: theology, the philosophy of
religion, the sociology of religion, the history of ideas and culture,
ethics, the philosophy of history, and even political analysis. Hence,
the search for a continuous thread in his thought as a whole is almost
hopeless. In the second place, the developmental character of his
thought presents the student of Troeltsch with special hermeneutical difficulties: each of his works seems to represent only his
tentative position, which he then supplemented or revised after
further scrutiny. For example, Troeltsch wrote the following concerning his *magnum opus, Die Soziallehren der christlichen
Kirchen und Gruppen* (1912): "Of course, on the whole, even this is
a preparatory study and is not my real work."/11/ In the third place,
Troeltsch's early death left his lifework a gigantic torso. Thus he was
no longer able to complete the second volume of *Der Historismus
und seine Probleme* (1st vol. 1922), in which he planned to unfold his
own material philosophy of history and ethics,/12/ not to mention his
"first love" *(erste Liebe)*/13/ and "real work,"/14/ namely, the philosophy of religion. Given this state of affairs, something similar to
what M. Ermarth calls the "Dilthey problem"/15/ is true of
Troeltsch. The treatment of Troeltsch's thought as a whole is a highly
technical task. The researcher faces a fundamental difficulty when
he/she attempts to comprehend the whole of Troeltsch's thought in a
systematic way. One may thus speak of a "Troeltsch problem." Such
work nevertheless needs to be done, for Troeltsch himself affirms
that "a systematic unified thought" *(ein systematischer
Einheitsgedanke)* underlies all his writings./16/

The aim of this study is precisely to identify what Troeltsch
himself described as the "systematic unified thought" of his work,
and thus to understand the full spectrum of his thought in a unified

way. To my knowledge, no conscious attempt has yet been made to specify the systematic unified thought underlying Troeltsch's entire work. Some attempts have been made, however, at interpreting the full spectrum of Troeltsch's thought in a unified way. Let us take a brief look at a few of these interpretations.

One classic example is Paul Tillich's short, but very instructive, interpretation of Troeltsch's lifework. According to Tillich, who considered himself a special pupil of Troeltsch, the core *(Kern)* of Troeltsch's *Lebensproblematik* is the "tension between the absolute and the relative" *(Spannung von Absoluten und Relativen)* that was not merely a mental preoccupation but, above all, a passionate experience in his life. All the writings of Troeltsch were infused with his strenuous effort to overcome this tension. Throughout his life, Tillich contends, Troeltsch desperately sought to find the absolute in the stream of the relative. Hence it would be false to construe Troeltsch's professional shift from the chair of systematic theology at Heidelberg to that of philosophy of culture at Berlin simply as Troeltsch's path from the absolute to the relative. Quite the contrary. After he had destroyed false absolutes in theology, Troeltsch fought even more passionately for the genuine absolute on the ground of philosophy./17/ Thus Tillich holds that Troeltsch "was the philosopher as a theologian and remained the theologian as a philosopher."/18/

Heinrich Benckert also maintains the "necessity of making an attempt to comprehend Troeltsch as a whole."/19/ He contends:

> It has become clear not only that ethics also played a role for Troeltsch, but that it was in fact of central significance. Thus, it must be said that an overall evaluation of Troeltsch's lifework that refuses to renounce a unified viewpoint must take ethics as its vantage point *(perspektivische Mitte)*. From the perspective of the religious-philosophical problems which are generally central to the first period, one cannot comprehend him as an organic whole, because they are only a part of the whole for him. However important they may be, they have as their object only one aspect of the cultural life of human being, which is comprehended completely by ethics. Nor can the philosophy of history (second period) serve as the foundation for a general interpretation, for according to Troeltsch's intention, it should be nothing other than the substructure for ethics. Thus only from the perspective of ethics can his achievements both in the phi-

losophy of history and in the philosophy of religion be viewed simultaneously./20/

Thus Benckert takes ethics as Troeltsch's central academic concern in terms of which the whole of his scientific endeavors can be properly evaluated. Benjamin A. Reist pays special attention to Troeltsch's own account of "the underlying unity" of his diversified literary activity in the Foreword to *Die Soziallehren*. According to Reist, "the integrating principle" of Troeltsch's research "should be clearly recognizable as the result of his training under Ritschl," who had evoked Troeltsch's "'twofold interest: the analysis of classical Protestantism *(Altprotestantismus)* and the analysis of the modern world.'" This twofold research was, however, "intrinsic to 'the solution of the systematic task,'" namely, "'to think through and formulate independently the Christian world of ideas and life with unreserved involvement in the modern world.'" In view of these statements by Troeltsch, Reist boldly asserts:

> Thus Troeltsch's endeavors revolved around three foci: (1) the probing of the past, particularly classical Protestantism, (2) the attempt to grasp as precisely as possible the profiles of the contemporary, modern world, and (3) in the light of these insights, and in a way that continually nourished the passion to broaden and perfect them, the attempt to think through and articulate what might be called the theology of involvement./21/

Hence Reist regards Troeltsch as "the first real *contextual* theologian" and his legacy as "a theology of involvement."

In his Tübingen theological dissertation/22/ Katsuhiko Kondo attempts to interpret the whole range of Troeltsch's thought in terms of a theology of *Gestaltung*. According to him, the *Gestaltungslehre* is the leitmotif of Troeltsch's entire thought. Kondo contends that Troeltsch developed the notion of a theology of *Gestaltung* in connection with his theory on the essence of Christianity. That is, Troeltsch's considerations on the essence of Christianity led through the concept of ideal *(das Wesen als Idealbegriff)* eventually to the *Gestaltungslehre*. Thus "in striving to re-establish the relation between the ideal and history and after the modification of the idealism of historical development, Troeltsch took up the *Gestaltungslehre* as his own position."/23/ Hence Kondo asserts that it is insufficient to describe Troeltsch's position after this time as well as in his third period at Berlin as mutual correction of Hegel and

Schleiermacher, as some have maintained. Kondo's bold thesis is therefore that the *Gestaltungslehre*, or a theology of *Gestaltung*, is the central frame of reference in terms of which the full spectrum of Troeltsch's diversified thought can and should be understood. Gerhold Becker's study of Troeltsch aims at drawing Troeltsch out of the neglect into which he has fallen by demonstrating "a far-reaching consistency immanent in his work."/24/ Calling attention to a perspective thus far neglected in the study of Troeltsch, namely, the theory of modernity, Becker attempts to show that this theory constitutes for Troeltsch a "structural principle not only of his philosophy of religion but also of his entire work."/25/ He contends:

> To what degree Troeltsch's thought is motivated by a unified impulse; and to what degree it is indebted to the program which is, despite all further development, so definite from the outset . . .: this becomes clear when one recognizes the question of the essence and origin of modern times to be a specifically philosophical question and exalts it to the formal structural principle of Troeltsch's thought, in relation to which stands materially the question of the essence and significance of Christian religiosity in modern times./26/

Hence Becker identifies "Troeltsch's basic problem" as "the question of the possibility of mediating specifically modern subjectivity and Christian-religious consciousness."/27/ His thesis is therefore that "Troeltsch's entire work is structured by the attempt to lay the foundation of a philosophy of religion which seeks to integrate in itself the specifically modern problem and can be worked out only in exact correspondence to it."/28/

Finally, Karl-Ernst Apfelbacher presents another possibility for viewing the whole range of Troeltsch's thought in its totality. He begins with the simple assumption that there is a correlation between the religious thinker's thought and his/her piety, and that the former is to some extent the reflection or expression of the latter. This is especially true of Troeltsch, he thinks. Apfelbacher thus maintains "the thesis that Troeltsch's scientific work is a consistent consequence of his personal religious life-position."/29/ This encourages him to examine Troeltsch's thought in the context of his biography, where his piety expresses itself in its naiveté./30/ Apfelbacher identifies Troeltsch's personal religious position as in line with the Christian-mystical tradition./31/ Hence the whole of Troeltsch's scientific work is regarded as a kind of "mystical theology." His philosophy of religion, ethics, and philosophy of history are all seen in the light of his "theological program," which arises from the Christian-mystical tradition. Thus he proposes his fundamental thesis that "the 'rote Faden' and the 'geistige Band' in Troeltsch's lifework is the question of obtaining a scientifically responsible Christian-religious life-position."/32/

I should now like to make a brief critical comment on each of these distinctive Troeltsch-interpretations. (Further critique will be indirectly presented by this study itself.)

Tillich discriminatingly perceived that the whole range of Troeltsch's work is permeated by his religious passion as well as by his earnest pursuit of truth. There is no doubt that the tension between the absolute and the relative, as Tillich saw it, forms the core of Troeltsch's lifework. However, this depiction is a bit too formal a formulation. This core alone does not exhaust the entire profile of Troeltsch's thought. Tillich's thesis must be therefore illustrated by a material study of Troeltsch's thought./33/

Benckert's interpretation is conspicuously one-sided. It is true that ethics is one of the most important fields of study for Troeltsch. Troeltsch himself held that his material philosophy of history, which was the later Troeltsch's preoccupation, should flow into ethics./34/ But Troeltsch did not publish his own ethics. Most of his scientific endeavors consisted of theological, religious-philosophical, philosophico-historical, and historical investigations. One must therefore examine the interrelationship of the disciplines in which Troeltsch worked rather than emphasize only one aspect of his academic pursuits.

In contrast, Reist rightly discerned the "underlying unity" and the "three foci" of Troeltsch's diversified literary activity. But should "the integrating principle" of Troeltsch's research be regarded as "the result of his training under Ritschl," as Reist simply presupposed? One of the fatal defects of Reist's study of Troeltsch is the lack of historical insight into Troeltsch's intellectual development, which is, in my judgment, indispensable to every serious study of Troeltsch. Because of this essentially unhistorical treatment of Troeltsch's thought, his early theological writings lie completely out of the scope of Reist's perspective, and Troeltsch's theology is discussed only in its phase of "collapse" or "failure." Such a treatment is, as this study will presently show, obviously unfair. Furthermore, is it possible to construe Troeltsch's systematic endeavors, as Reist did, as "the attempt to think through and articulate *what might be called the theology of involvement*" (emphasis mine)?/35/ All in all, Reist seems to me to have loaded too much of his own theological agenda into Troeltsch's thought. Kondo's discovery of the motif of *Gestaltung* in Troeltsch cannot be applauded too much. Indeed, the *Gestaltungslehre* can serve, in my judgment, to fill the missing link between Troeltsch the theologian at Heidelberg and Troeltsch the philosopher of history and culture at Berlin. Basically I stand on the same ground as Kondo, insofar as I put special emphasis upon the notion of *Gestaltung* as a continuous thread in Troeltsch's thought. Nevertheless, I do not want to assert the consistency and/or unity immanent in Troeltsch's entire work on the basis of a single viewpoint. I will pay more serious attention to Troeltsch's theological program than Kondo did.

Becker's interpretation explains Troeltsch's lifelong struggle well. There is no question that Troeltsch's entire scientific endeavor rose out of a vital problem of the modern world, namely, the fatal clash between modern scientific, historical thinking and traditional Christian piety. To this extent, the *"Neuzeit-Thematik"* is, as Becker rightly insists, one of two organizing points of Troeltsch's thought. However, this is not *the* structural principle of his entire work. Becker seems to me to place a bit too much emphasis upon the theme of modernity. In any event, Becker's interpretation, excellent though it is, must be supplemented by a study that pays more serious attention to what he considers the other organizing point of Troeltsch's thought, namely, his Christian-religious consciousness. In this sense Apfelbacher's study of Troeltsch is exemplary. It is to Apfelbacher's credit that he called attention both to Troeltsch's theological program as well as to his personal religious position. But the perspective on the theme of modernity, which played a decisive role in Becker's study of Troeltsch, is deficient, though not absent, in Apfelbacher's interpretation. Accordingly, each interpretation must be supplemented by others./36/ Furthermore, an insight into the moment of *Gestaltung*, as Kondo discriminatingly perceived it, is lacking in both cases. Apfelbacher should also have extended his interpretive thesis to Troeltsch's philosophy of history instead of confining it merely to his theology and philosophy of religion. As it is, a gap remains between the religious thinker and the philosopher of history and culture. In any event, Troeltsch's professional shift from theology to philosophy of history cannot be fully explained by Apfelbacher's thesis, which can only make a passing reference to the situation wrought by church politics which might have caused Troeltsch's move to the philosophy faculty./37/

In view of these different interpretive frames of reference, how, then, can we interpret the whole range of Troeltsch's thought in a unified way? Where can we find the "systematic unified thought" of Troeltsch's entire work? What features will it have? To answer these questions, we have to solve the following problems that trouble every student of Troeltsch's thought:

> (1) Is there any consistency in Troeltsch's central concern during his various periods? If so, what is the chief problem which occupied Troeltsch's mind all his life? When and in what way did it present itself to him?

> (2) Does Troeltsch have any scientific program by which his diversified academic activities can be systematized into a coherent unity? In what relation, if any, do theology, philosophy of religion, ethics, and philosophy of history stand to one another in his total academic plan?

> (3) How is the developmental nature of Troeltsch's thought compatible with its supposed consistency? Does not Troeltsch's professional shift of 1915, which has often led him to be branded as a wrecked theologian, mean that there was a radical break with theology, the field in which he had been professor for more than two decades?

Only the settlement of these problems can place us in a position to answer the question of what unified thought underlies Troeltsch's entire work. Though a full argument should be retained for the main body of this study, some provisional remarks are requisite here.

First of all, the problem of consistency in Troeltsch's central concern must be briefly discussed in relation to his intellectual development. If there is any consistent concern in Troeltsch's academic activities, then this must have taken its rise in the early phase of his intellectual development, no matter how undeveloped and immature it may have been. Extensive reading of Troeltsch's numerous writings reveals that his lifelong central concern was the settlement of the conflict between historical reflection and the determination of normative values, which was "a vital problem characteristic of the present stage of human development."/38/ This problem, as

Troeltsch himself states, presented itself to him at a very early stage./39/ However, it was first in his classic book on *The Absoluteness of Christianity*/40/ that this central theme took a clear shape. Troeltsch's real concern in this book was not to demonstrate the absoluteness of Christianity, as is often thought, but rather "to gain norms out of history."/41/ To use the phrase Troeltsch interpolated into the original text after a decade, this is the task of working out "an ever-new creative synthesis that will give the absolute the form *(Gestalt)* possible for it at a particular moment and yet remain true to its inherent limitation as a mere approximation of true, ultimate, and universally valid values."/42/ This idea clearly foreshadows the later Troeltsch's celebrated idea of a contemporary cultural synthesis *(die gegenwärtige Kultursynthese)*./43/ In any case, there seems to be a remarkable continuity in Troeltsch's central concern throughout his life. Nevertheless, there is no question that Troeltsch's intellectual development can be divided into several distinct periods. In this study Troeltsch's development is divided into three periods.

The first period is generally thought to have ended approximately with the year 1902. According to Troeltsch himself, his work on *The Absoluteness of Christianity* "forms the conclusion of a series of earlier studies and the beginning of new investigations of a more comprehensive kind in the philosophy of history."/44/ It therefore marks, as H. -G. Drescher correctly states, "the transition to the second period of his thought."/45/ It is also true, however, that this transition was not so abrupt and that the new beginning was still somewhat latent in this work. It is thus more appropriate to follow Kondo in thinking that Troeltsch's second period began with the publication of his significant essay on the essence of Christianity, for it is here that he first anchored his own theological position with his *Gestaltungslehre*. Hence I hold that the second period of Troeltsch's development covers approximately the time from the year 1903 till the end of his professorship in the chair of systematic theology at Heidelberg. Needless to say, the third period of his development is his Berlin period (1915–1923). (See Chapter III for the details.)

As will be elucidated below, the *Gestaltungslehre*, namely, Troeltsch's peculiar conception that "to define the essence [of Christianity] is to shape it afresh" *(Wesensbestimmung ist Wesensgestaltung)*,/46/ is a fundamental theory both for his theology in the second period and for his philosophy of history in the third

period. It can serve, in my judgment, as the link that connects the
systematic theologian at Heidleberg (the second period) with the
philosopher of history and culture at Berlin (the third period).
The Troeltsch of the second period becomes very clear about the
task he has to accomplish as a theologian. His lifework is now
composed of two parts: the historical task and the systematic task.
The historical task, in turn, is double in nature: analysis of the
ecclesiastical dogmatic tradition of Protestantism, on the one hand,
and analysis of the intellectual and practical situation of the modern
world, on the other hand. Hence the "twofold interest" (Doppelseitigkeit) of Troeltsch's historical research. All this research,
however, is only intended "to serve the solution of the systematic
task of thinking through and formulating independently the Christian world of ideas and life with unreserved involvement in the
modern world."/47/ Thus the principal concern of Troeltsch's academic activities lies not in the field of historical research but in that
of systematic research. Therefore, his achievements in the historical
field cannot be properly evaluated without reference to his systematic concern. (This is even true of his magnum opus, Die
Soziallehren der christlichen Kirchen und Gruppen.) In any case,
his systematic concern is "to formulate the Christian world of ideas
in the manner that corresponds to the intellectual situation of the
present day,"/48/ or simply, "a new formation" (Neuformung) of the
Christian world of ideas and life,/49/ "a new shaping" (Neugestaltung) of our religious ideas and life./50/ Here the motif of
Gestaltung is very clear. The same theme dominates Troeltsch's
thought in his Berlin period. The creative shaping of the future
(Zukunftsgestaltung) is the leitmotif of his philosophy of history./51/
His celebrated idea of a contemporary cultural synthesis must be
seen in this light. In any event, the main body of this study will
present a much more consistent picture of Troeltsch as thinker than
has hitherto been produced.

What about the second problem specified above? Troeltsch does
have his own scientific program by which his diversified academic
activities can be systematized into a coherent whole. Troeltsch no
longer considers systematic theology to be "a simple task of handing
down tradition and apologetics." Its proper task is rather one "of
orienting the tradition in view of the intellectual and religious life of
the present day." This work will someday necessarily result in a

"new shaping" of religious thought and its institutions./52/ Hence Troeltsch asserts:

> For us the central field of study shifts to the philosophy of religion, which defines the essence and significance of Christianity from the perspective of philosophy of history, and to general ethics, which elaborates the ultimate goal of humanity, a goal which can be comprehended only from a religious point of view./53/

On the other hand, "dogmatics" (or "Glaubenslehre") and "moral theology" (or "the Christian ethics") become "branches of practical theology in the narrower sense."/54/ What is of decisive significance for the intellectual and religious situation of the present day is the philosophy of religion and general ethics./55/ Christian theology (dogmatics and Christian ethics) must be developed within the horizon of the general science of religion (the philosophy of religion) and the humanities (ethics). In view of this conception of theology, one speaks of "Ernst Troeltsch's attempt to found theology in the human sciences" (*Ernst Troeltschs geisteswissenschaftliche Grundlegung der Theologie*)/56/ with reason. Whether such a conception of theology as a human science be proper or not, it is a fact that Troeltsch attempted to ground theology in the philosophy of religion and ethics, which, in turn, are grounded in the philosophy of history. The transition in Troeltsch's career is characteristic of a gradual shift of his principal concern from a more practically oriented discipline to a more fundamental discipline *within* the larger map of his scientific program. This understanding of his academic program accounts well for his professional shift from the chair of systematic theology to that of the philosophy of history and culture in the year 1915.

With regard to Troeltsch's scientific program, two things must be mentioned here. First of all, his scientific program was originally conceived in the context of an attempt to rescue theology of his time from the predicament in which it found itself. That is to say, Troeltsch found "the real main basic problem" of scientific theology in the nineteenth century in "the juxtaposition of a purely scientific historical theology and a practical mediating dogmatics."/57/ His proposed solution was intended to provide a common stem and thus a common presupposition for both branches of theology. In his view, a philosophy of religion which tackles the main question of theology concerning the validity of Christianity in a scientific way from the perspective of a general theory of religion *is* in a position to give a common stem to both historical theology and dogmatics./58/ Here Troeltsch appeals to the theological program Schleiermacher sketched out in his *Brief Outline*./59/ Whether or not Troeltsch's reference to his great master's program is justifiable, what is important here is to recognize that Troeltsch's philosophy of religion is intended to perform a constitutive function for theology. Philosophy of religion thus functions as *fundamental theology (prinzipielle Theologie)* in Troeltsch's scientific program.

In the second place, Troeltsch's change of profession from theology to the philosophy of history must be seen in terms of the total map of his scientific program. In view of this map, we can understand that this change of chair in the year 1915 does not mean a break with theology. Rather, this change should be seen as a shift *within* the map. In fact, even during the time when he concentrated on solving burning problems in the philosophy of history, Troeltsch showed great interest in religion. In the autobiographical sketch of his intellectual development written shortly before his death, Troeltsch disclosed his wish to return to the religious sphere:

> If life and strength remain, I would then like finally to return to the religious sphere and bring my philosophy of religion to completion. That is my first love, and the religious element remains at the center even in the present cultural synthesis which has to be drawn by the philosophy of history. Without this religious element there is no naiveté and freshness./60/

Furthermore, his philosophy of history was intended to solve "the problem of further formation of historical life from the historical viewpoint of the present."/61/ "To dam and shape the stream of historical life" *(Dämmung und Gestaltung des historischen Lebensstromes)* is the task his philosophy of history aimed at performing./62/ Thus the philosophy of history, conceived in this way, flows into ethics or "an ethical formation of the future" *(ethische Zukunftsgestaltung)*/63/ In any case, Troeltsch suggested the possibility of pursuing the reverse direction, namely, a reverse move from the philosophy of history through ethics to the philosophy of religion. These observations are positive evidence that theology, philosophy of religion, ethics, and philosophy of history are all organically connected in a definite order in Troeltsch's own academic total plan.

Thus not only from the viewpoint of his central concern but also from that of his scientific program we can conclude with good grounds that Troeltsch was right to speak of a systematic unified thought underlying all his work. What, then, is the material content of "the systematic unified thought"? Does the existence of such a thought mean that Troeltsch had his own proper system? Or does it simply mean that his entire academic activities were from beginning to end guided and penetrated by some distinctive primal theme? The answer to these questions can only be formulated at the conclusion of this study.

The main body of this study is composed of five chapters. Each chapter is basically arranged in chronological order. In the opening chapter we will discuss the early Troeltsch's theological concerns and his theological development toward a theology of *Gestaltung*. His thought up to 1903 (the first period) will therefore be examined here. The second period is the most prolific and fruitful period in Troeltsch's entire career. In this period he worked intensely not only in the field of theology proper but also in the philosophy of religion, ethics, the sociology of religion, and the history of ideas and culture. A fullscale analysis of his rich and diverse thought in this period is not possible owing to limitations of space. Accordingly, the chapters which deal with the second period of Troeltsch's development aim mainly at reviewing his scientific program as well as clarifying the constitutive significance of his historical research for the systematic task. In accordance with Troeltsch's intention, his understanding of Christian history will first be examined with special attention being given to its significance for the systematic task of theology (Chapter II). Following this examination of Troeltsch's understanding of history, his theological program will be explicated with reference to his systematic concern (Chapter III). Thereby discussion of the specific problems involved in each discipline which constitutes the total map of Troeltsch's scientific program is not intended. Chapter IV deals with Troeltsch's thought of the third period. Here both the theological implications of his philosophy of history and the problem of his professional shift will be examined. Finally, in the light of the results of the preceding chapters both the significance and the problem of Troeltsch's thought as a whole will be critically discussed (Chapter

Ernst Troeltsch

V). Our question concerning the "systematic unified thought" of his work will be answered in this closing chapter.

NOTES

/1/ R. R. Niebuhr, *Schleiermacher on Christ and Religion* (New York: Charles Scribner's Sons, 1964), p. 11.

/2/ J. L. Adams, Foreward to *Chrisis in Consciousness*, by Robert J. Rubanowice (Tallahassee: University Press of Florida, 1982), p. ix.

/3/ H. R. Niebuhr, Introduction to *The Social Teaching of the Christian Churches*, by Ernst Troeltsch, trans. Olive Wyon (New York: Harper & Brothers, 1960; reprint ed., Chicago: University of Chicago Press, 1976), p. 11.

/4/ W. Pannenberg, *Basic Questions in Theology*, trans. George H. Kehm (Philadelphia: Westminster Press, 1983), vol. 2, p. 67.

/5/ K. -E. Apfelbacher, *Frömmigkeit und Wissenschaft: Ernst Troeltsch und sein theologiches Programm* (Munich-Paderborn-Vienna: Verlag Ferdinand Schöningh, 1978), p. 27.

/6/ J. L. Adams, "Why the Troeltsch Revival?," *The Unitarian Universalist Christian* 29 (1974):5.

/7/ Pannenberg, *Basic Questions in Theology*, vol. 2, p.66

/8/ T. Rendtorff, "17.2.1865-17.2.1981 Warum Ernst-Troeltsch-Gesellschaft," pamphlet, Augsburg: Ernst-Troeltsch-Gesellschaft, 1981.

/9/ R. J. Rubanowice, *Crisis in Consciousness*, with a Foreword by J. L. Adams (Tallahassee: University Press of Florida, 1982), p.xxi.

/10/ H. R. Niebuhr, Introduction to *The Social Teaching*, p. 8.

/11/ E. Troeltsch, *Briefe an Freidrich von Hügel 1901–1923*, with an Introduction and edited by K. -E. Apfelbacher and P. Neuner (Paderborn: Verlag Bonifacius-Druckerei, 1974), p. 93 (hereafter cited as *Briefe*).

/12/ Ibid., p. 138.

/13/ E. Troeltsch, *Gesammelte Schriften*, vol. 4: *Aufsätze zur Geistesgeschichte und Religionssoziologie*, ed. H. Baron (Tübingen: J. C. B. Mohr, 1925; reprinted ed., Aalen: Scientia Verlag, 1966), p. 15 (hereafter cited as G.S. IV).

/14/ Id., *Briefe*, p. 93.

/15/ H. Ermarth, *Wilhelm Dilthey: The Critique of Historical Reason* (Chicago: University of Chicago Press, 1975), pp. 3–12.

xxvi

/16/ Troeltsch, G.S. IV, p. 18

/17/ P. Tillich, *Gesammelte Werke*, ed R. Albrecht, vol. 12: *Begegnungen. Paul Tillich über sich selbst und andere* (Stuttgard: Evangelisches Verlagswerk, 1980), p. 166.

/18/ Ibid., p. 176.

/19/ H. Benckert, *Ernst Troeltsch und das ethische Problem* (Göttingen: Vanderhoeck & Ruprecht, 1932), p. 7.

/20/ Ibid., pp. 15–16.

/21/ B. A. Reist, *Toward a Theology of Involvement: The Thought of Ernst Troeltsch* (Philadelphia: Westminster Press, 1966), p. 17.

/22/ K. Kondo, "Theologie der Gestaltung bei Ernst Troeltsch" (Inaugural-Dissertation, University of Tübingen, 1977).

/23/ Ibid., p. 41.

/24/ G. Becker, *Neuzeitliche Subjektivität und Religiosität: Die religionsphilosophische Bedeutung von Heraufkunft und Wesen der Neuzeit im Denken von Ernst Troeltsch* (Regensburg: Verlag Friedrich Pustet, 1982), p. xi.

/25/ Ibid.

/26/ Ibid., p. 83.

/27/ Ibid., p. 91.

/28/ Ibid., pp. 91–92.

/29/ Apfelbacher, *Frömmigkeit und Wissenschaft*, p. 37.

/30/ Hence Apfelbacher's study of Troeltsch can be characterized, as he himself remarks, as "the description of his [Troeltsch's] way of religious experience in the experience of life and his time, the articulation of his 'biography before God,' . . . the attempt at 'mystical biography'" (Apfelbacher, *Frömmigkeit und Wissenschaft*, p. 271).

/31/ Ibid., p. 44; in greater detail on pp. 155–160.

/32/ Ibid., p. 58.

/33/ Hiroshi Obayashi's study of Troeltsch may be regarded as one example of such a material study. See H. Obayashi, *Troeltsch and Contemporary Theology* (Tokyo: Shinkyo Shuppan, 1972). It is to Obayshi's credit that he perceived the same issue that the early Troeltsch struggled to solve in his classic work on *The Absoluteness of Christianity* in the later Troeltsch's two writings on *Historismus*—no matter how transformed it may be. The issue at stake in both cases is certainly the same. It is the problem of how we can obtain absolute norms from the relative stream of history. The problem with Obayashi's study is, however, that he did not pay any attention to the motif of *Gestaltung* in Troeltsch at all. Furthermore, Troeltsch's great achievements in the field of church history, the history of culture, and European intellectual history, which constitute half of his entire work, play no significant role in Obayashi's interpretation. Besides Obayashi and most recently, Helmut Thielicke employed the same interpretive frame of reference. In his notable history of modern theology and philosophy of religion, he has discussed Troeltsch under the heading of "The Unconditional That Narrowly Escapes from Relativism" (H. Thielicke, *Glauben und Denken in der Neuzeit: Die Großen Systeme der Theologie und Religionsphilosophie* [Tübingen: J. C. B. Mohr, 1983] pp. 553–579).

/34/ E. Troeltsch, *Gesammelte Schriften*, vol. 3: *Der Historismus und seine Probleme: Erste Buch: Das logische Problem der Geschichtsphilosophie* (Tübingen: J. C. B. Mohr, 1922; reprint ed., Aalen: Scientia Verlag, 1961), p. 79. Throughout this study this work will be referred to as *Der Historismus*. Reference in the notes will be indicated by G. S. III.

/35/ It is highly problematic to regard Troeltsch as simply a harbinger of "a theology of involvement," as Reist boldly asserts. For the support of his own thesis Reist appeals to Troeltsch's allegedly crucial phase "*mit rückhaltslosem Eingehen auf die moderne Welt die christliche Ideen-und Lebenswelt zu durchdenken und zu formulieren.*" I have no objection to translating this significant phrase, as Reist does, as "to think through and formulate independently the Christian world of ideas and life *with unreserved involvement in the modern world*" (Reist's emphasis). I even employ his translation in this study when this phrase must be cited. Nevertheless, I cannot follow Reist so far as to espouse a "theology of involvement" as the goal and legacy of Troeltsch's theology. The reasons for this will be explicated in the course of this study.

/36/ In fact, Apfelbacher himself admits the necessity of supplementing his study by Becker's. Cf. K. -E. Apfelbacher, Review of *Neuzeitliche Subjektivität und Religiosität*, by Gerhold Becker, *Mitteilungen der Ernst-Troeltsch-Gesellschaft* 1 (1982):53–58.

/37/ Apfelbacher, *Frömmigkeit und Wissenschaft*, p. 81.

/38/ E. Troeltsch, *Christian Thought: Its History and Application*, trans. by various hands, ed., with an Introduction and Index by Friedrich von Hügel (London: University of London Press, 1923), p. 6 (hereafter cited as *Christian Thought*).

/39/ Ibid., p. 4.

/40/ E. Troeltsch, *Die Absolutheit des Christentums und die Religionsgeschichte* (Tübingen and Leipzig: J. C. B. Mohr, 1902). The second edition of this book (Tübingen: J. C. B. Mohr, 1912) is considerably revised and enlarged. The changes which took place between the first and the second edition are not insignificant, though Troeltsch himself states that they are "merely stylistic" (2d ed., p. v). Admittedly, Troeltsch's basic position is the same in both editions. Nevertheless, special attention is given here to the changes in the editions in order that we might grasp Troeltsch's theological development precisely. Hereafter the first edition is cited simply as *Absolutheit*, while the second edition is cited as *Absolutheit* 2d ed.

/41/ Ibid., p. x.

/42/ Id., *Absolutheit* 2d ed., p. 58 (an interpolation from the year 1912).

/43/ In fact, Troeltsch himself upholds our view. According to him, the question of "how the way from the historical-relative to valid cultural values can be found," with which *Der Historismus und seine Probleme* (1922) deals, is "the old problem of the absoluteness now taken up in a much broader context and in view of the whole of cultural values, not merely of the religious position" (G. S. IV, p. 14).

/44/ Troeltsch, *Christian Thought*, p. 4.

/45/ H. -G. Drescher, "Ernst Troeltsch's Intellectual Development," in *Ernst Troeltsch and the Future of Theology*, ed. John Powell Clayton (Cambridge: Cambridge University Press, 1976), p. 13.

/46/ E. Troeltsch, *Gesammelte Schriften*, vol. 2: *Zur religiösen Lage, Religionsphilosophie und Ethik* (Tübingen: J. C. B. Mohr, 1913; reprint ed., Aalen: Scientia Verlag, 1962), p. 431 (hereafter cited as G. S. II).

/47/ E. Troeltsch, *Gesammelte Schriften*, vol 1: *Die Soziallehren der christlichen Kirchen und Gruppen* (Tübingen: J. C. B. Mohr, 1912; reprint ed., Aalen: Scientia Verlag, 1977), pp. vii–viii. Throughout this study this work will be referred to as *Die Soziallehren*. References in the notes will be indicated by G. S. I.

/48/ Id., *Absolutheit* 2d ed., p. viii (an interpolation from the year 1912).

/49/ Id., G. S. II, p. vii; cf. ibid., pp. 860–861.

/50/ Ibid., pp. 227–228. n. 11.

/51/ The reader of *Der Historismus* will be struck by Troeltsch's frequent use of the expression "Zukunftsgestaltung" and the related terms. See Troeltsch, G. S. III, pp. 79, 83, 114, 118, 125, 132, 137, 148, 169, 178, 235, 272, 296, 337, 364, 388, 417, 487, 704, and 710.

/52/ Troeltsch, G. S. II, p. 227. n. 11.

/53/ Ibid., p. 767.

/54/ Ibid.; cf. id., *Briefe, p. 93*.

/55/ Ibid., p. vii.

/56/ W. Pannenberg, *Wissenschaftstheorie und Theologie* (Frankfurt am Main: Suhrkamp Verlag, 1977), p. 105.

/57/ Troeltsch, G.S. II, p. 221.

/58/ Ibid., pp. 222–223.

/59/ Ibid., p. 225.

/60/ Id., G.S. IV, pp. 14–15.

/61/ Id., G.S. III, p. 79.

/62/ E. Troeltsch, *Der Historismus und seine Überwindung*. *Fünf Vorträge*, with an Introduction by Friedrich von Hügel (Berlin: Pan Verlag Rolf Heise, 1924; reprint ed., Aalen: Scientia Verlag, 1966), pp. 33, 37, 41, 44, 59, 60 (hereafter cited as *Überwindung*). In passing, *Christian Thought* is the English translation of *Überwindung*. I will cite from both according to the need in this study.

/63/ Id., G.S. III, pp. 79, 83.

CHAPTER 1

THE EARLY TROELTSCH'S THEOLOGICAL CONCERNS

The Beginning of Troeltsch's Theologizing

The whole of Troeltsch's life and thought is permeated by a distinctive antithetical character. Many contradictory interests are combined in his personality./1/ The inner tension thus produced informs not only "the secret of the fruitfulness of his thought and of its stimulating quality" but also "that constant change in his philosophical position which makes the analysis of his ideas so difficult a matter."/2/ The fundamental antithesis that yields such dynamism and fluidity in his thought is, in my view, the intrinsic polarity of his existential concern. This contrariety would be best characterized as the polarity of a deeply religious thrust *(Frömmigkeit)* and an insatiable hunger for knowledge *(Wissenschaft)*./3/ Raised in a Christian family which sustained "a mild religious rationalism,"/4/ and having received a thorough humanistic education in a cultural setting strongly colored by Lutheran tradition, Troeltsch was determined—throughout his life—by the heritage of Christian humanism, the ideal of which is the integration of Christian piety and classical virtue in the unity of personality./5/ Thus, interests "of different kind"/6/ occupied his mind with equal intensity: "an originally strong religious craving"/7/ and "zeal for truth."/8/ This as such would not have been so serious a problem had Troeltsch lived in a pre-modern age when "the disintegration of our religion by new science"/9/ had not yet begun. Troeltsch, however, lived and thought as a modern man in the fully modernized world where "the place of the principle of Christian piety within the scientific revolutions of the last centuries"/10/ had become more and more problematic. Furthermore, Troeltsch was extraordinarily sensitive to changes in intellectual and cultural trends. He has been compared to "a 'seimograph' which reacted to the slightest movements."/11/. As the valedictory speech that Troeltsch gave on graduating from the Anna-Gymnasium indicates, he, already at a very early age, keenly perceived the coming of a subjectivistic, relativistic, nihilistic age./12/ Given this extraordinary sensitivity to the changed modern intellectual climate, it is understandable that theologians of Lutheran neoorthodoxy at Erlangen (such as Frank, Zezschwitz, and Zahn), under whose guidance Troeltsch began his theological studies, did not impress the young Troeltsch./13/

The theologian who really first won Troeltsch for theology was Albrecht Ritschl. In fact, this towering theologian's influence on the young Troeltsch was momentous./14/ H. R. Niebuhr, for instance, considers Troeltsch's relation to Ritschlianism to be "to a large extent the key to the understanding of his own theological position."/15/ As this chapter will show, it would hardly be an overstatement to say that the entire course of Troeltsch's theological development was strongly determined by his Oedipean struggle to overcome the flaws which he exposed in his great teacher's doctrines. A remarkable statement Troeltsch made in the Foreword to *Die Soziallehren* supports this view:

> Trained in the school of Ritschl, I learned very early that two elements were united in the impressive teaching of this energetic and great scholar: a distinct conception of traditional dogma by means of which modern needs and problems were met, and just as decided a conception of the modern intellectual and religious situation, by means of which it seemed possible to accept and carry forward the teaching of tradition, understood in the Ritschlian sense. The question arose, therefore, quite naturally, first, whether this conception was true to dogmatic tradition in its actual historical sense, and, second, whether the present situation was being interpreted as it actually is. Then it became clear that from both sides a certain process of assimilation had been completed which did not correspond with actual factors and which did not permit the real contrast to appear in its full actuality. Thus I found myself confronted by a twofold task: to make clear to myself both the ecclesiastical dogmatic tradition of Protestantism in its own historical sense, and the intellectual and practical situation of the present day in its true fundamental tendencies. Hence the twofold interest of my researches—the analysis of early Protestantism and the analysis of the modern world. All this research, however, was only intended to serve the solution of the systematic task of thinking through and formulating

independently the Christian world of ideas and life with unreserved involvement in the modern world./16/ Thus, Troeltsch himself recognized not only the starting point but also "the integrating principle of his research" /17/ in his initial training under Ritschl. Seen against the background of his critical attachment to Ritschl's theology, the selection of his dissertation topic—the title of Troeltsch's Göttingen dissertation was "Reason and Revelation in Johann Gerhard and Melanchthon: An Investigation of the History of Early Protestantism"—is quite understandable. Looking back on the earliest phase of his own theological development, Troeltsch states the following:

> Despite basic studies of the history of early Christianity, the ancient church, and the Middle Ages, what attracted me above all was the theme of the rise of the modern situation and its problem, a theme which, at the same time, led to that of the conflict and confrontation of the traditional religious forces with the new intellectual forces which expressed themselves, above all, in philosophy./18/

The basic question was: "When did the whole of the modern intellectual situation in general arise, a situation in which an autonomous secular culture prevails over the theologically constrained culture?"/19/ This formulation of the question itself reveals Troeltsch's critical stance toward the Ritschlian synthesis of the ecclesiastical tradition and the modern scientific spirit. In any event, Troeltsch demonstrated through the investigation of the beginnings of Protestant orthodoxy in his dissertation that the Protestant theologians of the sixteenth and seventeenth centuries basically continued, though with some Protestant modifications, the supernaturalistic dualism of human and divine truth—the dualism of reason and revelation, natural and supernaturally revealed knowledge—so characteristic of great medieval Scholasticism.

For Troeltsch this insight involved, at least potentially, a twofold refutation of his teacher Ritschl's theological position. On the one hand, the modernizing of the Reformation and especially Luther as practiced by Ritschl and his following was revealed as untenable from a historical viewpoint. As Troeltsch's study in the history of Protestant orthodoxy implied, Luther and his Reformation did not represent the beginning of the modern world, but, seen on the whole, still belonged to the medieval sphere of life and thought. Hence Troeltsch accused Ritschl of understanding the whole of

Luther's religious and ethical thought "with the eyes of a modern man, not with those of Luther himself."/20/ On the other hand, Ritschl's hostility to apologetics, metaphysics, and natural theology was indirectly refuted from a systematic viewpoint. Such hostility was groundless because historical research showed that the Reformers to whom Ritschl generally resorted had presupposed both the Stoic idea of natural law and Aristotelian natural theology. Furthermore, the dogmatics of Protestant orthodoxy as such, like all dogmatics and dogma itself, took its rise out of "the apologetic needs to set the positive ideas of religion into relationship with the other knowledge of a cultured people."/21/

In view of these points, W. Bodenstein is not altogether wrong when he regards Troeltsch's "initial work of 1891" as "an attempt to gain independence form Ritschlian theology."/22/ Nevertheless, Troeltsch's departure from his teacher was not as dramatic as Bodenstein seems to think./23/ The fact is rather that Troeltsch was never a whole-hearted Ritschlian. It is true that Troeltsch "considered himself as wholly the student of Ritschl"/24/ and that he at one time aligned himself with the 'Ritschlian school.'/25/ In fact his earliest theological position was, as we will shortly see, strongly colored by Ritschlian traits, at least as far as his view on the absoluteness of Christianity is concerned. Yet Troeltsch, already as a student, had "two basic doubts" concerning his teacher's doctrines (if his own account in the Foreword to his Kant study is an authentic portrayal of the facts). These doubts were concerned, in the first place, with Ritschl's radical separation between theoretical and practical reason (the severing of faith and knowledge), and, in the second place, with his dubious linking of religious ideas and historical data (the residual supernaturalism)./26/ Nor did Troeltsch ever share Ritschl's aversion to philosophy and metaphysics. In his "Promotionsthesen" (1891) he already asserted the necessity of metaphysics and a philosophy of religion for theology./27/ These "Promotionsthesen" as well as his Göttingen dissertation of the same year are, therefore, strong evidence that Troeltsch did, from the beginning, assume a critical stance towards Ritschl's theological position at its pivotal points. In his postcard to Bousset of 16 June 1893 Troeltsch even wrote: "Basically and definitively I no longer have anything to do with the Retschlians now."/28/ But it is too rash to conclude from these considerations that by the middle of 1893 at the latest Troeltsch had gotten out of the spell of Ritschlianism under which he had fallen. For the standpoint which Troeltsch advocated concerning the absoluteness of Christianity in his first long essay on "The Christian World-view and the Scientific Counter-currents" (1893/94)/29/ was, as Troeltsch himself admits, nothing other than "the standpoint of the Ritschlian school."/30/ His break with the Ritschlian school was rather gradual, and his next longer essay on "The Independence of Religion" (1895/96)/31/ first marked, in my judgment, a decisive step in his departure from Ritschlianism. In this essay Troeltsch, "fundamentally following Dilthey," tried to "assert the originality and underivability of religious phenomena on the basis of a purely historical and psychological analysis of religion."/32/ At this phase of Troeltsch's theological development, his "departure from the Ritschlian method" or "departure from Ritschl's practical basic conceptions" was openly attacked with good reason by the main camp of the Ritschlian school./33/ F. Kattenbusch, for example, commented on "younger 'Ritschlians'" as follows:

> There are certainly residua of Ritschl in Troeltsch, Johannes Weiss, and others. But the central point of their interests, the method of their thought, and the leitmotif of their research do not originate from Ritschl. Thus, the name "Ritschlians" is, in the historical viewpoint, indeed retained for us older ones, be it an honorable or a contemptuous name./34/

In the face of such criticism, Troeltsch for his part openly declared his break with Ritschlianism and demanded the thorough application of the *religionsgeschichtliche* method to theology:

> My theological teacher was Ritschl; but gradually I have come to see that there are two things in the Ritschlian system which I cannot accept. The first is its supernaturalism, which appeared to me to be not maintainable in the face of history-of-religions research either within the field of Christianity or outside it. The second is the much too simple resolution of the problems of natural philosophy and metaphysics through the theory that nature is merely phenomenal, a solution which proved inadequate as I studied philosophical literature further./35/

Given this state of affairs, the importance of Troeltsch's initial work on J. Gerhard and Melanchthon should not, as H. -G. Drescher rightly asserts, be overplayed *with reference to his reaction to or departure from Ritschl.*/36/ Nevertheless, Drescher is wrong in underestimating the *latent* importance of this work. For Troeltsch's work in question does have, in my judgment, "a programmatic importance" for his subsequent theological development. One cannot, however, properly assess the real import of this work as long as one sticks to the general perspective of either Troeltsch's dependence on or his departure from Ritschlian theology. What is important with regard to this work is not Troeltsch's deviation from his teacher, but rather the question of how integral this historical study was to the systematic task which occupied his real interest./37/ The concluding remarks of this work are very significant in this respect. Troeltsch writes:

> We no longer have any of those old foundation-pillars, and yet we have no new foundation-pillar fitting for us. What we have in common with the old theologians stands on different ground among us, insofar as we have any ground under our feet at all. In all these respects, despite all the various progress, the old theology is by far superior to us. Direct continuity with it is no longer possible at all. But we shall be able to claim a share in its heritage only if we make at least some progress towards *solving the basic problem of dogmatics in a manner which corresponds to our modern needs.*/38/

Here the achievements of Troeltsch's historical research are directly related to his systematic concern. Historical insight into the complete transformation of the intellectual climate in modern times requires that theology must submit itself to a revolution corresponding to this intellectual change. In this case, however, the modern intellectual and cultural situation determines the form that theology should take. In other words, the *context* in which the contemporary Christianity must find its new expression conditions the *form* of theology (the legitimacy of such a conception of theology will be argued in Chapter V). In any case, the systematic concern expressed in this initial work to "make at least some progress towards solving the basic problem of dogmatics in a manner which corresponds to our modern needs" does provide a guideline to Troeltsch's subsequent development. His academic efforts were henceforth directed to the twofold task which resulted from this first study. The one is the historical task, first, of explicating the intellectual and cultural situation of the modern world in its true fundamental tendencies, and, second, of elucidating the ecclesiastical dogmatic tradition of Protestantism in its own historical sense. Most of Troeltsch's energy in the historical field was directed to the former in his first period (the latter was to be the main task of Troeltsch's historical research in the second period). The other is the systematic task of reformulating the world of Christian ideas to conform to the general intellectual climate of the modern world.

The main results of Troeltsch's historical research into the modern intellectual history are now contained in the fourth volume of his *Gesammelte Schriften:* "The Enlightenment" (1897), "Deism" (1898), "German Idealism" (1900), "Leibniz and the Beginnings of Pietism" (1902), and "The English Moralists of the Seventeenth and Eighteenth Centuries" (1903)./39/ This series of historical studies convinced Troeltsch that the Enlightenment was the real watershed between medieval and modern periods. "The Enlightenment is," Troeltsch asserts, "the beginning and foundation of the intrinsically modern period of European culture and history, in contrast to the hitherto regnant, ecclesiastically and theologically determined culture."/40/ For it offered "the first comprehensive and fundamental opposition to the dualistic-supernaturalistic form of religion."/41/ Troeltsch did not consider the break of modern scientific thought with the old dualistic-supernaturalistic theory to be a detrimental development. Rather, in Troeltsch's view, with the Enlightenment "a fundamentally new, anti-supernaturalistic foundation has been laid down for theology and the science of religion as well as for all the sciences."/42/ Thus for Troeltsch the bankruptcy of traditional supernaturalism "is no misfortune at all; it only urges us to formulate the question in a new fashion from the standpoint of the new scientific situation, under its presuppositions, and with its means."/43/ Troeltsch tackled this task in a series of essays: "The Christian World-view and the Scientific Counter-currents" (1893/94), "The Independence of Religion" (1895/96), "History and Metaphysics" (1898), and "On the Historical and Dogmatic Method of Theology" (1900), as well as in his little but significant book, *The Scientific Situation and Its Claims on Theology* (1900)./44/ Finally, *The Absoluteness of Christianity and the History of Religions* (1902) "forms the conclusion of a series of earlier studies and the beginning of new investigations of a more comprehensive kind in the philosophy of history."/45/

With this introductory survey of the early phase of Troeltsch's theological development, we are now in a position to elucidate Troeltsch's early theological thought as set forth in these writings.

The Conception of a Religionsgeschichtliche Theology

Troeltsch's theology was from the beginning determined by an apologetic concern. According to Troeltsch, the task of dogmatics lies neither "in the promotion of general knowledge and science" nor "in the quickening and deepening of religion as such," but in "the tormenting efforts to tie the knot between 'faith and knowledge'."/46/ Theology (Dogmatics) not only makes the coexistence of secular culture and religious truth possible but also seeks to solve the difficulties which inevitably arise from this coexistence. For this reason theology is "a kind of necessary evil."/47/ "The church can neither do without theology nor endure it."/48/ The apologetic task of relating the Christian message to rational knowledge of the day forms the prime concern of theology. Hence the question of whether and how secular culture and religious truth are compatible with each other is "the really cardinal question of dogmatics."/49/ "To demonstrate this compatibility *(Zusammenbestehbarkeit)* has always been the pivot and the proper business of all theology."/50/ What is really important for contemporary theology is the question of whether the Christian world-view as a whole is compatible with modern scientific thought. Since the new trends of thought have expressed themselves mainly in non-ecclesiastical literature, theology must go out of the church and confront this popular secular literature. Compared with this struggle, "the discussion of the problems in the field of theology proper" is like "a harmless enjoyment of conventicles," "a childish quarrel in a house on fire."/51/ Now "the real battle is fought not within the narrow walls of theology, but on the huge open field of general scientific thought."/52/ Theologians must acknowledge the complete change of intellectual climate after the eighteenth century. Since then human history has moved into "a clearly perceptible new stage."/53/ An enormous revolution has been taking place in religion and morality. The general mood has radically changed from otherworldliness to thisworldliness. Above all, human knowledge, both in its methods and in its results, has been fundamentally transformed. Modern science has shaken the basic ideas of traditional Christianity and has thus caused the religious crisis in which Christianity finds itself. The scaffoldings of thought which upheld Christian faith until now seem to have fallen apart./54/ "Everything is tottering" *(Es wackelt alles)*./55/ Such was Troeltsch's picture of the theological situation of his time and his conception of theological tasks demanded by this situation.

In the face of this situation, Troeltsch held that "a radical remolding of theology is inevitable"/56/; like all other sciences, "theology also must learn afresh"; "with solid confidence that its subject-matter can be approached only in another way, theology must seek a new path."/57/ How, then, and in what way can the subject-matter of theology be properly approached? How can the radical remolding of theology be carried out? According to Troeltsch, the way has been long pioneered by such great thinkers as Hume, Locke, Leibniz, Semler, Gottfried Arnold, Herder, Lessing, Kant, Jacobi, Fichte, Schelling, Goethe, Schleiermacher, Hegel, and others. Most of these "fathers of modern theology"/58/ were not professional theologians *(Fachtheologen)* but rather leaders of German Idealism or pioneers of modern philosophy. Nevertheless, they were, in Troeltsch's judgment, "non-theologians who drove forward theology."/59/ Their works can be characterized as "the theology not belonging to the guild" *(die unzünftige Theologie)* in contrast to professional theology, which Troeltsch called "the theology belonging to the guild" *(die zünftige Theologie)*./60/ He held that the impulse to the "revolution and new formation"/61/ of theology comes mainly from these non-theologians outside the guild of professional theologians. In any case, a new path for theology had been charted out by the great thinkers of the eighteenth and nineteenth centuries. Troeltsch argues:

> A really new construction of theology is therefore only possible when we go back to the common conceptual work of the science of religion and theology of the last two centuries, and when we make conspicuous its outlines and motifs and continue the work which stands under its influence./62/

What then is the legacy of these scientific thinkers of the last two centuries upon which a new structure of theology should be constructed? Troeltsch considered "psychological observation of religion" and "comparative study of the history of religion" to be such. Hence he attempted to reconstruct theology by means of psychological and historical reflection upon religion.

With all his "basically idealist outlook,"/63/ Troeltsch was convinced that positive religions or the history of positive religions must be "the basis of all theological work."/64/ Both psychology of religion and comparative study of the history of religions had a voice in this matter. According to Troeltsch, psychology of religion "inquires about the place, the origin, and the significance of religion in human consciousness and so is alone in a position to say what can be said about the truth of religion."/65/ From this psychological viewpoint, the religious theory of the Ritschlian theologians was utterly impossible. It was nothing but a disguised supernaturalism which was no longer tenable from the viewpoint of the modern science of religion./66/ On the other hand, Troeltsch was also very critical of any kind of reductionist account of religion, whether it be Feuerbach's illusionistic theory, the positivists' psychological immanentism, the Neo-Kantian view of religion as a moral postulate, or Hegel's thoroughly intellectualistic view of religion. Troeltsch asserted that religion cannot be explained away as a projection of human desires and needs; nor can it be deduced from the ethical or the aesthetic./67/ "Religion is not just a [logical] inference *(Erschließen)* or a [moral] postulate *(Postulieren),*" he says, "but rather a life in the intuition of great divine powers. . . ."/68/ It takes its rise "out of an inner contact with the supersensual world."/69/

Contra all these pseudo-scientific accounts of religion, Troeltsch held that "religion is a *unitary* phenomenon which moves according to its own laws in connection with the whole of spiritual and intellectual life."/70/ The conclusion of his lengthy discussion about psychology of religion is:

> Religion is something which is completely indepenedent in its kernel and is based on the interconnection of the human being with the supersensual world. In the piety which grows within the particular circles of religion and provides the foundation for this circle we always see that religion is based on fundamental intuition or experience of God, be it sometimes more reproductive and other times more productive in nature. It is true that religion stands in close interconnection with the whole of the spiritual and intellectual situation in general and can be influenced, limited, and controlled by the latter. But in every place where religion is internally living and actual we recognize a genuinely factual, undeductible relation to the self-disclosure of the deity, in which every being and life is included, and which

reveals itself sometimes more in an original way, sometimes more through the medium of the tradition./71/ On the other hand, the comparative study of the history of religions, as Troeltsch conceived it, "inquires about the laws and connections in the historical varieties of religion, and the basis of a criterion for the evaluation of these varieties."/72/ According to Troeltsch, there is no "*a priori* ready-made criterion"/73/ by which actual historical developments can be judged. However, history is not chaos; rather, divine reason operates in history and progressively reveals itself therein./74/ "The criterion grows in and with history itself."/75/ All that we need to do, in his view, is to search, with complete trust in this divine reason, for the driving force or the inner tendency of religion in the actual course of the history of religions, and to measure the latter according to the former. Troeltsch took the following as a consequence of the history of religions:

> The inner dialectic of the religious idea points in the direction of the perfectly individual and therefore universal religion of redemption. The religion of redemption can be perfectly individual and universal only because it is perfectly spiritualized and moralized. . . . There can be no doubt about this even with the most strict scientific objectivity. It is evident that Christianity is the most profound, the most powerful, and the richest expression of the religious idea.
> . . . Christianity has the most living and adaptable revelational basis, because it reverences in the personality of its founder and prophet the guarantee and model of its truth and yet depends not on external and mechanical authority but on the purely religious and moral significance of Jesus and his inner communion with God./76/

Be that as it may, what is important here is the fact that Troeltsch considered it both necessary and possible to establish, by psychological and historical reflection upon religion, first an empirical and rational basis for religion in general and, second, the supremacy or prime validity of Christianity in particular. In this way theology was incorporated into the general science of religion which treats religion historically and psychologically./77/ This is what is called the program of a *religionsgeschichtliche Theologie* (a theology based on the history of religions). But it must be emphasized here that by this Troeltsch did not intend to transform theology into the general science of religion or the comparative study of religion. Already in

his "Promotionsthesen," he made his intention very clear as to this
point:

> Thesis 1: Theology is a discipline based on the history of
> religions (eine religionsgeschichtliche Disziplin), though not
> in the sense that it is a constituent part of the construction of
> the universal history of religions, but in the sense that it
> defines the content of Christian religion through the com-
> parison with a few great religions of which we have more
> precise knowledge./78/

As shown clearly by this thesis, Troeltsch had no intention of trans-
forming theological faculties into faculties for the study of the history
of religions. "The issue in question is," he says, "certainly not the
history of religions in general, but *normative* knowledge acquired
through the scientific study of religion."/79/ What was important
was therefore "to derive this normativeness from the history of
religions instead of from scholastic theories of revelation or apologetics against philosophical systems."/80/ For Troeltsch, the history
of religions was thus *a function* of theology, not vice versa./81/ To use
Troeltsch's own words, "the universal history of religions is only a
preliminary and auxiliary discipline as far as theology is concerned"
(*nur Voraussetzungs- und Hilfswissenschaft der Theologie*)./82/

But strong objections were raised from different camps against
Troeltsch's program of a *religionsgeschichtliche* theology. Above all,
J. Kaftan, one of the most prominent Ritschlian theologians and
Troeltsch's one-time teacher at the University of Berlin, leveled
severe criticism against his former student./83/ In response to Kaftan's attack on him, Troeltsch contended that "the real difference"
between Kaftan and himself is their "different position on supernaturalism."/84/ For all his seemingly serious application of the
historical critical method to the Christian tradition, Kaftan's description of Christianity was, in Troeltsch's eyes, "through and through
dogmatic."/85/ Kaftan represented, in the last analysis, the supernaturalistic standpoint which "affirms a supernaturalistic moment
only *in Christianity*, a supernaturalistic moment that is distinguished in a special way from the mere ethico-religious super-
naturalness."/86/ This "supernaturalism which, from the outset,
gives Christianity a completely distinct position within the history of
religions"/87/ was out of the question for Troeltsch. He argues:

> Only one who roams through the history of religions simply
> as an apologetic hunt and is merely on the lookout for
> illustrations of arguments for the inferiority of non-Christian

religions, but not one who goes through this sublime world of marvels as a hushed and reverential wander, is able to bring home one's supernaturalism intact from such disputatious expeditions./88/ But this does not mean, contra a common misunderstanding, that Troeltsch denied any form of supernaturalism. He did affirm a form of supernaturalism which "acknowledges . . . a supernatural moment in *religion in general* and in Christianity in particular."/89/ This is the standpoint which was designated as "inner supernaturalism"/90/ in his preceding essay and which he will later define as "inclusive supernaturalism" *(inklusiver Supernaturalismus)* in distinction to "exclusive supernaturalism" *(exklusiver Supernaturalismus)*, which he rejected./91/ What he denied is therefore not 'supernaturalism' as such, but the specific form of supernaturalism which "presupposes and shows that Christianity is *toto genere* different from non-Christian religions."/92/ The point he wanted to make is simply that "the question concerning the place and truth of Christianity must be raised from an overview of the total phenomenon of religion."/93/

With this position, Troeltsch considered himself the heir of the authentic—this means non-ecclesiastical—Schleiermacher who "constructed his theology on the basis of his ethics and [who] through his analysis of religion and its historical development pioneered the way first to the understanding and then to the justification of Christianity."/94/ By proceeding from a philosophy of history and of human consciousness, Schleiermacher laid the foundation of this conception of a theology based on the history of religions. But "this is," so Troeltsch says, "exactly what my essays also intended."/95/ "In the face of the scientific situation only the trail which Schleiermacher has blazed remains."/96/ Thus, for Troeltsch, "the idealism of historical development" *(der entwickelungsgeschichtliche Idealismus)* in the Schleiermacherian sense, which is, in turn, based on "a metaphysics of history or of human spirit" *(eine Metaphysik der Geschichte oder des menschlichen Geistes)*, was "the only possible starting-point" for theology./97/ According to him, such a metaphysics of history or of human spirit was demanded by the general intellectual situation, which was characterized by what the so-called *Historismus* has brought about:

Playful relativism, for which everything is growth and decay, conditional and approximate, the . . . renunciation of every

personal conviction, the asphyxiation of all productiveness
and . . . simple confidence in generally valid standards, the
disintegration of scholarship in the creation of endless du-
plication of what has already formerly passed, the habitua-
tion to the destitute routine of historical specialization,
these are the oppressive defects of *Historismus*, which are
now and then so strident that they can make one apprehen-
sive about the continuation of our civilization./98/
The theological scene at the turn of the twentieth century reflected
this general situation. *Historismus* had long ago put its merciless
hands on theology. It prompted genuine historical studies of Christianity and produced many significant and original works. At the
same time, however, it made dogmatics harder and harder. In the
face of this situation, Troeltsch did not believe for a moment that the
present theological predicament could be remedied by "a renunciation of history" or by "a return to supernaturalism."/99/ The solution
he recommended was different: "*Historismus* will not let itself be
shaken off again, and supernaturalism will not be called back again.
The danger of the situation can be overcome only by a metaphysics
of history."/100/
    Troeltsch now gained a sense of vocation for the task of actualiz-
ing a "latent theology of *Historismus*."/101/ Thus he recommended
the historical method as the alternative to the dogmatic method of
old supernaturalism.
    In his classic essay "On the Historical and Dogmatic Method of
Theology," Troeltsch offered a clear account of the historical method
which he identified as his own "theological method."/102/ According to him, the historical method operates with three indissolubly
connected principles: "criticism," "analogy," and "correlation." The
first principle denotes that historical study renders only "probable
judgments." The application of historical criticism to the religious
tradition requires that the latter be critically treated in exactly the
same way as profane tradition for the measurement of the degree of
probability appropriate to it. Historical criticism is made possible by
the second principle, analogy. Analogy with our ordinary experi-
ences is the key to criticism. Agreement with normal, customary, or
otherwise attested occurrences is the criterion for the probability of
an event. This "omnipotence of analogy," however, presupposes the
"fundamental similarity" (*prinzipielle Gleichartigkeit*) and "common nature" (*Gemeinsamkeit*) of all historical occurrences. Hence
the third principle, correlation. Correlation denotes "the mutual

effect of all occurrences of human life," that is, the conception that "all events stand in a continuous, correlative interconnection and must necessarily constitute a single flow in which each and all hang together, and every event stands in relation to others."/103/ Thus, no single historical fact as such can be isolated and absolutized; it should rather be understood in the total context./104/

The consequence of applying the historical method to theology is revolutionary. Troeltsch illustrated it with striking metaphors. "Whoever has given a little finger to it [historical method] must also give it the whole hand."/105/ "Once the historical method is applied to biblical studies and to church history, it is a leaven that alters everything and, finally, bursts apart the entire form of theological methods hitherto employed."/106/ Thus "the historical method, once trained on a given point, necessarily draws everything into its wake and implicates everything in one comprehensive interconnection of correlative effects and metamorphoses."/107/ Because of this thoroughgoingness and radicalness, partial appropriation of the historical method in accommodation to the traditional dogmatic method was utterly impossible for Troeltsch. "A peeling away to some kind of unhistorical inner kernel"/108/ or an appeal to "something that is history of a higher order"/109/ was entirely out of the question. For Troeltsch, there was only one option: "One must carry through with the historical method in full seriousness."/110/ This being the case, a total revolution of theology both in method and in conception was inevitable.

> There arises the demand for a construction of theology based on a historical method conceived in terms of universal history; and since our concern is with Christianity as both religion and ethic, this means that the method will have to be that of the history of religions./111/

Thus, Troeltsch's early theological reflection culminated in the advocacy of a *religionsgeschichtliche* theology, which applies the historical method to all the corners of the Christian tradition in an unreserved way and thus aims at actualizing the "latent theology of *Historismus*."

The Problem of the Absoluteness of Christianity

The problem of the absoluteness of Christianity assumed overwhelming importance for Troeltsch when he demanded that

Christianity be studied historically, with special attention being given to its total context. But neither the interlacing of Christianity in the universal history of religions nor the resultant problem of the absoluteness of Christianity presents a theoretical advancement by Troeltsch. Rather the involvement of Christianity in the general history of religions is the undeniable result of the modern comparative study of religions, and the problem of the absoluteness of Christianity "grows directly out of the modern conception of history as such."/112/ Troeltsch only explicated these issues. As we have already seen, the modern science of history had radically called into question the old apologetic form of ecclesiastical philosophy and theology. It broke down "the apologetic barrier"/113/ which had separated Christianity from other religions. "With this, however, there [was] no longer any way to isolate Christianity from the rest of history and then, on the basis of this isolation and its formal signs, to define it as an absolute norm."/114/ Confronted by this impossibility, the great thinkers of German Idealism attempted to establish the absoluteness of Christianity by yet another path. Proceeding from the idea of a total history of humanity as a single whole, in which the ideal of religious truth was deemed to move toward its realization in gradual stages, they held Christianity to be the realization of the general principle of religion and therefore the absolute religion. This concept of Christianity, pioneered by Lessing, Kant, and Herder, and then developed into a refined form by Schleiermacher and Hegel, became the foundation of modern apologetics. "The term 'absoluteness' derives," Troeltsch argues, "from this kind of modern evolutionary apologetic and has a precise meaning only under its presuppositions."/115/ In any case, the problem of the absoluteness of Christianity is a specifically modern problem, conditioned by the modern understanding of history.

This problem of the absoluteness of Christianity became all the more urgent and serious for Troeltsch because the idealistic-evolutionary theory, which had been the only alternative to the supernaturalistic-orthodox apologetic in the modern form, also seemed to him untenable in the face of the modern science of history and religions. Hence the task of establishing the supremacy or prime validity of Christianity became a tormenting problem for Troeltsch. He tried to attain this goal through psychological and historical reflection on religion and religions.

A not insignificant shift on the problem of the absoluteness of

Christianity may be discerned in the early phase of Troeltsch's theologizing. In his first long essay on the Christian world-view and its counter-currents, Troeltsch still advocated a Ritschlian standpoint with respect to the problem of absoluteness. There he asserts:

> Christianity stands in sharp opposition to all other religious developments. It is not the highest point of a continual progression that shows itself as a final result of the historical development thus far, but stands as a fundamentally new one in opposition to the totality of non-Christian religions./116/

Christianity as a "purely spiritual and ethical world religion" was thus set in sharp opposition to all other religious developments as "the religion of nature."/117/ The basis for this judgment was "our personal conviction" or "the confession of being virtually overwhelmed by the Christian principle."/118/ In the even longer essay that followed, Troeltsch was much more free from the "dogmatic bias"/119/ which still dominated the preceding essay. He was now more aware of the methodological problem involved in the discussion of the absoluteness of Christianity. The central problem for the history of religions was now taken to be that of the "criterion of judgment" *(Beurteilungsmaßstab)* according to which a large variety of religious developments should be measured./120/ That is to say, the question was now not *whether* Christianity is the absolute religion, but *how* it can be asserted that Christianity is the absolute religion, should this be the case. Troeltsch's approach to this question is characterized by a peculiar combination of empirical (psychological and historical) study of religions and a metaphysical conviction of a basically idealist outlook. Proceeding from the general standpoint of an 'idealism of historical development' and yet rejecting a Hegelian "*a priori* construction of the history of religions,"/121/ he tried to establish the supremacy or prime validity of Christianity, as it were, *from below* through comparison of the "basic conceptions" *(Grundkonzeptionen; Grundanschauungen)*/122/ of each religion which were discerned by comparative study of religions. He argued that "nothing remains for us but to follow *a posteriori* the actual historical development and to infer the goal and yield from its course, which has its basis in God."/123/ Troeltsch limited the scope of his investigation to the religious developments in the Indo-European and Semitic cultural sphere. He justified such a delimitation with a sort of monadological idea:

We must be satisfied with this: namely, that we, having
complete and sincere confidence in the divine reason which
governs and maintains everything, seek the driving forces
(die treibenden Kräfte), the developmental tendencies *(die
Entwickelungstendenzen)*, and the inner movement *(den
inneren Zug)* of religion in the fragmentary pieces available
to us; and we must console ourselves by thinking that we
know the highest product of this development thus far, as far
as it is measured by these tendencies known to us . . .
However, . . . what we have before us is not a mere mean-
ingless fragment, but a fragment in which the most profound forces of the whole certainly have already had their
most significant effect./124/

The result of his research was this: "The inner dialectic of the
religious idea points in the direction of the perfectly individual and
therefore universal religion of redemption," because this religion of
redemption alone is "perfectly spiritualized and moralized"; "it is
evident that Christianity is the most profound, the most powerful,
and the richest expression of the religious idea."/125/

There is no great change in Troeltsch's position between the
essay just discussed of 1895–96 and the book entitled *The Absoluteness of Christianity and the History of Religions* (1902), as far as
his conclusion as to the place of Christianity among the world
religions is concerned. To set forth his conclusion in advance, Christianity was still regarded as "the strongest and the most concentrated revelation of religious forces."/126/ Christianity represents,
Troeltsch asserted, "the only complete break with the limits and
conditions of the religion of nature" and "the only depiction of the
higher world as infinitely valuable personal life that conditions and
shapes everything else." It "not only occupies a unique position in
principle, . . . but in this unique position it also synthesizes separate tendencies and suggestions into one common goal."/127/ Thus
Christianity was understood "not only as the culmination point
(Höhepunkt) but also as the convergence point *(Konvergenzpunkt)*
of all the developmental tendencies that can be discerned in religion." In other words, Christianity was taken to be "the focal
synthesis *(die zentrale Zusammenfassung)* of all religious tendencies" and "the disclosure of what is a qualitatively new way of life"
(die Eröffnung eines prinzipiell neuen Lebens)./128/ Hence, Christianity was said to be "the highest religious truth that has relevance
for us."/129/

For Troeltsch, however, this was not the same thing as to assert

that the Christian religion is the absolute religion. What could be
demonstrated by the modern science of history was no longer the
'absoluteness' of Christianity in the strict sense, but the "simple
normative validity" (die blosse normative Geltung)./130/ Be that as
it may, demonstration of the absoluteness of Christianity was not
Troeltsch's main purpose in this book. His real intention was rather
to call in question the validity of any such attempt through critical
examination of all such undertakings in the past. In his view, only
two great theories called for special attention: the supernaturalistic-
orthodox apologetic in the modern form which "relies on the absolute miracle of an inner renewal that transcends all natural powers,"
and the idealistic-evolutionary theory which "finds its support in the
realization of the essence of religion in Christianity, defending this
concept by reference to the historical development."/131/ But the
former was simply out of the question for him, given the modern
understanding of history. Consequently, only the latter deserved
serious critical consideration./132/
    According to this idealistic-evolutionary theory,

> There exists, in reality, only one religion, namely the princi-
> ple or essence of religion, and this principle of religion, this
> essence of religion, is latent in all historical religions as their
> ground and goal. In Christianity this universally latent es-
> sence, everywhere else limited by its media, has appeared
> in untrammeled and exhaustive perfection. If Christianity is
> thus identical with this principle of religion that is
> elsewhere implicit and that comes to complete explication
> only in Christianity, then the Christian religion is of course
> normative religious truth./133/

The basic ideas of this theory are clear: first, it subordinates history
to "the concept of a universal principle" (Allgemeinbegriff); then, it
elevates this concept of a universal principle to "the principle of a
norm and ideal" (Norm- und Idealbegriff); and thirdly, it binds
these two concepts together by means of "a theory of evolutionary
development" (Entwickelungstheorie)./134/ Troeltsch's fundamental
criticism of this procedure is as follows: first, history knows no
universal principle by which the content and sequence of events
might be deduced (it knows only concrete, individual phenomena,
always conditioned by their context); second, it knows no values or
norms that coincide with actual universals (it knows them as universally valid ideas which invariably appear in individual form and
make their universal validity known by their resistance to the

merely existent); third, it knows no evolutionary development in which an actual, law-regulated universal principle produces universally authentic values; and finally, it knows no absolute realization of such a universal principle within the context of history./135/ After all, "it is impossible," in Troeltsch's judgment, "to construct a theory of Christianity as the absolute religion on the basis of a historical way of thinking or by the use of historical means."/136/ Judged from the historical standpoint, Christianity is a 'relative' phenomenon.

> Christianity is in every moment of its history a purely historical phenomenon, subject to all the limitations to which any individual historical phenomenon is exposed, just as are the other great religions. It is to be investigated, in every moment of its history, by the universal, verified method of historical research./137/

But acknowledgment of this relativity or historical conditionality of Christianity did not necessarily mean a loss for theology. For "the historical and the relative are identical."/138/ An unlimited relativism was not the inevitable consequence of this acknowledgment. Rather, "the idea of relativity" simply meant

> that all historical phenomena are unique, individual configurations acted on in varying degrees of immediacy by influence from the total context; therefore, that proceeding from every construct of history, a perspective evolves which ranges to a broader context and thus finally embraces the whole; and that only the survey of all historical phenomena as a whole *(Zusammenschau im Ganzen)* makes valuation and judgment possible./139/

For Troeltsch relativity did not mean denial of historical values. "History does not exclude norms. On the contrary," he says, "its most important work is exactly the production of norms and the striving for a synoptic synthesis of these norms."/140/ The task of the science of history was to identify "something *common and universally valid*" that dwells in historical configurations, or "the *goals and ideals* that find individually conditioned realization in every form of life."/141/ The convergent lines evident in the basic features of dynamic historical progress suggested a universally valid goal. However, "to wish to possess the absolute in an absolute way at a particular point in history," he says, "is delusion. This wish shatters not only because of its impracticability but also because it stands in internal contradiction to the nature of every historical religion."/142/ For, from the scientific and philosophical viewpoint, "absolute, unchanging value, conditioned by nothing temporary, exists not within but beyond history and can be perceived only in presentiment and faith."/143/ Troeltsch believed that Christianity also supports this judgment. According to him, its central basic thought teaches us that "absolute truth belongs to the future and will appear in the judgment of God and the cessation of earthly history."/144/

In conclusion, for Troeltsch the absolute lay beyond history. Within history it could be apprehended only in individual and conditioned forms as "a normative and universally valid goal floating before the eyes trained on the whole" (*ein dem Ganzen vorschwebendes allgemeingiltiges, normatives Ziel*)./145/ The real problem of history was not that of "making an either/or choice between relativism and absolutism" (*das Entweder-Oder von Relativismus und Absolutismus*) but that of combining the two, namely, the problem of "discerning, in the relative, tendencies toward the absolute goal" (*das Herauswachsen der Richtungen auf absolute Ziele aus dem Relativen*)./146/ Or, to put it more accurately,

> How does one work out an ever-new creative synthesis (*die immer neue schöpferische Synthese*) that will give the absolute the form possible for it at a particular moment and yet remain true to its inherent limitation as a mere approximation of true, ultimate, and universally valid values? This is the gist of the problem./147/

As clearly perceived here, the problem Troeltsch tackled under the theme of the absoluteness of Christianity was nothing other than the task of working out "an ever-new creative synthesis that will give the absolute the form (*Gestalt*) possible for it at a particular moment." This idea of a creative synthesis, though spelled out first in the revised second edition of 1912, is already inherent in his discussion of the absoluteness of Christianity in the first edition of 1902 and provides a guideline for his subsequent theological development. Not only can his later celebrated idea of a contemporary cultural synthesis be seen in this light, but also the true meaning of the Troeltschian idea of *Gestaltung* (shaping; configuration; formation), which will occupy us next, is illuminated from this perspective.

The Way to a Theology of Gestaltung/148/

So far in this opening chapter, we have discussed the formation and the characteristic features of Troeltsch's *religionsgeschichtliche* theology. As we have seen, the main concern of such a theology based on the history of religions was the establishment of the normativeness or prime validity of the Christian religion through scientific religious-historical investigation. Troeltsch took this to be the only way to solve the basic problem of theology in a manner which corresponds to our modern needs. However, this "attempt to gain the normative from history,"/149/ as Troeltsch gradually realized, could only be accomplished through "an ever-new creative synthesis that will give the absolute the form *(Gestalt)* possible for it at a particular moment." This, theologically speaking, was nothing but the task of "formulating the basic Christian idea in a manner corresponding to the present" *(die der Gegenwart entsprechende Gestaltung des christlichen Gedankens),*/150/ or simply, that of a "Neugestaltung" (new shaping)/151/ of Christianity. Hence, along with the task of "gaining *normative* knowledge through the science of religion,"/152/ the task of a *Neugestaltung* of the Christian world of life and ideas became a more and more central theme for Troeltsch. For example, in the second edition of *The Absoluteness of Christianity* he asserts:

> What is important, therefore, is, in the first place, to gain this normativeness [of Christianity] from the history of religions instead of from scholastic theories of revelation or apologetics against philosophical systems, and then, *in the second place, to give to the Christian world of ideas a form that will correspond to the present religious and intellectual situation.*/153/

Seen from the bibliographical viewpoint, this emphasis by Troeltsch on the *Neugestaltung* or "Neuformung" (new formation)/154/ of Christianity found its first clear formulation in his significant essay, "What Does 'Essence of Christianity' Mean?" (1903). There he clearly set forth his theory of *Gestaltung* in relation to the concept of the essence of Christianity. In my view, Troeltsch first secured his own theological position with this theory, and hereafter he developed his theological and philosophical thought along this line. Now let us examine, first, his understanding of the essence of Christianity, and then, in relation to this, his theory of *Gestaltung*.

According to Troeltsch, the whole expression "the essence of Christianity" is linked to modern, critical, and evolutionary history. The expression, as it first emerged in Chateaubriand's *Génie du*

Christianisme, has its source in the historical way of looking at things and in the art of Romanticism, but the problem as such had already been sensed by Lessing and Herder. They did not understand Christianity as the teaching of the New Testament, the teaching of Jesus, or the doctrine of the Church, but rather as "the totality of Christian life, to be understood in the fulness of the historical manifestations resulting from a driving idea."/155/ Therefore the expression involves "the application of a basic methodological idea and an extremely widely maintained presupposition of modern history in general."/156/ The 'essence' is "the abstract idea, *the abstraction peculiar to history*, by means of which the whole known and precisely researched context of related formations is understood in terms of the basic driving and developing idea."/157/

This being the case, definition of the essence of Christianity involves as its presupposition the renunciation of the dogmatic method. "The essence must be sought with determination through modern historical thinking."/158/ However, one more point must be mentioned. Definition of the essence is, indeed, a 'purely historical' task, but it involves more than simply descriptive history. The definition of the essence "grows out of the method and spirit of empirical-inductive historical writings" but it "goes beyond the ordinary accounts of inductive-empirical history." The task lies "at the point of transition from empirical-inductive history to the philosophy of history."/159/ These were the preliminary considerations which led into the detailed discussion of the problem involved in the definition of the essence.

If the definition of the essence is an abstraction from the total extent of historical manifestations down to the present, and if one's intention is to single out and formulate the driving forces (*die treibenden Kräfte*), then one may think it possible to solve the problem by considering all manifestations as arising in accordance with a driving force inherent in the basic ideas or with a law of development contained in such a driving force. In fact, the Hegelian school understood the historical development of Christianity as teleologically necessary revelations of the essence. But, even apart from purely historical thinking, Protestant conviction reacts against this view in principle. For it is impossible for Protestantism to consider the development from the primitive church to Catholicism to be the teleologically necessary, organic one./160/ Within history there emerges not only something essential but also what is inessential or contrary to the essence. There is also something contingent or accidental in history. This being the case, definition of the essence must involve criticism. Thus the concept of the essence is at the same time criticism *(Kritik)*.

> It is *not merely an abstraction from the manifestations, but at the same time criticism of the manifestations*, and this criticism is *not merely an evaluation of something not yet complete in the terms of the driving ideal but a discrimination between what corresponds to the essence and what is contrary to it./161/*

This criticism is called immanent criticism. "The historical is measured by the historical, the individual formation is measured against the spirit of the whole conceived intuitively and imaginatively."/162/ Admittedly, the subjective and personal element is increased here. For this very reason, the task of the definition of the essence demands "important scientific and spiritual resources, a personality at one and the same time trained in the exactness of history and disciplined in religion and ethics."/163/ In this sense the definition of the essence is "a matter of historical competence."/164/

If the first task of the definition of the essence is to make fundamental distinctions between the essential and the unessential, then where is the pre-eminently important revelation of the essence to be found? This is the second problem. Generally speaking, the classical revelation is to be found in the origins, where the whole set of ideas is still in its freshness and purity. Troeltsch had no objection to this commonly held view. The original meaning of a historical phenomenon is indeed contained most powerfully and purely in its origin. This is also altogether true of Christianity. But the question is: "what is it in the initial period which contains the truly classical element?"/165/ In Troeltsch's view, the initial period is in no sense a completely unified complex. One already finds here the basic difference between the preaching of Jesus and that of Paul, which, though capable of being harmonized, has also had a distinctive influence on the whole history of Christianity./166/ Besides, since the original time is after all only the seminal form of the further development, and if there exists no absolute gap between the original time and the further development, then the further development is also of fundamental importance for the definition of the essence. In reality, Christianity has developed by assimilating a great variety of elements, such as Platonism, Stoicism, humanism, and so forth. Therefore the identification of the essence cannot be exclusively based on the initial period and on the preaching of Jesus as was Harnack's procedure. Instead, "the essence has to be an entity with an inner flexibility and a productive power for new creation."/167/ It cannot be characterized by one word or one doctrine. Rather

> it *must be a developing spiritual principle,* a 'germinative principle' as Caird calls it, a historical idea in Ranke's sense, that is to say, not a metaphysical or dogmatic idea, but a driving spiritual force which contains within itself purposes and values and which elaborates these both consistently and accommodatingly./168/

The essence of Christianity must bear "opposites and tensions" within itself. It must contain within itself "an oscillation between several basic ideas."/169/ For example, the religiously utterly transcendent and eschatological ethical idea of the preaching of Jesus is in continuous inner tension with the immanent ethic of the later world church. Thus "the formula for the essence of Christianity can by no means be a simple concept such as sonship of God, spiritual religion, personal religion, belief in God as Father, or something similar."/170/ To sum up,

> the essence of Christianity contains a polarity within itself, and an expression of it must be dualistic. To take over an image which Ritschl used in a rather different sense, it is like an ellipse which does not have one center like a circle but rather two foci./171/

In the third place, a perspective on the future is indispensable in the definition of the essence. For when it is a question of summarizing such a large and important area as Christianity under unified concepts, history can never altogether avoid thinking of the future, drawing out existing lines into the future, and illuminating the present and the past by means of this projected continuations. For this reason the definition of the essence of Christianity is strongly conditioned by one's personal attitude toward Christianity. For those who no longer believe in the validity of Christianity, there is no longer any motive to ascribe to the essence a maturer or purer idea yet to be worked in the future. On the other hand, those who affirm Christianity and who strive to work out such an idea will at the same time see the essence in the light of this idea and emphasize that moment in the past which is amenable to the possibilities of the future. Accordingly, the identification of one's personal position with reference to the value and truth of Christianity is one of the prerequisites of a definition of the essence. In any case, the definition of the essence must take up within itself the future form *(zukünftige Gestaltung)* which is to be effected by our work or the ideal of Christianity as we understand it. Troeltsch states:

> The future development will have to be counted in with the developing essence, and since the future development is controlled by our insight into how it ought to be according to the essence and driving force of the Christian idea, *the essence changes quite automatically from being an abstracted concept to being an ideal concept.*/172/

The most difficult problems involved in the definition of the essence of Christianity arise out of this unavoidable transition from an abstracted concept to an ideal concept. These difficulties are attributable to the fact that the position taken toward Christianity, despite all the accompanying objective considerations of a philosophico-historical and metaphysical-speculative kind, is in the last analysis a thoroughly personal matter conditioned by personal religious acceptance and appropriation of the Christian idea in the living context of the present. The question is "how the starting point of a purely historical approach, chosen precisely with a view to an objective clarification, is related to this recognition of the strongly subjective factors which contribute to the results."/173/ It was exactly at this point that Troeltsch found "the real knot of the whole problem."/174/ However, this knot, he asserted, cannot be undone at all. Rather we have to seek an ever-new union of the subjective and the objective with full consciousness and care. This can never be achieved by theory, but only by the living act, which, in spite of their theoretical incompatibility, always combines the objective and the subjective in itself. This is therefore a "creative act" *(schöpferische Tat).*/175/

But if the definition of the essence is an act, then it is no longer merely a judgment about history but rather itself part of history. It is itself "a constituent element of the continuing historical development and indeed one of the most important and crucial means by which it takes place."/176/ In this sense "to define the essence is to shape it afresh" *(Wesensbestimmung ist Wesensgestaltung).*/177/

> The definition of the essence is the elucidation of the essential idea of Christianity in history in the way in which it

ought to be a light for the future, and at the same time it is a
living view of the present and future world together in this
light. The definition of the essence for a given time is the
new historical formulation of Christianity for that time (*die
jeweilige historische Neugestaltung des Christentums*)./178/
The above has summarized the main lines of Troeltsch's argument as to the methodological problems involved in the definition of
the essence of Christianity. His proposition was, in a word, thus:
"The essence is an intuitive abstraction, a religious and ethical
critique, a flexible developmental concept, and the ideal to be
applied in the work of shaping and recombining for the future."
With all this in mind, Troeltsch designated the definition of the
essence as "the crown and at the same time the self-abrogation of
historical theology," "the unification of the historical element of
theology with the normative element or at least the element which
shapes the future."/179/ In this unification, however, Troeltsch saw
the same problem that he had tackled in his *Absoluteness of Christianity*, namely, "the major, general problem of the relationship
between history and normative thought."/180/ After showing the
untenability of the three major solutions presented up to that
time,/181/ he contended that "there remains no other solution than
. . . the doctrine of an ever renewed, purely factual and irrational
combination of what is recognized to be necessary and true with
historical tradition and experience."/182/ This doctrine of an ever-
new combination of the objective (universally valid) and the subjective (historical-conditional) as a creative act is what we have designated as his theory of *Gestaltung* (*Gestaltungslehre*). Thus, Troeltsch
eventually found in this doctrine of *Gestaltung* his long-sought
proper solution to that problem of the relationship between history
and norms which had tormented him so heavily from the outset of
his intellectual pilgrimage.

In any case, with this doctrine of *Gestaltung* the whole of
Troeltsch's theology and philosophy was now focused on the new
shaping and formulation of the Christian world of life and ideas. The
demand for a "rejuvenation" (*Verjüngung*) of Christianity, which had
been one of his central concerns from the beginning, was now made
on the basis of a more solid methodology./183/ This theme of a
rejuvenation of Christianity then led to the advocacy of "a free
Christianity" (*ein freies Christentum*) in due course of time. In some
paragraphs interpolated when the original essay was incorporated

into the second volume of his collected writings, Troeltsch spells out this demand. According to him (Troeltsch around the year 1913), free Christianity with its acceptance of the whole universal-historical way of thinking, as compared with older Protestantism, does indeed involve something new. Defining the essence differently with living involvement in the historical powers of the present day, it represents "the second act of Protestantism, which corresponds to the completely changed overall situation."/184/ Far from having lost the essence, as some opponents of liberal theology declare to be the case, the advocates of this free Christianity, in Troeltsch's view, do only what older Protestantism itself did, that is, they are formulating a new expression of the essence. Thus the "Neo-Protestantism" of which Troeltsch was a champion is alleged to represent "nothing other than the attempt to formulate anew the essence of Christianity."/185/ Whether or not Troeltsch's assertion here is justifiable from the authentic Christian viewpoint, it is important to recognize that *Gestaltung* will be the leitmotif of Troeltsch's theology and philosophy from now on. With this recognition, however, we have already left the early Troeltsch far behind us and have stepped into his second period.

NOTES

/1/ Walther Köhler characterizes Troeltsch's theology and philosophy as one of "balance." He asserts that to keep the unconditional and the conditional, the valid and the historical, the ideal and the real in balance is "the legacy of Ernst Troeltsch." "The *coincidentia oppositorum* as such is certainly of decisive importance for him and is thus the basic element of his world-view." W. Köhler, *Ernst Troeltsch* (Tübingen: J. C. B. Mohr, 1941), p. 414.

/2/ H. R. Niebuhr, "Ernst Troeltsch's Philosophy of Religion" (Ph.D. dissertation, Yale University, 1924; Ann Arbor, Mich.: University Microfilms, 1965), p. 5.

/3/ It is to K. -E. Apfelbacher's credit that he made a comprehensive analysis of Troeltsch's theological and religious-philosophical thought in view of this polarity of *Frömmigkeit* and *Wissenschaft*. K. -E. Apfelbacher, *Frömmigkeit und Wissenschaft: Ernst Troeltsch und sein theologisches Programm*, Beiträge zur ökumenischen Theologie 18 (Munich-Paderborn-Vienna: Verlag Ferdinand Schöningh, 1978).

/4/ E. Troeltsch, "Die 'kleine Göttinger Fakultät' von 1890," *CW* 34 (1920): 281; cf. id., *Briefe*, p. 100.

/5/ The valedictory speech Troeltsch gave on 6 August 1883 well documents this:
"Only (!) those who take the positive axioms of religion as the guide in the world of ideas remain protected from a wrong way; and furthermore: only those who know the classical heathen world with its sometimes imperceptible, sometimes perceptible, yearning for knowledge; only those who are aware of the questions which it first put to the world: only they can attain in the highest way the highest thing that ever exists, namely, the truth through searching."
Quoted in G. Wünsch, "Ernst Troeltsch," in : W. Zorn, ed., *Lebensbilder aus dem bayerischen Schwaben*, vol. 9 (Munich: Verlag Max Hueber, 1966), pp. 386–387.

/6/ E. Troeltsch, "Die Selbständigkeit der Religion," *ZThK* 5 (1895): 361 (hereafter cited as "Selbständigkeit").

/7/ Id., G.S. IV, p. 4.

/8/ A phrase in Troeltsch's valedictory speech. Quoted in H. Renz and F. W. Graf, eds., *Troeltsch-Studien: Untersuchungen zur Biographie und Werkgeschichte* (Gütersloh: Gütersloher Verlagshaus Gerd Mohn, 1982), p. 28 (hereafter cited *Troeltsch-Studien*).

/9/ Troeltsch, "Selbständigkeit," 5:361.

/10/ Ibid.

/11/ Köhler, *Ernst Troeltsch*, p. 2.

/12/ Troeltsch, "Absolventenrede," 6 August 1883, quoted in *Troeltsch-Studien*, p. 24. Here Troeltsch spoke as follows: "The age of discontent comes when the entire world of ideas seems to lose itself into nothingness and when a house of cards seems to break down."

/13/ Looking back on his school days at Erlangen after three dozen years, Troeltsch wrote as follows:
"The faculty members who were very influential at that time, such as Frank, Zezschwitz, and Zahn, could hardly attract us [Bousset and Troeltsch]. We had cool respect for the professors, feeling in our hearts that they were antiques from the time of the German Confederation, relics of the battle between neo-pietism and the Enlightenment. Our interests were different, lying partly in the political and social problems of the time and partly in the world-view of the natural sciences then current" (Troeltsch, "Die 'kleine Göttinger Fakultät' von 1890," p. 282).

/14/ Troeltsch studied three semesters (1886–1888) at the University of Göttingen, where he attended Ritschl's lectures on dogmatics and theological ethics. How striking Ritschl's impression on the young Troeltsch was is perceived from the latter's retrospective remarks on his teacher. Troeltsch states:
"Ritschl really won us [Bousset and Troeltsch] for theology for the first time.

His powerful personality drew us up to Götingen. With fellow students yet to be mentioned, we formed his last school." Today one can hardly imagine the authority, dignity, and power with which this weighty, but utterly unromantic, admittedly unpoetic man impressed us through his intellectual sharpness, the grandiosity and strictness of his systematic conception, and the integrity and excellence of his character" (Troeltsch, "Die 'kleine Göttinger Fakultät' von 1890," p. 282).

/15/ Niebuhr, "Ernst Troeltsch's Philosophy of Religion," p. 15.

/16/ Troeltsch, G.S. I, pp. vii–viii.

/17/ Reist, *Toward a Theology of Involvement*, p. 17.

/18/ Troeltsch, G.S. IV, p. 7.

/19/ Ibid.

/20/ E. Troeltsch, *Vernunft und Offenbarung bei Johann Gerhard und Melanchthon: Untersuchung zur Geschichte der altprotestantische Theologie* (Göttingen: Vandenhoeck & Ruprecht, 1891), p.212. Strictly speaking, this work is not identical with Troeltsch's theological dissertation submitted to the Georg-August-Universität at Göttingen in 1891. It is an expanded version of his dissertation. This work is hereafter cited as *Vernunft und Offenbarung*.

/21/ Ibid., pp. 1–2.

/22/ W. Bodenstein, *Neige des Historismus: Ernst Troeltschs Entwicklungsgang* (Gütersloh: Gütersloher Verlaghaus Gerd Mohn, 1959), pp. 7–15.

/23/ Hans-Georg Drescher blames Bodenstein for ascribing "a programmatic importance to Troeltsch's work on Johann Gerhard and Melanchthon." He states the following:
"The importance of this work of Troeltsch is clearly overplayed here. It was less dramatic than that. . . . In this largely historically oriented investigation Bodenstein tends to perceive the systematic insights which Troeltsch conceived later . . . If Troeltsch's argument had already gone as far as Bodenstein seems to think, his further theological development would be difficult to understand" (H. -G. Drescher, "Ernst Troeltsch's Intellectual Development," in *Ernst Troeltsch and the Future of Theology*, ed. J. P. Clayton [Cambridge: Cambridge University Press, 1976], pp. 5–6).
It is true that Troeltsch's break with Ritschl was not so dramatic and abrupt. As far as his view on the absoluteness of Christianity is concerned, Troeltsch defended a Ritschlian position in his earliest long essay on the Christian world-view. But Drescher seems to me to underestimate the significance which this historical study by Troeltsch had for his systematic task.

/24/ E. Troeltsch, *Das Historische in Kants Religionsphilosophie. Zugleich ein Beitrag zu den Untersuchungen über Kants Philosophie der Geschichte* (Berlin: Verlag von Reuther & Reichard, 1904), p. v.

/25/ Cf. id., "Die 'kleine Göttinger Fakultät' von 1890," p. 282; id., *Absolutheit* 2d ed., p. 145.

/26/ Id., *Das Historische in Kants Religionsphilosophie*, pp. v–vi.

/27/ Id., "Thesen welche mit Genehmigung der theologischen Lizentiatenwürde an der Georg-August-Universität zu Göttingen Sonnabend den 4. Februar 1891 11 Uhr öffentlich vertheidigen wird Ernst Troeltsch Predigtamtskandidat," reprinted in *Troeltsch-Studien, pp. 299–300* (hereafter cited as "Promotionsthesen"). The assertion in question is found in Thesis 15.

/28/ Ernst Troeltsch to Wilhelm Bousset, 16 June 1893, quoted in *Troeltsch-Studien*, p. 121.

/29/ E. Troeltsch, "Die christliche Weltanschauung und die wissenschaftlichen Gegenströmmungen," *ZThK* 3 (1893):493–528; 4 (1894):167–231 (hereafter cited as "Weltanschauung").

/30/ Id., G.S. II, p. 324 n. 20.

/31/ Id., "Die Selbständigkeit der Religion," *ZThK* 5 (1895): 361–436; 6 (1896):71–110, 167–218.

/32/ Id., "Zur Religionsphilosophie. Aus Anlaß des Buches von Rudolf Otto über 'Das Heilige' (Breslau 1917)," *Kantstudien* 23 (1919):65–66; cf. id., "Selbständigkeit," 5:415–416; 6:169.

/33/ G. Ecke, *Die theologische Schule Albrecht Ritschls* (Berlin: Reuther & Reichard, 1897), pp. 124–125.

/34/ F. Kattenbusch, "In Sache der Ritschlschen Theologie," *CW* 12 (1898):77.

/35/ E. Troeltsch, "Geschichte und Metaphysik," *ZThK* 8 (1898):52 n. 1 (hereafter cited as "Metaphysik").

/36/ See note 23.

/37/ Already in his proposal for his qualifying examinations of 3 November 1889, "Gesuch des Predigtamtskanditaten Ernst Troeltsch um Zulassung zur Lizentiatenprüfung und zur Habilitation," Troeltsch made it very clear that his real interest lay in systematic theology. There he states the following:
"If I should successfully pass this examination, then I obediently beg you, most honored faculty, to allow me to become a lecturer in the field of church history and the history of doctrine, from which I hope then to move on to systematic theology to which my real intention is directed" (Quoted in *Troeltsch-Studien*, p. 89).

/38/ Troeltsch, *Vernunft und Offenbarung*, p. 213 (emphasis mine).

/39/ The original sources of these essays are: *Realencyklopädie für protestantische Theologie und Kirche*, 3d ed., s.v. "Aufklärung," "Deismus,"

"Idealismus, deutscher," and "Moralisten, englische" by Ernst Troeltsch;
id., "Leibniz und die Anfänge des Pietismus," in *Der Protestantismus am
Ende des XIX, Jahrhunderts in Wort und Bild*, ed. C. Werckshagen (Berlin:
Verlag Wartburg, 1902), pp. 353–376.

/40/   Troeltsch, G.S. IV, p. 338.

/41/   Ibid., p. 339.

/42/   Id., "Metaphysik," p. 40.

/43/   Id., *Die wissenschaftliche Lage und ihre Anforderungen an die Theologie* (Tübingen: J. C. B. Mohr, 1900), p. 9 (hereafter cited as *Lage*).

/44/   The first and fourth of these essays are now, with sundry revision and
supplements, contained in the second volume of his *Gesammelte Schriften*.
For specific bibliographical information on each of these works, see the note
concerned on previous pages.

/45/   Troeltsch, *Christian Thought*, p. 4.

/46/   Id., *Vernunft und Offenbarung*, p. 2.

/47/   Ibid., p. 3; cf. id., "Selbständigkeit" 5:420.

/48/   Id., "Selbständigkeit" *ZThK* 6 (1896):109; cf. E. Troeltsch, "Thesen
welche mit Genehmigung der theologischen Lizentiatenwürde an der
Georg-August-Universität zu Göttingen Sonnabend den 4. Februar 1891,
11 Uhr öffentlich vertheidigen wird Ernst Troeltsch Predigtamtskandidat,"
reprinted in *Troeltsch-Studien*, pp. 299–300. Thesis 16 reads as follows:
"Theology is just as difficult for the church to endure as to do without."

/49/   Id., *Vernunft und Offenbarung*, p. 3.

/50/   Id., "Weltanschauung," 3:495.

/51/   Ibid., 3:504.

/52/   Ibid., *ZThK* 4 (1894):230.

/53/   Id., *Lage*, p. 3.

/54/   Ibid., pp. 3–8.

/55/   W. Köhler suggests that this phrase, if rightly understood, could be
taken as the leitmotif of Troeltsch's theology and philosophy. He reports the
following interesting anecdote:
"The 'Friends of the Christian World' gathered in Eisenach in 1896; Julius
Kaftan from Berlin had just completed a learned, somewhat scholastic
lecture on the meaning of the logos-doctrine. With the opening of general
discussion, there leaped with youthful elan to the rostrum a young man who
began his statement with the words: 'Gentlemen, everything is tottering'
(*Meine Herren, es wackelt alles*)—Ernst Troeltsch. Then he went on to
outline with large, firm strokes a picture of the situation which was to

confirm his judgment. The older scholars were appalled. As their spokesman Ferdinand Kattenbusch rebuked him for 'paltry theology' (*schofelen Theologie*), Troeltsch got up and left the assembly room, slamming the doors behind him. But we younger ones picked up our ears." W. Köhler, *Ernst Troeltsch*, p. 1.

/56/   Troeltsch, "Weltanschauung," 4:230.

/57/   Id., *Lage*, p. 9.

/58/   E. Troeltsch, "Religionswissenschaft und Theologie des 18. Jahrhunderts," *Preußische Jahrbücher* 114 (1903):31.

/59/   Ibid.

/60/   Ibid., pp. 30–31. See also E. Troeltsch, "Theologie und Religionswissenschaft des 19. Jahrhunderts," *Jahrbuch des Freien deutschen Hochstifts Frankfurt am Main 1902* (Frankfurt am Main: Druck von Gebrüder Knauer, 1902), p. 91.

/61/   Id., "Theologie und Religionswissenschaft des 19. Jahrhunderts," p. 91.

/62/   Id., "Religionswissenschaft und Theologie des 18. Jahrhunderts," p. 56.

/63/   Id., "Selbständigkeit," 5:362, 415. In his first long essay, "The Christian World-view and the Scientific Counter-currents" (1893/94), Troeltsch points out that the basic trends of modern thought by which his theology will be able to orient itself are: "metaphysical idealism on an epistemological basis, an idealist ethics which elaborates a unitary viewpoint of imperative and goal, a theism based on the total phenomenon of religion and its development, and our German science of history with its basis in a cautious theory of development." Troeltsch, "Weltanschauung," 3:506.

/64/   Id., "Selbständigkeit," 5:364.

/65/   Ibid., 5:370. The psychology of religion, as Troeltsch understands it, however, does not intend "to ignore speculative efforts concerned with the object of religion" (ibid.).

/66/   Troeltsch states the following:
"To apply Feuerbach's theory to non-Christian religions and at the same time a supernaturalistic theory of revelation to Christianity is an extremely dangerous experiment. Not many people will be able to find the truth of Christianity in any form secured by this. These are all attempts to exempt Christianity from the fundamental ideas of the philosophy of religion. Those who have themselves for a while made grateful use of this gambit for isolating Christianity as a way out of theological difficulties know only too well how far the wish is father to the thought here" (ibid., 5:375).

/67/   Ibid., 5:392–393; 5:400–406, 6:79–80.

/68/   Ibid., 6:96.

/69/   Id., "Zur theologischen Lage," *CW* 12 (1898):630.

/70/   Id., "Selbständigkeit," 5:369–370.

/71/   Ibid., 5:431.

/72/   Ibid., 5:370.

/73/   Ibid., 6:167.

/74/   E. Troeltsch, "Ueber historische und dogmatische Methode der Theologie," *Theologische Arbeiten aus dem rheinischen wissenschaftlichen Predigerverein*, n.s. 4 (1900):102 (hereafter cited as "Methode").

/75/   Id., "Selbständigkeit," 6:78; cf. 5:373.

/76/   Ibid., 6:200.

/77/   Troeltsch takes this as the first and fundamental claim which the present scientific situation makes on theology. See id., "Lage," p. 47.

/78/   Id., "Promotionsthesen," p. 299.

/79/   Id., *Absolutheit*, p. iv (emphasis original).

/80/   Ibid. A significant clause is added to the sentence just cited in the second edition of 1912. It reads: "and then, in the second place, to give to the Christian world of ideas a form that will correspond to the present intellectual situation *(diejenige Gestaltung der christlichen Ideenwelt zu schaffen, die der heutigen geistigen Lage entspricht)*" (id., *Absolutheit* 2d ed., p. viii).

/81/   See F. W. Graf, "Der 'Systematiker' der 'Kleinen Göttinger Fakultät.' Ernst Troeltschs Promotionsthesen und ihr Göttinger Kontext," *Troeltsch-Studien*, p. 287.

/82/   Troeltsch, *Absolutheit*, p. vi.

/83/   Under the title of "The Independence of Christianity" (1896) he attacked Troeltsch's theological position as set forth in "The Independence of Religion" (1895/96). Troeltsch responded to Kaftan with his essay "History and Metaphysics" (1898), to which Kaftan then replied with his "Reply: (1) Method; (2) Supernaturalism" (1898). Two years later, Troeltsch added to this controversy another very significant essay "On the Historical and Dogmatic Method of Theology" (1900) which, though motivated directly by Niebergall's attack on him, was at the same time indirectly his final word to Kaftan. Troeltsch's relation to Kaftan is worthy of note. In the academic year 1885–86, as a student at the Friedrich-Wilhelm-University of Berlin, Troeltsch attended all the lectures and seminars that Kaftan offered. This suggests that Kaftan's theology greatly attracted the young Troeltsch. Their personal relationship must have begun during this period. Kaftan reviewed Troeltsch's initial work *Vernunft und Offenbarung* (*ThLZ* 2 [1892]:208–212).

But their relationship, both theological and personal, cooled down after a decade. In his letter to W. Bousset of 27 May 1896, Troeltsch still showed his "great personal gratitude" to Kaftan. However, the confrontation at the annual meeting of the 'Friends of the Christian World' in Eisenach in the fall of the same year did fatal damage to their relationship (see Köhler, *Ernst Troeltsch*, p. 1). It caused "a decisive break with Kaftan and even with Herrmann" (Troeltsch to Bousset, 4 January 1896 [1897]). Soon after this, Troeltsch wrote: "Anyway, I am personally finished with Kaftan and want to know nothing more about him" (Troeltsch to Bousset, 27 January 1897). See *Troeltsch-Studien*, p. 55; E. Troeltsch, "Briefe aus der Heidelberger Zeit an Wilhelm Bousset 1894–1914," ed. E. Dinkler-von Schubert, *Heidelberger Jahrbücher* 20 (1976):31–32 (hereafter cited as "Briefe an Bousset").

/84/   Troeltsch, "Metaphysik," pp. 3, 25.

/85/   Ibid., p. 14.

/86/   Ibid., p. 4.

/87/   Ibid., p. 9.

/88/   Ibid.

/89/   Ibid., p. 4.

/90/   Id., "Selbständigkeit," 5:363.

/91/   E. Troeltsch, "Religionsphilosophie," in *Die Philosophie im Beginn des zwanzigsten Jahrhunderts. Festschrift für Kuno Fischer*, ed., W. Windelband, vol. I (Heidelberg: Carl Winters Universitätsbuchhandlung, 1904), p. 133 (hereafter cited as "Religionsphilosophie").

/92/   Id., "Metaphysik," p. 25.

/93/   Ibid.

/94/   Ibid., p. 28.

/95/   Ibid., p. 27.

/96/   Ibid., p. 40.

/97/   Ibid., pp. 40–41.

/98/   Ibid., pp. 68–69.

/99/   Ibid., p. 69.

/100/   Ibid.

/101/   Ibid.

/102/   Id., "Methode," p. 87.

/103/   Ibid., p. 89.

/104/   Ibid., pp. 93–94.

/105/ Ibid., p. 92. The English translation is based on the revised text in the *Gesammelte Schriften*. Cf. G.S. II, p. 734.

/106/ Ibid., p. 88.

/107/ Ibid., pp. 91–92.

/108/ Ibid., p. 95.

/109/ Ibid., p. 106.

/110/ Ibid., p. 95; cf. p. 94.

/111/ Ibid.

/112/ E. Troeltsch, "Thesen zu dem am 3. Oktober in der Versammlung der Freunde der Christlichen Welt in Mühlacker zu haltenden Vortrage über die Absolutheit des Christentums und die Religionsgeschichte," *CW* 15 (1901):923.

/113/ Id., *Absolutheit*, p. 5.

/114/ Ibid.

/115/ Ibid., p. 9. The second edition contains the following statement: "The expression 'absoluteness' signifies the perfect self-comprehension of the idea that strives for complete clarity, the self-realization of God in human consciousness. It is the speculative substitute for the dogmatic supernaturalism of the church." Id., *Absolutheit* 2d ed., pp. 15–16.

/116/ Id., "Weltanschauung," 4:224.

/117/ Ibid., 4:224–226.

/118/ Ibid., 4:222. But Troeltsch could no longer maintain this standpoint after two decades. He states the following:
"Today I can no longer advocate this standpoint, which was asserted at that time. . . . The absoluteness of Christianity thus asserted is based on too narrow and too flimsy grounds: self-assertion and the proof that the concept of development as such is incapable of laying the basis for the positive content of life . . . However, . . . no revelational faith equivalent to the ecclesiastical dogma can be grounded on skepticism toward the concept of development, emphasis on the self-assertion of Jesus and the church, and inner experience of this self-assertion." G.S. II, p. 324 n. 20.

/119/ Id., *Lage*, p. 51 n. 1.

/120/ Id., "Selbständigkeit," 6:167.

/121/ Ibid., 6:94. Against Hegel, Troeltsch contends that there exists "no *a priori* ready-made criterion" for the history of religions (ibid., 6:167). Rather, "the criterion grows in and with history itself, since a higher

phenomenon carries in itself the certitude of its greater strength and depth"
(ibid., 6:78).

/122/   Ibid., 6:101.

/123/   Ibid., 6:167.

/124/   Ibid., 6:169. The thought dominant in this paragraph is not merely
Dilthey's idea of historical individuality but also a Lotze-Leibnizian monadological idea. Troeltsch's later idea of a universal history of Europeanism
based on a Leibnizian monadology is foreshadowed here.

/125/   Ibid., 6:200.

/126/   Id., *Absolutheit*, pp. 77–78. This passage is slightly modified in the
second edition. The phrase "religious forces" is replaced by "personalistic
religiosity" (id., *Absolutheit* 2d ed., p. 86). It is one of the characteristic
features of Troeltsch's second period that much more emphasis is laid on the
personalistic nature of the Christian religion.

/127/   ibid., p. 78.

/128/   Ibid., p. 80.

/129/   Ibid., p. 73.

/130/   Ibid., p. 17.

/131/   Ibid., p. 21.

/132/   Ibid.

/133/   Ibid, p. 7 (emphasis original).

/134/   Ibid., p. 27.

/135/   Ibid., pp. 27–28.

/136/   Ibid., p. 23.

/137/   Ibid., p. 49.

/138/   Ibid.

/139/   Ibid., p. 53. It is noteworthy that Troeltsch derives a notion of
universal history from the principle of historical relativity. For example, he
states:
> "The historical method relativizes everything . . . in the
> sense that every moment and every construct of history can
> be conceived only in connection with others and finally with
> the whole, that the construction of every gauge of value
> cannot be based on isolated particulars but only on a survey
> of the whole *(Ueberschau des Ganzes)*. This relativizing and
> the view of the whole *(der Blick auf das Ganze)* belong
> together . . ." (id., "Methode," p. 94).

/140/   Ibid., p. 54.

/141/   Ibid., p. 62.

/142/   Ibid., p. 86.

/143/   Ibid., p. 54.

/144/   Ibid., p. 82.

/145/   Ibid., p. 63.

/146/   Id., *Absolutheit*, 2d ed., p. 58. Both this quotation and the next, which are of vital importance to this study, are interpolations that were made in the revised second edition, and are therefore not found in the first edition. This fact suggests that the idea of a creative synthesis of the absolute and the relative as a solution to the problem of the absoluteness of Christianity took on clearer shape during the period between the first and second edition of *Absoluteness*.

/147/   Ibid.

/148/   The German term "Gestaltung" is difficult to render into English. The German verb "gestalten" of which it is a nominalization is often translated as "to shape," "to form," or "to configure." It is therefore possible to translate the term as "shaping," "formation," "configuring," or "configuration." These translations, however, do not necessarily suggest the original term's intimate association with the word "Gestalt," though this association is crucial for Troeltsch's thought. Since the term "Gestaltung" not only has a specific Troeltschian meaning but also is of pivotal importance for his thought, it is best left untranslated in some cases. The specific Troeltschian meaning of this term will be further elucidated in the following.

/149/   Troeltsch, *Absolutheit*, p. x.

/150/   E. Troeltsch, "Was heißt 'Wesen des Christentums'?," *CW* 17 (1903): 443–446, 483–488, 532–536, 578–584, 650–654, 678–683; here col. 644 (hereafter cited as "Wesen").

/151/   Id., G.S. II, pp. 227–228 n. 11.

/152/   Id., *Absolutheit*, p. iv (emphasis mine).

/153/   Troeltsch, *Absolutheit*, 2d ed., p. viii (emphasis mine). Though the paragraph cited constitutes part of the foreword to the first edition of *The Absoluteness of Christianity*, comparison of the first edition with the second and third reveals that the sentence underlined in this quotation is an interpolation from the year 1912. The sentence *"in zweiter Linie darum, die jenige Gestaltung der christlichen Ideenwelt zu schaffen, die der heutigen geistigen Lage entspricht"* is therefore missing in the original text. This suggests that Troeltsch had not yet developed, at least not yet clearly, the motif of *Gestaltung* when he first published his *Absoluteness*. The interpolation does, however, also suggest that this book does contain the germ of what would lead to his subsequent *Gestaltungslehre*.

/154/   Id., "Wesen," col. 682; G.S. II, pp. vii, 860–861.

/155/   Ibid., col. 483.

/156/   Ibid., col. 484.

/157/   Ibid.

/158/   Ibid., col. 488. However, this does not mean the exclusion of the world of non-Christian religions from the scope of investigations. On the contrary, "the essence of Christianity can only be ascertained insofar as Christianity is thought of as part of an overall religious and cultural development" (ibid., col. 486). Hence the comparative history of religions and the history of culture in general must be taken into consideration.

/159/   Ibid., col. 486.

/160/   In the second version of this essay, now contained in the second volume of the *Gesammelte Schriften* (pp. 386–451), Troeltsch raised another objection to this teleological view on the basis of the results of his *Soziallehren*. There he states that the sects and mysticism also invalidate such a teleological view. While the one-sided ecclesiastical perspective on Christianity, which dominates not only Catholic but also Protestant historiography, holds Jesus, Paul, the ancient church, Catholicism, the Reformation, and modern Protestantism to be the main lines of Christian history, the sects and mysticism assert their own meaning and independent relationship to the Gospel and to original Christianity. There can be no question that they are also living forms of the Christian idea alongside its expression in the church. Or rather, from their viewpoint the 'church' in all its forms must be viewed as contrary to the essence of Christianity. Given this state of affairs, the teleological concept of the essence of Christianity also meets with critique from this quarter.

/161/   Ibid., col. 534 (emphasis original).

/162/   Ibid.

/163/   Ibid.

/164/   Ibid., col. 535.

/165/   Ibid., col. 580.

/166/   In the second, revised version Troeltsch clearly sets this forth: "The essence of Christianity has had from the beginning two distinctive accents, if not indeed two altogether distinct elements" (G.S. II, p. 416).

/167/   Id., "Wesen," col. 581. A slight change is found in the second, revised version. It reads: "the essence has to be an entity with an inner, living flexibility and a productive power for new creation and assimilation" (G.S. II, p. 418).

/168/   Ibid.

/169/   Ibid., col. 583.

/170/   Ibid.

/171/   Ibid.

/172/   Ibid., cols. 651–652.

/173/   Ibid., col. 652.

/174/   Ibid., cols. 652–653.

/175/   Ibid., col. 653.

/176/   Ibid.

/177/   Ibid., col. 654.

/178/   Ibid.

/179/   Id., G.S. II, p. 433. The original text is slightly different. It reads: "The definition of the essence is the crown of historical theology; it is the unification of the historical element of theology with the normative element" (id., "Wesen," cols. 678–679).

/180/   Id., "Wesen," col. 679.

/181/   These are, to use Troeltsch's classification, the rationalistic, the supernaturalistic, and the idealistic, evolutionary-historical solutions. The first solution assumes a self-evident, universally acknowledged judgment on the part of thinking individuals about how things ought to be and regards history as the more or less sullied execution of this idea. The second solution recognizes normative truth to reside in an authority itself recognizable by miracle, divine revelation, and institutions. The third one, proceeding from history, draws its norms from history by seeing therein the traces of objective reason. Each of these contains a grain of truth. But they all have fatal shortcomings. The first fails, according to Troeltsch, to perceive the historical conditioning of all truth and of our spiritual conditions. The second is impossible for a modern scientific mind, insofar as it appeals to the miraculous. The third wrecks not only on the folly, sinfulness, and apathy of human beings but also on the irrational and contingent factuality of history.

/182/   Troeltsch, "Wesen," col. 679.

/183/   See id., "Selbständigkeit," 5:362, 364; E. Troeltsch, "Christentum und Religionsgeschichte," Preußische Jahrbücher 87 (1897):441.

/184/   Id., G.S. II, p. 447.

/185/   Ibid.

CHAPTER II

TROELTSCH'S UNDERSTANDING OF CHRISTIAN HISTORY

Reflections on the Salient Features and Method of Troeltsch's Historical Investigations

According to Troeltsch's autobiographical sketch of his intellectual development, "his drive for knowledge was directed from the beginning toward the world of history."/1/ Along with this historical interest, however, "another, just as original interest" preoccupied his mind throughout his life, that is, "the interest in reaching a vital and effective religious position."/2/ Thus the subtle combination of this twofold interest—the one is historical, the other religious-metaphysical in nature—informs the stimulating quality of Troeltsch's thought. According to his own account, Troeltsch became a theologian because theology appeared to him to furnish the only access to metaphysics and at the same time to get one involved in exciting historical problems. "Metaphysics and history were," he says, "certainly the two stimulating problems which, from the beginning, fascinated me at one and the same time as well as in their reciprocal relation."/3/ Nevertheless, he continues to say, for him "history was, in the last analysis, only a means by which to penetrate into the core of religious-metaphysical consciousness."/4/ This observation touches the essence of Troeltsch's thought, insofar as the inner relationship between historical and systematic interests is concerned. It is true that the essential feature of Troeltsch's work was characterized—throughout his career—by "the equilibrium of historical and systematic interests."/5/ And yet all his historical research was, in the last analysis, "only intended to serve the solution of the systematic task of thinking through and formulating independently the Christian world of ideas and life with unreserved involvement in the modern world."/6/ However, to put this state of affairs positively, the historical research was *intrinsic* to the solution of the systematic problem toward which Troeltsch's real interest was directed. His historical research thereby involved "a twofold task," namely, the elucidation of "the ecclesiastical dogmatic tradition of Protestantism in its own historical sense" and the explication of "the intellectual and practical situation of the present day in its true fundamental tendencies."/7/

Closely related to Troeltsch's combination of historical and systematic interests was the contemporary and therefore ethical orientation of his historical investigations. For Troeltsch every science was bound up with the presuppositions of the thinker./8/ The study of history was no exception. "With all its striving for precision, appropriateness to the subject matter, and scholarly specification, the study of history too is," Troeltsch argues, "bound up with such presuppositions." He saw the fundamental presupposition of historical scholarship in its unavoidable correlation with "the present experience." According to Troeltsch, history becomes meaningful only from the "retrospective vantage point" that understands the causal relations of past occurrences in view of "analogy with the present-day life." That is to say, "we . . . always set the course of things in relation to the total effects which lie in the present," and that "we always draw particular or general consequences from the past *with a view to shaping the present for the future (auf unsere Gestaltung des Gegenwärtigen für die Zukunft).*" Objects lacking a bearing on the present belong to the "autiquary"; studies which completely and fundamentally set aside such a bearing are of worth only for the "dilettante."/9/ Thus, Troeltsch regarded "the understanding of the present" as "the ultimate goal of every history."/10/

Troeltsch's conflation of the historical and ethical tasks was repeatedly attacked with good reason by professional historians. B. Schmeidler, for example, criticized Troeltsch's ethicized conception of history as follows: Such a conception of history is "nothing other than a characteristic and adequate expression of the modern spirit lustful of creation" and is "diametrically opposed to the simplest understanding of the basic procedures for authentically historical creation."/11/ Accordingly, "the whole mental attitude of a man who wants to create something new for the future and to give the first impetus to it does not fit the business of an intellectual activity that intends to revive something past."/12/ Less severe, but to the same point, was F. Meinecke's criticism of Troeltsch. This celebrated historian, who was both Troeltsch's colleague and close friend at

Berlin, criticized his comrade for bringing "historical science and life" or "contemplation and creation" into too direct correlation. He argues:

> If one sets historical science directly to the task of formulating a practical cultural program as Troeltsch intends to do, then one burdens historical science all too soon with practical interests that threaten to obfuscate its genuine efforts at reaching truth./13/

Against such criticism and suspicion, Troeltsch constantly asserted that "there is no purely contemplative view of history that does not flow into the understanding of the present and the future."/14/ On the contrary, "the merely contemplative view of history is," he argues, "something unnatural and senseless" and inevitably "leads to a base *Historismus*."/15/ Whether or not Troeltsch's attempt to bridge the gap between historical scholarship and the ethical standpoint—Troeltsch considers this to be the main cause of the contemporary crisis of historical scholarship—through the creative act of the historian is justifiable in view of the practice of historical scholarship, the most important consideration for this study is that the notion of *Gestaltung*, which we have characterized as the leitmotif of Troeltsch's theology, is operative here. In any event, this contemporary and ethical orientation of Troeltsch's historical investigations as well as his subtle combination of historical and systematic (religious-metaphysical) interests indicates the *constructive* nature of his historical thought, no matter how dubious they may be in the eyes of a historian who clings to the ideal of pure empiricism.

Another, just as salient feature of Troeltsch's historical investigations is said to be his methodological novelty./16/ What, then, is his method of historical inquiry? And what is new about it? It is generally held that "the sociological formulation of the question"/17/ and the ideal-type analysis, as Troeltsch exemplified them in writing *Die Soziallehren*, inform his method in historical investigations./18/ Thus understood, Troeltsch's method is, however, nothing new in itself but "a prominent borrowing from Weber."/19/ In that case, Troeltsch's novelty and originality, if any, would lie at most in his "expansion of Weber's church-sect ideal-type construction into the scheme of church-sect-mysticism"/20/ and/or in his application of the Weberian ideal-type analysis "beyond the limits of Weber's researches, vast though they were."/21/ In fact, Troeltsch himself frankly confessed his great indebtedness to his friend, colleague,

and former cotenant at Heidelberg/22/ in an obituary tribute to this
great German sociologist as follows:

> Max Weber was one of the few great men of contempo-
> rary Germany, one of the utterly few real geniuses that I
> have met in my life. . . .
> Such a man was unable to remain without exerting
> strong influence upon others, and he gathered a great circle
> of friends of varying degrees of intimacy around him-
> self. . . . As for myself, I want only to remark that for years I
> experienced the immensely stimulating vigor of this man in
> daily communication, and that I am conscious of being
> indebted to him for a great part of my knowledge and
> ability./23/

In the autobiographical sketch of his own intellectual development,
Troeltsch reported his 'fruitful intellectual intercourse' with Weber
in greater detail:

> Because of certain new problems which forced themselves
> upon me I was carried away almost tempestuously into new
> historical investigations into the nature and history of Chris-
> tianity . . . I plunged myself into sociological studies,
> which, indeed, are less a ready knowledge than a new mode
> of observing. The whole range of ideas in the philosophy of
> history and theory of development, which had to date been
> one-sidedly ideological, as with Hegel and Dilthey, but
> which had to play so important a role in every philosophy of
> religion, was now transformed. New problems emerged out
> of all the previous solutions. At the same time I came into
> the sphere of influence of such an overwhelming personality
> as Max Weber, to whom these surprises dawning upon me
> had long since been obvious facts. And at this point I was
> captivated with the greatest force by the Marxist doctrine of
> infrastructures and superstructures. Not that I simply con-
> sidered it correct, but it does involve a mode of questioning
> which can never be evaded, . . . The formulation of the
> question, consequently, was this: To what extent is the
> origin, development, change, and modern plight of Chris-
> tianity sociologically conditioned, and to what extent is
> Christianity itself an actively forming sociological principle
> *(ein aktiv gestaltendes soziologisches Prinzip)?* These were
> extraordinarily difficult questions and scarcely any useful
> preliminary studies had been done on them. And yet it was
> no longer possible to speak of a purely dogmatic and ide-
> ological treatment of the history of Christianity, once this
> problem had been grasped./24/

Given this grandiose acknowledgment by Troeltsch himself of his indebtedness to his comrade, it is hardly possible to deny Weber's momentous influence on Troeltsch's construction of Christian history as exemplified in *Die Soziallehren*. Nevertheless, overemphasis of the Weber-Troeltsch association or simple identification of Troeltsch's historical tools with Weber's sociological method and ideal-type analysis is misleading. The final result of such moves is always either the reduction of Troeltsch to the parrot or medium of Weber or else what is bemoaned as the "Troeltschian syndrome," that is, "a misdirected focusing upon Troeltsch's use of these [church-sect] concepts in developing a 'sociological formulation' for solving a theological problem, rather than on the sociological problem itself."/25/ The latter, in turn, "leads to the misconstrual of the ideal type as a methodological device and thereby to the concomitant reification of the original constructs."/26/ In either case, it is easy to come to the conclusion, as H. Herring, for example, does, that "Troeltsch did not understand Max Weber in the depth of the latter's thought and, from his standpoint, was certainly unable to understand Weber."/27/ But such a judgment is clearly a one-sidedly distorted picture of the relationship between Weber and Troeltsch. Although at the present stage of both the Weber and the Troeltsch studies we cannot go so far as to state with certainty that "there was a genuine cross-fertilization of ideas and not merely a one-way influence"/28/ between them (such is most likely the case, though), it is clear that a bias which is from the outset in favor of Weber hardly permits an understanding of the depth of Troeltsch's thought in its own terms./29/ In view of this consideration, it must be our foremost task to identify Troeltsch's own method of historical investigations without taking Troeltsch's complete reliance on Weber for granted in advance.

In response to Felix Rachfahl, who had attacked his deviation as well as his scientific dependence on Weber with bitter sarcasm,/30/ Troeltsch wrote the following: "It is completely misleading, if it appears, as it does to Rachfahl, as if we, Weber and I, are both carrying on a common scientific business"/31/; while "Weber's study proceeds from a purely economic-historical formulation of the question" and aims at reaching a psychological-genetic understanding of certain main forms of capitalism, "my own investigations have a completely different field of material and a completely different goal of knowledge. They are essentially religious-historical investigations."/32/ In the Introduction to *Die Soziallehren* Troeltsch once again made this point very clear. There he remarked that his investigations are mainly concerned with "the formulations of the problem in principle, from the point of view of an ethical, theological, or cultural-philosophical interest," whereas Weber's work relates to "the region of sheer facts, from the standpoint of economic history and of social history."/33/ Furthermore, Troeltsch stated in *Die Soziallehren* that "his researches did not start from those of Weber." According to Troeltsch, all the previous interests independent of Weber flowed into this monumental work on the history of Christian social thought. Such were: 1) "the sociological-phenomenological interests in the conception and nature of the Church, which resulted from the well-known doctrine of Rothe" (Troeltsch's bibliographical reference is to his essay "Religion and Church"[1895]), 2) "the interests in the history of the Christian ethics" ("The Basic Problems of Ethics" [1902]), 3) "my researches into the meaning of the *lex naturae*" (a number of treatises from his initial study on the *Reason and Revelation in Johann Gerhard and Melanchthon* onwards), and finally 4) "the program which in 1901 [1900] I outlined in my review of Seeberg's *Lehrbuch der Dogmengeschichte*."/34/ These alone would be sufficient indication of the independent value of Troeltsch's historical achievements. But to convince the reader of Troeltsch's significant independence from Weber, we should like finally to call attention to Troeltsch's assessment of the worth of sociology for historical scholarship.

In *Der Historismus*, which dealt with 'the logical problem of the philosophy of history,' Troeltsch sets a limit to the extent to which sociology and the generalizing social sciences are useful tools for historical investigations. With regard to these disciplines, Troeltsch remarks:

> All these abstract-historical sciences of laws and types are for true, descriptive history indeed only auxiliary disciplines, formulations of questions, categories, models, ways to observe and to classify, but furnish in themselves no picture and understanding of the world of history at all./35/

The universal-historical construction of human history by means of sociology may be, Troeltsch thinks, a possible task. But "such a sociology is then just for this reason neither history nor the philosophy of history, but a generalizing auxiliary discipline of both."/36/

After all, "it is the historian," he says, "who shows the primordial phenomena of history to the psychologist and sociologist, and not vice versa."/37/ This view of sociology as an auxiliary, supplementary discipline to historical scholarship is strong evidence that Troeltsch's method of historical research cannot be simply identified with the Weberian sociological method.

What, then, is Troeltsch's own method of historical research? We could characterize it as a "history-of-culture method" *(kulturge-schichtliche Methode)*. As early as 1895 Troeltsch identified his method as such, saying:

> At present I am working on the most recent theology, and that according to my method, that is to say, not as the sum of book analyses but from the viewpoint of church history and the history of culture *(kirchengeschichtlich und kulturge-schichtlich)*./38/

In what relationship does this method stand with "the history-of-religions method" *(die religionsgeschichtliche Methode)*, which is generally regarded as Troeltsch's theological method? His answer was this: "The *religionsgeschichtliche* method must always be a *kulturgeschichtliche* method that, to be sure, includes the *sozialgeschichtliche* method, when the historical life in general is sufficiently known in its total phenemena."/39/ Since the modern historical method, as Troeltsch understands it, "has made every-thing fluid, mobile, and relative" and, above all, "has placed in the foreground the great cultural and intellectual contexts, on which the actual, definite sphere of governing religious structures of thought depends,"/40/ the study and assessment of Christianity must hence-forth take place "in the context of the history of religion and the history of culture."/41/ Thus Troeltsch demanded that there should be "a history of Christianity which places its object much more firmly in the general history of culture and in intellectual history, as well as in the history of the real and material presuppositions of thought" [than Harnack's *History of Dogma* did]. There is no ques-tion that Troeltsch's *Soziallehren* intended to be such "a truly dif-ferent account"/42/ of the history of Christianity. For *Die Soziallehren* was, by design, an effort "which places side by side with the eminent, essentially *ideological-dogmatic* presentation of Christianity that Harnack has produced an essentially *sociological-realistic-ethical* one."/43/ In this sense it was "a full parallel to Harnack's *History of Dogma*." In *Die Soziallehren* Troeltsch indeed "treated all religious, dogmatic and theological issues only as *the basis of their effects in social ethics* or as *a mirror and reflex of the sociological contexts*, varying in intensity according to the period."/44/ In conscious opposition to the traditional, essentially *ideological-dogmatic* account of the history of Christianity which is *"interested only in the development of the ideas of belief,"* Troeltsch thus recommended an essentially *sociological-realistic-ethical* account of Christian history which "comprehends the ethical and religious ideas in their *close relationship* with the various Christian social formations and in their *interaction* with the secular forces of society."/45/ This method, characteristic of *Die Soziallehren*, is precisely Troeltsch's own method of historical inquiry which we have characterized as the *kulturgeschichtliche* method. Such a method was admittedly "a new method of writing church history," as Roland Bainton rightly asserts./46/ It was in essence a modification of the Marxist social-historical method, though. Troeltsch accepted the Marxist doctrine of infrastructure and superstructure with qualifications. Instead of presenting the whole of Christianity exclusively as the ideological mirror-image of economic developments, he affirmed the "interaction" between the religious and the economic, the "very close, but variously mediated, fairly complicated relationships."/47/ Such a reciprocal relationship, however, implies "not only the dependence of the religious on the social, but also conversely the dependence of the social on the religious."/48/ That is to say, "the purely ideological and the sociological stand in a constant interplay."/49/ Given this mutual effect between the religious and the socio-economic, the religious-historical phenomenon of Christianity, Troeltsch argues, can be adequately understood neither from the purely dogmatic and theological viewpoint nor from the exclusive viewpoint of socio-economic developments. And yet direct correlation of both perspectives is also out of the question. Consequently, Troeltsch drew attention to "a fundamental sociological schema" *(ein soziologisches Grundschema)*,/50/ which issues from universal religious ideas and then, in some way or another, exerts an influence upon all social relationships. Then Troeltsch formulates the question as follows:

> In the first place we shall have to inquire into the intrinsic sociological idea of Christianity, and its structure and organization. This will always be found to contain an ideal of a universal fundamental schema of human relationships in

general, which will extend far beyond the borders of the
actual religious community or Church. The problem then
will be how far this fundamental schema will be able to
penetrate into actual conditions and influence them; in what
way also it will feel the reflex influence of these conditions;
and to what extent in such a situation an inner life unity can
be, or is, actually created./51/
Such a fundamental sociological schema of Christianity is, however,
nothing other than what is generally called the Christian ethos.
Hence the researcher who applies the "sociological formulation of
the question"/52/ to the whole sweep of the history of Christianity
has to undertake the task of "representing the Christian ethos in its
inner interconnection with the general history of culture."/53/ Accordingly, "research into the history of the Christian ethos"/54/
became the central theme of Troeltsch's historical investigations.
Thereby, needless to say, such historical investigations, conceived as
research into the history of the Christian ethos, stood in close
relationship with ethics.

In view of this consideration, Schmeidler's criticism of Troeltsch
to the effect that the latter's historical research runs the danger of
falling into a "teleological view of history" *(Zweckgeschichte)* or a
"tendentious view of history" *(Tendenzgeschichte)* seems to be not
without reason./55/ In the long run, Troeltsch was much too preoccupied with Christian religious interests to be just an empirical
inductive historian. Indeed, the concern "to examine the present
situation and its significance for the fate of Christianity in the
modern world"/56/ was dominant throughout his historical investigations. Nevertheless, the fact that "Troeltsch sets about this
question [concerning the present situation] above all as *a historically interested theologian, as the historian of religion,"*/57/ is not at
all a disgrace to Troeltsch, as Herring seems to hold, but rather an
honor to him. For Troeltsch himself intended, in my view, to be
precisely such a theologian and historian until his death. In any
event, Troeltsch's strong Christian religious bias never hindered his
historical investigations, but rather drove them forward. This is the
main thing.

Protestantism and the Modern World

In the preceding section we have touched on the "twofold
interest" *(Doppelseitigkeit)* of Troeltsch's historical investigations.

Such was "the analysis of early Protestantism and the analysis of the modern world."/58/ Underlying this double nature of his historical research was his central concern with "the fate of Christianity in the modern world."/59/ Troeltsch's most famous thesis in this connection, which aroused a heated discussion among scholars, was the thesis concerning the sharp distinction between "early Protestantism" *(Altprotestantismus)* and "Neo-Protestantism" *(Neuprotestantismus)*, to which another no less important thesis on the periodization of Christian history was closely related. According to Troeltsch, Luther's Reformation was in essence "a reshaping *(Umformung)* of the medieval idea" and was therefore "medieval in character."/60/ "The dominant ideas" of the Reformers grew "directly out of the continuation and the impulse of the medieval idea" and were "only new solutions of medieval problems."/61/ "The modern elements which are undeniably contained" within the Reformation came into their own only after this "initial and classical form of Protestantism" had "crumbled away or disintegrated."/62/ In contrast, "the modern world" made its first appearance "with the transition from the seventeenth to the eighteenth century," but "its real starting point" was "the eighteenth century with its great conflicts and triumphs."/63/ That is to say, "the Enlightenment," not the Renaissance or the Reformation, was "the beginning and foundation of the intrinsically modern period of European culture and history in contrast to the hitherto regnant ecclesiastically and theologically determined culture."/64/ With the rise of the modern world, however, the context which the Reformers and their immediate successors had presupposed disappeared and, as a result of this disappearance of the presupposed context, Protestantism had to undergo deep-seated changes. In view of this shift in the context and its radical impact upon Protestantism, Troeltsch formulated the difference between pre-modern or classical Protestantism and modern Protestantism as follows:

> The early, authentic Protestantism of Lutheranism and Calvinism is, despite its anti-Catholic doctrine of salvation, through and through an ecclesiastical culture in the medieval sense, as far as it is seen in its total phenomenon. It intends to regulate the state and society, education and science, the economic and the juridical systems, according to the supernatural standards of revelation. And, as did the Middle Ages, it incorporates the conception of the *lex natu-*

rae within its own general framework, by considering the *lex naturae* as originally identical with the law of God. In contrast, modern Protestantism, beginning with the end of the seventeenth century, is everywhere transplanted to the ground of the nondenominational, or even religiously indifferent, state. It transferred in principle the whole activity of religious organization and the formation of religious communities to the realm of voluntarism and personal conviction. It did so under the influence of the basic acknowledgment of both the fact and the possibility of a pluralism of religious convictions and communities existing side by side. Furthermore, it acknowledged in principle the fact of a fully emancipated secular life existing alongside itself—a life that it no longer attempted to dominate either directly or indirectly through the intervention of the state. In connection with this it forgot, even to the point of complete lack of understanding, its old doctrine making possible and promoting this dominance, the identity of the *lex dei* and the *lex naturae*./65/

Hence Troeltsch asserted that "it is necessary for any genuinely historical consideration . . . to *distinguish clearly between early Protestantism and neo-Protestantism.*"/66/ He proposed this "fundamental thesis" as "the presupposition for any historical understanding of Protestantism."/67/

However, this seemingly negative assessment of the Reformation by Troeltsch does not necessarily mean its devaluation. Troeltsch, for instance, saw a much stronger potency of sociological productivity *(soziologische Produktivität)*/68/ in the Reformation than in the Renaissance. He argues:

> Individualism of the Renaissance is really a complete autonomy of the subject liberated from authority, who exercises full freedom in his artistic contemplation and is merely bound to the rules of logic in his intellectual activity. . . . Exactly for this reason, the Renaissance is, however, sociologically utterly unproductive. It is anarchistic and aristocratic in its smallest circles; otherwise it is completely dependent on the existing forces in the state and the church. Sociologically speaking, it creates the aristocracy of the educated and the salon but otherwise does homage to force and power. In contrast to this, individualism of the Reformation is only an internalization and spiritualization of the genuinely objective, supernaturally obligatory realities; it is by no means an unconditional religious autonomy. But for this very reason the sociological energy of the Reformation is quite extraordinary. It creates the territory churches

of Lutheranism and Calvinism. . . . It promotes the religious cohesion of the mass people. . . . And it fights against
heterodox governments for civil rights and the freedom of
faith. /69/

This fundamental difference between the Renaissance and the Reformation is, according to Troeltsch, best represented by the contrast of their ideal human types. While the Refomation combined
world affirmation and asceticism in its concept of vocation
(*Berufsbegriff*), the Renaissance knew no such concept.

> The ideal of the Renaissance is a man without vocation (*der*
> *berufslose Mensch*), who, either through dependence on
> ruling forces, through pension, or through his own exploita-
> tion of dominion, acquires freedom of developing and carry-
> ing through his own self in the universality of his strength
> and talent. Its goal is the *uomo universale*, der *galantuomo*,
> a man of intellectual freedom and education; this [ideal
> human type] is just the opposite of the man of vocation and
> profession (*Berufs- und Fachmensch*) [of the Reforma-
> tion]. /70/

This contrast between the *uomo universale* (or *der universale*
Bildungsmensch/71/) and the *Berufs- und Fachmensch* expresses
well the difference in potency of sociological productivity between
the Renaissance and the Reformation. Troeltsch's conclusion from
the above consideration was this: "the religious innovation of the
Reformation was by far the stronger principle"/72/; "the sociological
formative impulse and the forming power" (*der soziologische*
Bildungstrieb und die Formungskraft) of the Renaissance, in contrast, was "much too weak,"/73/ for the educated aristocracy of the
Renaissance had to "bear of sociological necessity something parasitic"/74/ in itself.

This being the case, how, then, can Troeltsch's emphasis on the
medieval character of Luther and his Reformation be related to such
a high assessment of the Reformation's potency of sociological productivity? This question touches a subtle point in Troeltsch's understanding of Christian history. Troeltsch did affirm the modern element in the Reformation. For instance, he argues as follows:

> Now, to be sure, throughout all of this "the New" (*das Neue*)
> must not be overlooked—that which Protestantism brought
> about and by means of which it became at least to some
> extent the creator of the modern world. But these new
> elements need throughout and first of all the dissolution of

their close connection with the Reformation's supernatural
ideas of the Church, authority, and culture, . . . in order
really to operate as "the New" in principle./75/

He continues to argue:

> . . . the new elements never lie, first of all, in the realm of
> general cultural effects of Protestantism. These cultural
> effects were, in the first instance, in reality limited to the
> one, but exceedingly important, fact of the severance of half
> of Europe from the Papal universal monarchy./76/

In the long run, "the really new elements are," he says, to be sought
only in "the positive religious ideas of the Reformation themselves."/77/ He spoke of "the dissolution of the concept of the
sacraments" in the authentically Catholic sense as the "central religious idea of Protestantism."/78/ All other important ideas were
consequences of this new basic idea. Such were: 1) the replacement
of magic and sacramental religion by spiritual and sentimental religion, 2) the religious individualism of universal priesthood, 3)
ethics of sentiment, 4) the affirmation of the world through the
acceptance of the concept of vocation as the central idea of Christian
ethics. Each of these four traits, reflecting the modern elements of
the Reformation, had their "common root" in "Luther's characteristic idea of God."/79/

But Troeltsch's emphasis upon these modern elements of early
Protestantism first appeared in the second edition of "Protestantisches Christentum und Kirche in der Neuzeit" (1909). In the first
edition (1906), Troeltsch's remarks on the modern elements were
merely passing comments. There he observed "ideas of the most
enormous significance"/80/ for modern thought in the doctrines of
the Reformers, but his point was rather to indicate the halfway
character of the Reformation as a modern phenomenon. For the
reference to the modern thoughts involved in the Reformers' basic
ideas was immediately followed by negative statements:

> However, the Reformers have indissolubly combined
> these fully modern thoughts with two completely un-
> modern ideas: first, with the binding of the redeeming
> knowledge of God to an absolutely objective supernatural
> authority and an ecclesiastical establishment handling this
> authority of no less supernatural character; secondly, with
> the most highly intensified doctrine of original sin, which
> isolates the Christian from the non-Christian, depreciates
> the presence of God in the creation and in the natural

goods, and permanently fixes the whole picture of the world
in the myth of the originally perfect, painless, immortal
world which is then lost and becomes sorrowful for the sake
of freedom./81/
In the second edition Troeltsch's delineation of classical Protestantism was more moderate and more well-balanced. Now he asserted
that the Reformation represents "not only a breakthrough affecting
the core of the Catholic system," but at the same time a breakthrough "in the direction that is a religious parallel to the emergent
basic tendencies of the modern world," such as intellectualism,
individualism, autonomy, immanence, and thisworldliness. Hence
he held it understandable that the religious communal life of Protestantism was "in the course of time easily combined and fused with
the modern intellectual world."/82/

Nevertheless, this new emphasis upon the modern elements of
Protestantism was still accompanied by severe qualifications. He still
spoke in the same breath of "the limitations of the congeniality [of
classical Protestantism] with the modern world." Why was Troeltsch
so negative about the Reformation? His reservations about the modern character of Protestantism were, in the last analysis, related to
his sociological-realistic-ethical orientation. Seen from this viewpoint, classical Protestantism, to be sure, still shared with medieval
Catholicism the "foregone conclusions and presuppositions (*Selbst-
verständlichkeit und Voraussetzungen*) which from the outset place
those modern tendencies of [classical] Protestantism within completely limited bounds."/83/ These facts that had been presupposed
as a matter of course by the Reformers were, in a word, "a complete
cultural idea" (*eine geschlossene Kulturidee*)/84/ of the ideal of the
Corpus Christianum. That is to say, classical Protestantism, despite
its modern elements, retained "the concept of a strictly ecclesiastical and supernatural culture"/85/ as a matter of course. In the
final analysis, classical Protestantism, especially Luther's Reformation, was "only a reforming (*Umbildung*) of Catholicism," "a continuation of the Catholic formulation of the question, to which a new
answer is given."/86/ It answered "only the old question of the
certainty of redemption." This question was, however, through and
through the old question which had been deeply engraved in our
hearts through education in Catholicism. The difference is only that
the Reformers answered this question "through reference to a simple, radical, and personal decision of faith"/87/ instead of appealing

to the hierarchical redeeming institution of the Church and to the *opus operatum* of the sacraments. But "the old basic idea of a thoroughly *authoritative, purely divine redeeming institution*" was retained by the Reformers. They "intended to reform the whole of the Church" and succeeded in errecting their own churches "only through compulsion."/88/ The reason why their churches became territorial churches is that the Reformers could carry through their ideal of the Church only with the help of the governments and therefore had to refrain from trying to accomplish their ideal beyond the boundaries of the territory. They did not, however, renounce "the idea of the Church as the supernatural redeeming institution of salvation and education" itself. They undoubtedly retained such idea and intended only to construct the Church "purely from the biblical viewpoint."/89/ The difference from Catholicism is therefore only that now the Bible took the place of the hierarchy and the miracle-working sacraments. Given this state of affairs, "the modern problem of the relationship between Church and state,"/90/ which is the most prominent feature of the modern world, did not exist for early Protestantism. The ideal of the *Corpus Christianum* remained intact. All this is, Troeltsch argues, positive evidence that classical Protestantism represented, as did medieval Catholicism, "the idea of the ecclesiastically controlled culture" *(die Idee der kirchlich geleiteten Kultur)*./91/ Hence he concludes as follows:

> All things considered, it is evident that [classical] Protestantism cannot directly mean the pioneering of the modern world. On the contrary, Protestantism appears, despite all its great new ideas, first of all, as the renovation and reinforcement of the ideal of the ecclesiastically compulsory culture *(Erneuerung und Verstärkung des Ideals der kirchlichen Zwangskultur)*, as a full reaction of medieval thought. . . ./92/

But this conclusion is not Troeltsch's final say with regard to the significance of Protestantism for the rise of the modern world. For he asserted at the same time that in view of the facts themselves "there can be no doubt" about Protestantism's having shared in the "production of the modern world." The paradoxical character of its relationship with the modern world can be deciphered only when one seeks its significant contribution to the emergence of the modern world "not in the general rebirth or rebuilding of the totality of life," but to a large extent "in the *indirect* and *unconsciously yielded*

consequences, yes, exactly in *accidental side-effects* or also in influ-
ences generated *against its will.*"/93/ Here Troeltsch took notice of
"those historical constructs which came to pass alongside classical
Protestantism and first attained their somewhat general acceptance
in Neo-Protestantism," but which "were internally sharply distinguished from classical Protestantism and had their own historical
effect": namely, "*humanistic*, historical-philological-philosophical
theology," "the free-churchly and sectarian Anabaptism," and "the
completely individualistic-subjective Spiritualism."/94/ All three of
those parallels to the Reformation involved such radical elements as
were to result in the total denial of the ecclesiastically compulsory
culture, which was the heart of the cultural philosophy of the
Reformers. For this very reason classical Protestantism felt from the
outset "an inner and fundamental opposition"/95/ to them and distinguished itself from them sharply and often with bloody violence.
These groups therefore had to undergo first "long and cruel oppres-
sion" before they "experienced the world-historical moment."/96/

> Only when Neo-Protestantism had lost sight of the idea of
> the ecclesiastical complete culture could it designate the
> moral demand of historical-philological criticism, the forma-
> tion of religious community as a free church or an associa-
> tion, and the doctrine of revelation as received in the inner
> personal conviction and illumination as the genuine Protes-
> tant principle, . . ./97/

According to Troeltsch, the decisive battle marking the turning
point from the medieval to the modern period was fought in England of the mid-seventeenth century. Thus, his argument culminates
in the depiction of the Puritan Revolution. In view of its critical
importance for a proper understanding of Troeltsch's entire argument, the paragraph concerned should be cited at full length.
Troeltsch argues as follows:

> Here [in England] these stepchildren of the Reformation
> *(Stiefkinder der Reformation)* in general eventually experi-
> enced their great world-historical moment. The Anabaptist
> idea of a free church, democratic and communist ideas,
> spiritualistic independence, pietistically radicalized Cal-
> vinism, classical ideas of Calvinism concerning the right for
> revolution, the sovereignty of the people, and the Christian
> state: all these were combined with the consequences of
> political catastrophes and the demands of old English
> rights. Out of this fusion, supported by the army of the

saints, there arose the demand for the Christian state, . . . The state of Cromwell, which obviously intended to be a Christian state, realized this idea for a short period. Though this grand construction endured only for so short a period, its world-historical effects are tremendous. For out of this prodigious episode sprang and remained such great ideas as *the separation of the Church and the state, the toleration of different religious communities existing side by side, the principle of voluntarism in the formation of the Church, the—of course in the first instance relative—freedom of conviction and opinion with respect to everything concerned with world-view and religion.* . . . Here the end of the medieval cultural idea is effected, and the beginning of the modern, ecclesiastically free, individual culture takes the place of the compulsory culture of the state church. . . . The English [Puritan] Revolution pioneered the way for the modern freedom with its religious energy. However this is not the work of Protestantism but a work of the Anabaptism and Spiritualism which were revived and fused with radicalized Calvinism. They received thereby too late a reward for the exorbitant sufferings which this religion of tolerance and moral conviction had to go through from all confessions in the sixteenth century./98/

The paragraph cited here involves the gist of Troeltsch's whole argument in question. First, Troeltsch regards England, not his homeland Germany, as the geographical locus in which the transition from the medieval to the modern period took place. Second, he considers neither the Reformers of the sixteenth century nor their lineal successors (Lutheranism and Calvinism), but the so-called "stepchildren of the Reformation" (humanistic theology, Anabaptism, and Spiritualism) to have played the leading part of the production of the modern world. Third, he sees the hallmark of the modern culture in such principles as the separation of Church and state, toleration, voluntarism in the formation of religious communities, freedom of conviction and opinion. Thereby he points out that these principles were produced in the Puritan Revolution by Cromwell. Fourth, he characterizes the turning to the modern period as a shift from the ecclesiastical compulsory culture to the modern ecclesiastically free, individual culture. Seen against the background of the third and the fourth points, Troeltsch's emphasis on the medieval character of early Protestantism is quite understandable. The main reason for this judgment is that Troeltsch finds "the idea of the ecclesiastically controlled culture" or the ideal of the

Corpus Christianum in the Reformers. Conversely, modernity, as Troeltsch understands it, implies both the disappearance of the previous context in which such "a complete cultural idea" held good as a foregone conclusion and the emergence of a new context in which the principle of the separation of Church and state gains currency./99/ The impact of this shift in the context was really drastic on modern Christianity. The full range of the impact, to be sure, is properly measured only when the sociological dimensions of this profound change are taken into account. But this is only possible for such sociologically-realistically-ethically oriented historical investigations as Troeltsch recommended. Thus, his method of historical research clearly had the advantage over the purely ideological-dogmatic method that it can cope with the difficult sociological questions concerning Christianity's involvement in the modern world. But historical research as such cannot solve the religious, theological, and metaphysical problems involved in such an involvement, no matter what method it employs. Historical research clarifies the context in which the problem requires a new solution, but the solution belongs to the specific business of systematic theological thought. Therefore, our next task must be an examination of Troeltsch's systematic achievements. Before we set about this task, however, we must discuss Troeltsch's analysis of the modern world more in detail. For all his systematic endeavors were attempts to rescue Christianity from its disfranchisement in the modern world.

The Modern Impasse of Christianity

As we have just seen, Troeltsch's thesis concerning the distinction between classical Protestantism and modern Protestantism implied a profound shift in the social and cultural context from the eighteenth century onward.

> With the eighteenth century, church history as a whole entered upon a new phase of existence *(unter neue Bedingungen)*. As a result of the dissolution of the unity of cultural life controlled by a state church, combined with the development of the independence of modern thought, it has since then no longer possessed a unified and fixed object./100/

Troeltsch's insistence on the replacement of the "ideological-dogmatic" treatment of Christian history by the "sociological-realistic-ethical" treatment of it as well as his advocacy of the *kulturgeschichtliche* method as a new appropriate method of writing church history, to be sure, finds its justification in the deep-seated changes in the modern context. However, the recommendation of the "sociological-realistic-ethical" treatment of Christian history itself presupposed as its starting point the modern predicament of Christianity./101/ The application of the *kulturgeschichtliche* method to its history only confirmed the impression, to use Reist's arresting expression, that Christianity "is involved in the modern world as a disenfranchised alien seeking for a home in a strange, new land with no possibility of return to familiar and comfortable surroundings."/102/ Seen from the sociological and cultural-historical viewpoint, the Enlightenment of the eighteenth century marked the real beginning of the intrinsically modern world. (Thereby the English Puritan movement of the seventeenth century was regarded as the transition from the medieval to the modern period.) Thus understood, the modern world from the outset involves, however, ominous implications for Christianity. Since the Enlightenment represents, in Troeltsch's opinion, not only "the first comprehensive and fundamental opposition to the dualistic-supernatural form of religion" but also "a total revolution of culture in the all realms of life,"/103/ the modern world is first of all characterized in its negative aspect as "the break with the ecclesiastical authoritative culture."/104/ Though this negative formulation should not be taken as denoting that the modern world took its rise in "the unitary and substantial opposition to the Christianity that dominated the older world,"/105/ it is undeniable that the modern world is no longer under the hands of the Church. What this simple fact implies is that the modern world lacks "the unity of origin and development." This is so because the modern world is, unlike the immediately preceding ages, no longer governed by a "single authoritative thought that can make everything bow before itself."/106/ In this view, the Enlightenment admittedly marked "not the beginning but the end of the European cultural unity."/107/ In any case, the modern world has "no unified principle," but knows only "an abundance of concurring, but at the same time contradictory developments."/108/

> Accordingly, all unitary constructions of the modern world from a *single* standpoint are likewise impossible, whether it be from the standpoint of anti-Christianity, individualism, this-worldliness, and immanence, or from that of

the pure progress or the disintegrating process of obsolete
cultures./109/

Given this state of affairs, one can only enumerate several
prominent features of the modern world. As such prominent features Troeltsch specifies: the expansion of the states and surrounding
worlds, combined with the increase in traffic and population; individualism based on the recognition of the supreme value of the
individual; this-worldliness in political and cultural activities; the
remarkable enhancement of criticism and scientific reflection; the
technical control of nature and its utilization in economic rationaliza-
tion; optimistic humanism; the construction of a powerful state with
its possible strongest national unity; the general world-view of the
continual and monistic world-process; and finally, above all, spiritual
freedom or the autonomy of thinking and moral action./110/ Thus he
considered both individualism and autonomy the most prominent
traits of the modern world, as far as the modern intellectual and
cultural climate is concerned. These two principles were tolerated
by the Christian standpoint as long as they remembered their
Christian religious origins. But as they were secularized to the point
of completely forgetting their religious roots, they became simply
the opposition to Christianity in any of its forms. After the eclipse of
"a definite epoch essentially determined by religious ideas," the
pendulum has now swung toward "an essentially secularly minded
and religiously weak epoch." Thus the modern world implies,
Troeltsch says, "a serious religious crisis."/111/ The question then
arises: What is the destiny of Christianity in the totally transformed
modern world? Does Christianity still have a future in its present
estrangement? Or, is it destined to be replaced by a new religion
that the modern world produces? Troeltsch formulated the question
in the following manner: a decision must be made "between no
religion, restoration of confessionalism, free further development of
Christianity, and the formation of a completely new religion."/112/
Troeltsch's own position as to this question was throughout very
decided. He maintained that "no matter what the modern world
may have brought about, it has not created something really new
(*wahrhaft Neues*) in the realm of religious life and can only shape
afresh (*neu gestalten*) the old possession." Hence, as seen in the
preceding chapter, the "shaping of Christianity for the future"
(*Zukunftsgestaltung des Christentums*) or the "new formation of the
Christian world of life" (*Neuformung der christlichen Lebenswelt*)

became Troeltsch's life-long program./113/ But exactly at this point, where the possibility of a "free Christianity" is at stake, the problem of his own theological position is also disclosed.

According to Troeltsch, "the modern world has perfectly done its work of shattering old religious restraints. But it *has not brought about any kind of really new strength.*"/114/ Consequently, Christianity should always be in the center of any discussion about the future of religion in the Western world. He was convinced that "a religious spirit that is proper to the modern world" has been nurtured on the Protestant ground./115/ In this respect he took notice of both "an essentially practical, dogmatically conservative, but not strongly interested Protestantism" of the Anglo-American countries and "the forces of German Idealism standing in close relation to Protestantism"/116/ on the Continent. Hence he concluded that "the religion of conviction and conscience of Protestant personalism is the religiosity that is congenial and corresponds to the modern individualistic culture."/117/ He also put the matter a bit differently as follows:

> The best [thing that the modern world has brought about] is a Christian spirit which, based upon the exclusively inner certainty of the revelation of God, nurtures and strengthens this certainty by means of history and causes an ethical deepening and renovation of both an individual and a corporate personality in the faith in this revelation./118/

However, to put the matter this way admittedly runs the risk of an impasse. For such a historical judgment implies, to use Troeltsch's famous three sociological types of the Christian idea, the endorsement of the priority of "Mysticism" over "the Church" and "the Sect" in the modern and contemporary context, because such a religion of conviction and conscience as Troeltsch recommends is nothing other than Spiritualism belonging to this Mysticism. At this point an attentive reader of Troeltsch's work would realize that two non-historical moments were at the same time at work on this historical judgment. The first moment at work is Troeltsch's *personal* religious position, whose mystical-spiritualistic bent is attested by Troeltsch himself and others./119/ The second is his *theological* interest in the possibility of a "free Christianity" (*freies Christentum*). An intimate religion of personal conviction, as Troeltsch endorses it, turns out to be identical with what Troeltsch outlined as the "essence" of free Christianity./120/ When these personal and theological interests are combined with a historical insight into the history of Christian thought, there arises what Troeltsch calls "my thesis," that is, the thesis that "modern philosophy of religion and theology stand, in the scientific construction of thought, in much closer relation to Spiritualism than they do to Luther's objective authoritative theology of the word and the natural religion of the Enlightenment."/121/ The reason why such a thesis runs the risk of an impasse is well documented in *Die Soziallehren*. First of all, Mysticism as the third type of Christian sociological forms, to which such a Spiritualism belongs, is completely *parasitic* in character.

> Mysticism in the widest sense of the word is nothing other than the pressing toward the direct, inner, and present character of religious experience. It presupposes the objectivizing of the religious life in cult, rites, myths, or dogmas, and it is either a reaction against this objectivizing, which it seeks to take back anew into the living process, or it is a supplementation *(Ergänzung)* of the traditional cult by means of a personal and living stimulus. Mysticism is thus always something intentionally reflective./122/

Second, this third type is "a radical individualism"/123/ and therefore lacks the "organizational impulse."/124/

> . . . Mysticism does not press toward a relationship of person to person, but toward a relationship to God. It turns all the historical, the authoritative, and the cultic into merely means of religious stimulation, which it can do without if need be. In particular, Spiritualism, in its intense emphasis upon first-hand experience, actually sweeps away the historical element altogether, and in so doing it eliminates the only center around which a Christian cult can be formed. Thus Spiritualism becomes ahistorical, cultless, and unsocial . . ./125/

Consequently, the third type is sociologically *impotent*.

> . . . of itself Spiritualism has no social effect on the general public. Its intimate circles do not penetrate into the mass, and its purely contemplative thought does not take hold in the common life, but works in a purely personal fashion or hovers in a literary manner over the whole. . . . It accompanies social conditions, but does not proceed out of them, nor does it influence them directly. Indirectly, however, the fact that it weakens the power and exclusiveness of the Church means that it has a very important social influence./126/

This being the case, to give priority to the Spiritualism of the third type, as Troeltsch did, implies a serious dilemma. Troeltsch, to be sure, was well aware of this dilemma. For instance, he remarks:

> The so-called *religionsgeschichtliche Schule* turns back completely to Spiritualism, and is, therefore, ecclesiastically "impotent." My theology is certainly spiritualistic, but for that very reason it seeks to make room for the historical element, and for the cultic and sociological factor bound up with it. Naturally I am well aware of the difficulties of such an undertaking./127/

Hence he spells out:

> The modern educated class . . . understands in general only Spiritualism. This is at the same time a reflection of the radical, atomizing individualism of modern culture in general, an individualism which, in the non-religious sphere of life, already begins to give in and change into its opposite. With the sublimation of community, cult, history, and social ethics, this Spiritualism, in spite of all the depth and inwardness of its thought, is also a weakening of the religious life, though this religious life must be upheld by the Church and the Sect in its concrete fullness of life so that an entirely individualistic Mysticism can spiritualize it at all. Thus, and one may not conceal it, this style of Christianity, which alone meets the needs of the modern educated class, presupposes alongside itself the continuation of other and more concrete Christian formations of life, and it can never be for all./128/

Whether one sees here Troeltsch's concession to the established Christian formations of the first and the second types or his matured wisdom of keeping the balance, the question for him was, in any case, a fusion of Church, Sect, and Mysticism. He boldly asserts:

> In the reciprocal penetration of the three basic sociological forms and their unification into a structure reconciling all these motifs lie the future tasks of Protestantism, tasks of a sociological-organizational nature which are more urgent than all the tasks of dogmatics./129/

The central problem here, as Troeltsch understands it, is concerned with the relationship between the Christian message whose ideal is, in his view, in essence transworldly, and historical and cultural values of this world. Troeltsch's typical stance on this question deserves special attention at this point. He was of opinion that:

> The Ethos of the gospel is an ideal which requires a new
> world if it is to be fully realized; it is this new world-order
> that Jesus proclaimed in his message of the Kingdom of
> God. But this is an ideal which cannot be realized within
> this world apart from compromise. Therefore the history of
> the Christian Ethos becomes the story of a constantly re-
> newed search for this compromise, and of fresh opposition
> to this spirit of compromise./130/

Troeltsch's trichotomy of Church, Sect, and Mysticism had mainly to
do with this question of the relationship to the world and its inevitable concomitant, compromise./131/ Accordingly, when a conflation
of the three sociological types is in question, the question of a new
compromise or a new supplementation naturally comes to the fore
(supplementation is the positive and creative aspect of compromise).
Troeltsch thereby considered supplementation of religious
onesidedness by means of an ethic of culture to be necessary. He
argues:

> Today, however, in the midst of a completely new cultural
> situation, the achievements of old supplementary processes
> have become impossible. A new supplementation *(eine neue
> Ergänzung)* is therefore necessary. The Christian Ethos
> cannot live for itself alone and be sufficient in a continuing
> world. The question now is: How can this supplement be
> shaped today? Here lies the task of a new Christian eth-
> ics./132/

Hence arose Troeltsch's program of "a Christian-social mastering of
the situation." For the purpose of realizing this program he called
for "new thoughts which have not yet been thought, and which
correspond to this situation." He asserted that such new thoughts
have to be developed "out of the inner impulse of the Christian idea
and its living and present new shaping *(lebendig-gegenwärtigen
Neugestaltung)*, and not solely out of the New Testament."/133/

Now sufficient documents are before us to enable us to make
our judgment on Troeltsch's historical achievements. In what follows, we shall in the main only confirm our previous judgments
made in the course of our discussion, especially in the opening
section of this chapter. First of all, what Troeltsch said about his
supposedly main work, *Die Soziallehren,* applies to the whole of his
historical achievements. As *Die Soziallehren* was for him "a preparatory work and not my real work,"/134/ so did all his historical
investigations have only preparatory and preliminary significance for

his systematic interest. His major concern in the realm of historical studies was, in the last analysis, to reach "something lasting and eternal" which might serve as "a guiding star for the present and for the future, something which would aid us not merely to understand *(Begreifen)* but also to shape *(Gestalten)* the situation./135/ This is precisely what we have characterized as Troeltsch's contemporary and ethical orientation. The paragraph just cited also shows, in the second place, where Troeltsch's systematic interest lay and what it was. His systematic concern, which all his historical investigations aimed at serving, was to carry through the program of a free Christianity. Thereby the problem of a new shaping and new formulation of Christianity *(Neugestaltung des Christentums)* came to the fore. In this connection genetic studies of Protestantism and the modern world not only informed Troeltsch of the distinction between classical Protestantism and modern Protestantism but also attested the necessity and the legitimacy of "the second act of Protestantism, which corresponds to the totally changed overall situation." Corroborated by historical investigations, he then elevated this *de facto* distinction to the *de jure* distinction. He asserted: with the advocacy of the free Christianity "we are doing only the same thing as classical Protestantism did, that is, we are formulating a new expression of the essence" of Christianity "with a living involvement in the historical forces of the present day"; "Neo-Protestantism" is indeed "nothing other than the attempt to formulate anew the essence of Christianity."/136/ (The legitimacy of such a bold assertion will be discussed in Chapter V.) Finally, Troeltsch's dilemma must be indicated here. His dilemma, which implies also the modern impasse of Christianity, is, in my view, attributable to his personal adhesion to Spiritualism. That is to say, Troeltsch characterized the third type (Mysticism) as not only derivative and parasitic in character but also sociologically impotent; nevertheless, he attempted "a Christian-social mastering of the situation" with special emphasis being laid upon the Spiritualism of the third type for the reason that Spiritualism is "the religiosity that is congenial and corresponds to the modern individualistic culture." This is obviously a dilemma—a dilemma which, in my judgment, was fatal to his entire scientific endeavor. Furthermore, how is "the reciprocal penetration" of Church, Sect, and Mysticism possible? On what conceptual basis can a new supplementary process, as Troeltsch attempted to perform, take place? Is "a Christian-social mastering of the situation" possible at all? If so, what "new thoughts" are necessary for its actualization? All these questions lead us to another realm of Troeltsch's investigations, namely, the realm of systematic and constructive reflection. Final assessment of Troeltsch's achievements is possible only after close examination of his systematic works. But if a "systematic unified thought" underlies all his work, including his historical studies, then our observation in this chapter certainly suggests not only the vigor but also the vulnerability of this "*enfant terrible*" of Protestant theology.

NOTES

/1/ Troeltsch, G.S. IV, p. 3.

/2/ Id., *Überwindung*, p. 63; cf. *Christian Thought*, p. 5.

/3/ Id., G.S. IV, p. 4.

/4/ Ibid., p. 5.

/5/ Id., G.S. II, p. 754.

/6/ Id., G.S. I, p. viii.

/7/ Ibid., p. vii.

/8/ For this reason Troeltsch regarded Max Weber's idea of *Wertfreiheit* as "utterly impossible" (id., G.S. III, p. 49 n. 21).

/9/ E. Troeltsch, *Die Bedeutung des Protestantismus für die Entstehung der modernen Welt,* Historische Bibliothek, vol 24 (Munich and Berlin: Druck und Verlag von R. Oldenbourg, 1911; reprint ed., Aalen: Otto Zeller Verlagsbuchhandlung, 1963), p. 5 (hereafter cited as *Bedeutung*).

/10/ Ibid., p. 6.

/11/ B. Schmeidler, "Zur Psychologie des Historikers und zur Lage der Historie in der Gegenwart," *Preußische Jahrbücher* 202 (1925):232.

/12/ Ibid., p. 237.

/13/ F. Meinecke, *Friedrich Meinecke Werke,* vol. 4: *Zur Theorie und Philosophie der Geschichte,* ed. E. Kessel (Stuttgart: K. F. Koehler Verlag, 1965), p. 378.

/14/ Troeltsch, G.S. III, p. 70.

/15/ Ibid., p. 68.

/16/ Because of its methodological novelty Roland H. Bainton regards Troeltsch's *Soziallehren* as "a pioneer endeavor of abiding significance."

According to Bainton, Troeltsch introduced "a new method of writing church history with a view to the impact of Christianity upon civilization and particular cultures." With regard to this point, Bainton argues as follows:

> "Troeltsch, to be sure, was not absolutely original—who ever is?—for he learned much from his colleague Max Weber. . . . But Troeltsch brought to the execution of the task much deeper grounding in philosophy and theology and for that reason may properly be regarded as the inaugurator of a new method in the field of church history" (R. H. Bainton, "Ernst Troeltsch—Thirty Years Later," *Theology Today* 8 [1951]:70).

/17/   Troeltsch, G.S. I, p. viii.

/18/   Reist, for example, takes this commonly held view as a matter of course. Cf. Reist, *Toward a Theology of Involvement*, pp. 106–141.

/19/   R. J. Rubanowice, *Crisis in Consciousness: The Thought of Ernst Troeltsch*, with a Foreword by J. L. Adams (Tallahassee: University Press of Florida, 1982), p. 45.

/20/   Ibid., pp. 46–47.

/21/   Reist, *Toward a Theology of Involvement*, p. 113.

/22/   The friendship between Weber and Troeltsch seems to have begun shortly after the former moved to Heidelberg in 1897 to become professor of economics. But since Weber was ill from 1898 to 1902, their close relationship might have started around 1902. Troeltsch's first reference to Weber is in the preface of *Political Ethics and Christianity* (1904). In the summer of the same year Weber and Troeltsch travelled together to the United States to attend the "Scientific World Congress" held in St. Louis. Their friendship deepened after this trip. In the spring of 1910, they began to share a large old house situated on the Neckar river, Weber taking the second and Troeltsch the third floor. Their cohabitation ended when Troeltsch left for Berlin early in the spring of 1915. On the unhappy end of their friendship, see Eduard Baumgarten, *Max Weber: Werk und Person* (Tübingen: J. C. B. Mohr, 1964), p. 624; W. Pauck, *Harnack and Troeltsch*, pp. 73–75.

/23/   E. Troeltsch, "Max Weber," in *Deutscher Geist und Westeuropa: Gesammelte kulturphilosophische Aufsätze und Reden*, ed. Hans Baron (Tübingen: J. C. B. Mohr, 1925; reprint ed., Aalen: Scientia Verlag, 1966), pp. 247–249.

/24/   Id., G.S. IV, pp. 10–11.

/25/   W. H. Swatos, Jr., "Weber or Troeltsch?: Methodology, Syndrome, and the Development of Church-Sect Theory," *Journal for the Scientific Study of Religion* 15 (1976):129.

/26/ Ibid., p. 130. In using the charge of the "Troeltschian syndrome"
Swatos blames subsequent 'church-sect' theorists for their misidentification
of "what Troeltsch himself calls a 'sociological formulation' of a theological
question" with "Weber's attempt to solve a sociological problem" (ibid., p.
133). Thus, he is not accusing Troeltsch with this charge. Instead, he
appreciates "the uniqueness of Troeltsch's contribution" (ibid.). His main
point is to call attention to "the difference between the two men's projects,"
so that "Weber's methodological contribution" may receive due recognition
(ibid., p. 134). Nevertheless, Swatos seems to imply that Troeltsch is partly
to be blamed for this "Troeltschian syndrome."

/27/ H. Herring, "Max Weber und Ernst Troeltsch," *Kantstudien* 59
(1968):433. It should be noted that this negative judgment of Troeltsch by
Herring is closely related to the latter's negative view of theology and
metaphysics. I agree with Herring when he asserts that the fundamental
difference between Weber and Troeltsch is that Troeltsch was, in the last
analysis, "a historically interested theologian" or "the historian of religion,"
while Weber was a social scientist who tried to reach objectively valid
knowledge in historical sciences. Troeltsch's academic endeavor, to be sure,
was directed not to the "investigation of the European social and economic
life from the viewpoint of its cultural and material grounds" but to the
"explication of the contemporary situation of Christianity" (ibid., p. 424).
His "inclination to metaphysics" (ibid.), as Herring indicates, is also undeniable. But all these facts are not the reason for the devaluation of Troeltsch's
endeavor. Such a devaluation reflects rather the general anti-metaphysical
and anti-theological trend of the day which Herring shares. Interesting in
this connection is Gertrud von le Fort's testimony concerning the relationship between Troeltsch and Weber. She wrote: "his [Troeltsch's] ultimate tie with Christianity disturbed his relation to his otherwise highly
respected friend Max Weber from time to time" (G. v. le Fort, *Hälfte des
Leben: Erinnerungen* [Munich: Ehrenwirth Verlag, 1965], p. 89). If this is
the case, it might be possible to reverse Herring's bold assertion and to
assert that Weber did not and could not understand Troeltsch in the depth
of his thought. However, this kind of argument is simply nonsense. Suffice
it to say that Weber and Troeltsch differed from each other in their ultimate
concerns.

/28/ Rubanowice, *Crisis in Consciousness, p. 45.*

/29/ Owing to lack of insight into theological and metaphysical problems,
Herring certainly did not uinderstand the depth of Troeltsch's thought. The
same is true of H. S. Hughes's well-received book. Hughes's biased judgment is, for example, documented in the following:
    "Besides the fact that Troeltsch was obviously Weber's intel-
    lectual inferior, there was the further difficulty that the
    former was dealing with material in which his own religious
    faith, his own value-system, were deeply involved. Unlike
    Weber, he was in no position to pursue the full relativist

implications of his method, to treat Christianity in as detached a fashion as though it were the religion of China" (H. S. Hughes, *Consciousness and Society* [Revised ed., New York: Vintage Books, 1977], p. 236). Apart from such bias, Hughes's view of Troeltsch is obviously based on secondhand sources, not on a firsthand reading of Troeltsch's writings.

/30/ F. Rachfahl, "Kalvinismus und Kapitalismus," *Internationale Wochenschrift für Wissenschaft, Kunst und Technik* 3 (1909); now reprinted in *Max Weber. Die protestantische Ethik*, vol. 2: *Kritiken und Antikritiken*, ed. Johannes Winckelmann (Gütersloh: Gütersloher Verlagshaus Gerd Mohn, 1982), p. 57–148.

/31/ Troeltsch, G.S. IV., p. 785.

/32/ Ibid., pp. 785–786.

/33/ Id., G.S. I, p. 15 n. 9.

/34/ Ibid., p. 950 n. 510.

/35/ Id., G.S. III, p. 66.

/36/ Ibid., p. 715.

/37/ Ibid., pp. 45–46.

/38/ Troeltsch to Bousset, 23 July 1895, "Briefe an Bousset," p. 29.

/39/ E. Troeltsch, *Augustin, die christliche Antike und das Mittelalter: Im Anschluß an die Schrift "De Civitate Dei,"* Historische Bibliothek 36 (Munich and Berlin: Druck und Verlag von R. Oldenbourg, 1915; reprint ed., Aalen: Scientia Verlag, 1963), pp. v–vi.

/40/ Id., G.S. IV, p. 741.

/41/ Id., G.S. II, p. 733. With regard to the relationship between the history of religions and the history of culture, Troeltsch remarks: "Without religion there is only the history of culture" ("Selbständigkeit," 6 [1896]:80). Accordingly, both must be distinguished from each other.

/42/ Ibid., p. 390.

/43/ Id., G.S. III, p. 369 n. 160 (emphasis mine).

/44/ Id., G.S. IV, pp. 11–12 (emphasis mine).

/45/ Id., G.S. II, p. 449 (emphasis mine).

/46/ Bainton, "Ernst Troeltsch—Thirty Years Later," p. 70.

/47/ Troeltsch, G.S. IV, p. 27.

/48/ Ibid., p. 32.

/49/ Ibid., p. 722.

/50/   Id., G.S. I, pp. 9–10.

/51/   Ibid., p. 14.

/52/   Ibid., p. viii.

/53/   Ibid., p. 3.

/54/   Id., G.S. II, p. 18.

/55/   Schmeidler, "Zur Psychologie des Historikers und zur Lage der Historie in der Gegenwart," pp. 234, 237.

/56/   E. Troeltsch, *Protestantism and Progress*, tr. W. Montgomery (London: Williams & Norgate, Ltd.; New York: G. P. Putnam's Sons, 1912; reprint ed., Boston: Beacon Press, 1958), p. vi.

/57/   Herring, "Max Weber und Ernst Troeltsch," p. 424 (emphasis mine).

/58/   Troeltsch, G.S. I, p. vii.

/59/   Id., *Protestantism and Progress*, p. vi.

/60/   E. Troeltsch, "Protestantisches Christentum und Kirche in der Neuzeit," in *Die Kultur der Gegenwart*, ed. Paul Hinneberg (Berlin & Leipzig: Teubner, 1906), I (IV/1): *Die christliche Religion: Mit Einschluss der israelitisch-jüdischen Religion*, p. 257. The second edition of this work is to a great extent revised and enlarged. Consequently, it is necessary to treat these two editions as different works and to give special attention to the changes between them. Reference to the first and the second edition will be respectively indicated by the shortened titles *Neuzeit* and *Neuzeit* 2d ed. Cf. E. Troeltsch, "Protestantisches Christentum und Kirche in der Neuzeit," in *Die Kultur der Gegenwart*, ed. Paul Hinneberg (Berlin & Leipzig: B. G. Teubner, 1909), I (IV/1): *Die Geschichte der christlichen Religion. Mit Einleitung: Die israelitisch-jüdischen Religion*, pp. 431–755.

/61/   Ibid., p. 258; cf. *Neuzeit*, 2d ed., pp. 438–439.

/62/   Ibid., p. 257; cf. *Neuzeit*, 2d ed., p. 436.

/63/   Troeltsch, "Religionswissenschaft und Theologie des 18. Jahrhunderts," *Preußische Jahrbücher* 114 (1903):32.

/64/   Id., G.S. IV, p. 338.

/65/   Id., *Bedeutung*, p. 25.

/66/   Ibid., p. 26 (emphasis mine).

/67/   Id., *Neuzeit*, p. 257; cf. *Neuzeit*, 2d ed., p. 436.

/68/   Id., G.S. IV, p. xxiii.

/69/   Ibid., p. 276.

/70/   Ibid., p. 281.

/71/ Ibid., p. 282.

/72/ Ibid., p. 286.

/73/ Ibid., p. 287.

/74/ Ibid., p. 288.

/75/ Id., *Neuzeit*, 2d ed., p. 454; cf. *Neuzeit*, p. 266.

/76/ Ibid., p. 455. Both this and the next paragraphs are lacking in the first edition.

/77/ Ibid.

/78/ Ibid., p. 456; cf. *Neuzeit*, p. 266.

/79/ Ibid., p. 466. With regard to these points, Troeltsch's revision and enlargement in the second edition are considerable. He has now assigned about sixteen pages (originally only two pages) to the delineation of the modern elements of early Protestantism. This shift seems to suggest that Troeltsch admitted that his emphasis on the medieval character of Luther and his Reformation in the first edition had been somewhat too onesided. With all this new emphasis on the modern elements of early Protestantism, however, Troeltsch's overall judgment of it remained the same in the second edition.

/80/ Id., *Neuzeit*, p. 268. As such ideas, Troeltsch enumerates the following:

> "It is the inner, personal, and spiritual character of religion; the autonomy, freedom, and wholeness of the morality arising out of surrender to God; it is the immanence and presence of God in his world and the consecration of all the natural as a divinely willed component of his creation; the overcoming of the evil will purely through knowledge of the divine determination of holiness and grace" (ibid.).

/81/ Ibid. Here Troeltsch's formulation admittedly suffers, as Reist justly criticizes him, from the limits of his own theological persuasion. But it is obviously unfair that Reist did not pay any attention to Troeltsch's much more positive assessment of the Reformer's thought as set forth in the second edition. Cf. Reist, *Toward a Theology of Involvement*, p. 99.

/82/ Id., *Neuzeit*, 2d ed., p. 470.

/83/ Ibid.

/84/ Ibid., p. 442; cf. *Neuzeit*, p. 261.

/85/ Id., *Bedeutung*, p. 26.

/86/ Ibid., p. 32.

/87/ Ibid., p. 33.

/88/   Ibid., p. 34.

/89/   Ibid., p. 35.

/90/   Ibid., pp. 35–36.

/91/   Ibid., p. 37.

/92/   Ibid., p. 44.

/93/   Ibid., p. 45 (emphasis mine).

/94/   Ibid., pp. 26–27. In the original version of this study as an article (1906), Troeltsch did not yet clearly distinguish between "Anabaptism" and "Spiritualism." There, for instance, he spoke of "the two," namely, both humanistic theology and "Anabaptism and Spiritualism," instead of "the three." He also used such expressions as "the Anabaptist-enthusiastic and Spiritualistic theories" and "Anabaptist subjectivism" (E. Troeltsch, "Die Bedeutung des Protetantismus für die Entstehung der modernen Welt," *Historische Zeitschrift* 97 [1906]:15–16, 28). The latter is, however, rephrased as "Anabaptist sectarian ideal" and "mystical subjectivism" in the second book version of the year 1911. Here "the Anabaptist-sectarian groups" and "mystics and Spiritualists" are clearly distinguished (*Bedeutung*, p. 28). This fact seems to suggest that Troeltsch did not yet clearly distinguish between the "sect-type" and "mysticism" in the year 1906.

/95/   Id., *Bedeutung*, p. 27.

/96/   Ibid., p. 28.

/97/   Ibid., p. 27.

/98/   Ibid., pp. 62–64 (emphasis original). Troeltsch's depiction of the 'English Revolution of 1649' in "The English Moralists of the 17th and 18th Centuries" (1903) did not yet appreciate the significant contribution of these "stepchildren of the Reformation" to this Revolution. Although he did already mention Spiritualism and Anabaptism, he ascribed the major significance for the Puritan Revolution to Calvinism (id., G.S. IV, pp. 394–400).

/99/   Indeed Troeltsch regards "the separation or at least the tendency toward *the separation of the state and the Church* as an essential feature of the modern religious situation" (id., G.S. IV, p. 328).

/100/   Id., G.S. I, p. 965. Here, as at many other points, the English translation by Olive Wyon involves a serious misreading. Obviously by misinterpreting the phrase "bis zum 18. Jahrhundert" as signifying "as far as [the end of] the eighteenth century" (because *Die Soziallehren* deals with the Christian social thought of the eighteenth century too), she has rendered the phrase "mit jenem Jahrhundert," which evidently refers to the "18. Jahrhundert" in the original context, into the expression "with the nineteenth century," so that her translation reads: "*With the nineteenth century* Church History entered upon a new phase of existence" (emphasis mine). But such a reading clearly contradicts Troeltsch's own understanding of Christian history.

/101/   Cf. id., G.S. IV, pp. 739–752.

/102/   Reist, *Toward a Theology of Involvement*, p. 106.

/103/   Troeltsch, G.S. IV, p. 339.

/104/   Ibid., pp. 330, 336.

/105/   Ibid., p. 331. Troeltsch holds such a view to be "fundamentally wrong." According to him, "not atheism or pantheism" but in the main "an inspired believing theism and the amalgam of Christian and classical-philosophical ideas as prepared by the Church" are "the starting point of the modern world" (ibid., pp. 331–332). To this extent, the modern world is "not an opposition to or a derivation from the ecclesiastical culture" but rather "its successor and heiress" (ibid., p. 334).

/106/   Ibid., p. 333.

/107/   Id., *Deutscher Geist und Westeuropa*, p. 218.

/108/   Ibid., p. 334.

/109/   Ibid., p. 336.

/110/   Ibid., p. 337.

/111/   Ibid., p. 329 (emphasis mine).

/112/   Ibid., p. 649.

/113/   Id., G.S. II, p. 860.

/114/   Id., G.S. IV, p. 328 (emphasis original).

/115/   Id., *Bedeutung*, p. 89.

/116/   Ibid., p. 92.

/117/   Ibid., p. 101.

/118/   Id., G.S. IV, pp. 328–329.

/119/   As regards his own religious position, Troeltsch remarks, for example: "Certainly I am personally Protestant and am rooted in a religious individualism which has grown out of Protestantism, though I do not otherwise fail to appreciate the significance of the idea of solidarity and continuity" (id., *Briefe*, p. 73). Troeltsch's own religious position was, to use his own expression, "a mysticism which is rid of strife and yet guides us actively into a battle, labor, and a formation of community" (ibid., p. 94). That such a mysticism informed Troeltsch's own religious position has been attested by his close friends and disciples. Gertrud von le Fort, for example, says: "When one spoke to him [Troeltsch] alone, he confessed his personal adherence to mysticism—a Silesian shoemaker Jakob Böhme was his most favorite" (G. v. 1. Fort, *Hälfte des Lebens: Erinnerungen* [Munich: Ehrenwirth Verlag, 1965], p. 89). Friedrich Meinecke, Troeltsch's comrade at Berlin, also testifies that Troeltsch's religiosity was "of active and ethical kind" (F. Meinecke, *Werke*, vol. 4, p. 378).

/120/   Troeltsch's outline of the essence of a free Christianity is: ". . . first, it replaces the tie to an authoritative Church by an inwardness that derives, freely and individually, from the strength of the common spirit of the tradition; second, it transforms what has been the basic idea of historic Christianity, namely, the idea of a miraculous salvation of a human race suffering from the mortal infection of sin, into the idea of a redemptive elevation and liberation of the person through the attainment of a higher personal life from God" (Troeltsch, G.S. II, p. 840).

/121/   Troeltsch, "Zur Religionsphilosophie," p. 75. See also id., G.S. I, p. 934. Here Troeltsch asserts that modern theology is "all along the line the renovation of classical spiritualism."

/122/   Id., G.S. I, p. 850.

/123/   Ibid., p. 864.

/124/   Ibid., p. 960.

/125/   Ibid., p. 864.

/126/   Ibid., pp. 960–961.

/127/   Ibid., p. 936 n. 540a.

/128/   Ibid., pp. 938–939.

/129/   Ibid., p. 982.

/130/   Ibid., p. 973.

/131/   Since I have elucidated the main points concerning the meaning and significance of the concept of "Kompromiß" in Troeltsch's usage in my previous study, I should like just to refer to it here. See T. Yasukata, "The Concept of 'Kompromiß' in Ernst Troeltsch," *Journal of Christian Studies* 2 (1979):104–118.

/132/   Troeltsch, G.S. I, p. 975.

/133/   Ibid., p. 985.

/134/   Id., *Briefe*, p. 93.

/135/   Id., G.S. I, p. 977.

/136/   Id., G.S. II, p. 447.

CHAPTER III

THE THEOLOGICAL PROGRAM OF TROELTSCH'S MATURITY

The Mid-Troeltsch and His Theological Program

The question of when the second period of Troeltsch's intellectual development began is still open among researchers. Some (e.g., E. Lessing, G. v. Schlippe) deem the end of his first period approximately 1900, others (e.g., J. Wendland, H. R. Niebuhr, K. Kondo) take the year 1903 as the beginning of the second period, and still others (e.g., R. Röhricht, H. -G. Drescher) hold yet other views./1/ But they are all at one at least in their view that Troeltsch's second period is characterized by his preoccupation with the transcendental philosophy advocated by the Windelband-Rickert school of Neo-Kantianism. Troeltsch provides a basis for this commonly held view when he says that "the changes in the later works lie . . . , crudely stated, in a shift of philosophical standpoint from Dilthey and Lotze to Windelband and Rickert."/2/ But exactly what is the *terminus a quo* of Troeltsch's second period? In determining its starting point most researchers appeal to Troeltsch's own statements. For example, in the second volume of his *Gesammelte Schriften* Troeltsch states:

> My treatises on the 'Absoluteness of Christianity' and on the concept of 'the essence of Christianity' . . . made use of Rickert's philosophy of history and especially of its doctrine concerning the relation between empirical study of history and the philosophy of history as the most important means to solve the problems that burdened me./3/

Or:

> The whole line of thought of this present study [the essay "What Does 'Essence of Christianity' Mean?"] is based considerably on what I have learned from Rickert. Under this influence I have also turned away from the more Hegelian definition of the essence which I earlier set out in the essay "History and Metaphysics."/4/

It is rash, however, to conclude from these statements that Troeltsch was already under the influence of Rickert when he wrote (the first edition of) *The Absoluteness of Christianity*./5/ For Troeltsch wrote the following in his original essay, "Modern Philosophy of History" (1903), which appeared as a critical review of Rickert's *Die Grenzen der naturwissenschaftlichen Begriffsbildung* (1902):

> . . . my book, *The Absoluteness of Christianity and the History of Religions* (1901), is also indeed considerably on good terms with Rickertian propositions. Had I, in writing my book, already known the main part of Rickert's work, then several points in my book would have been clearer and more precise. In any case, however, this coincidence testifies to the significance of such studies for theology too./6/

This being the case, it would be wrong to see Rickert's influence upon Troeltsch in the first edition of *The Absoluteness of Christianity*. (The current edition is considerably revised and supplemented from the Rickertian standpoint, though.) In my judgment, Troeltsch's real commitment to Rickert first took place through the reading of the latter's insightful book mentioned above, though his initial encounter with this Neo-Kantian logician can be traced back to the year 1899./7/ Troeltsch's main ideas in the original version of *The Absoluteness of Christianity* certainly run parallel to Rickert's./8/ But we had better take this parallel as a "coincidence." This Kantian philosopher's influence on Troeltsch first took clear shape in the latter's above-mentioned critical review. Troeltsch appropriates Rickert's basic ideas in his own manner and then developed his scientific doctrine of *Gestaltung* in the essay "What Does 'Essence of Christianity' Mean?" (1903). Therefore, we have good reason to regard the year 1903 as the *terminus a quo* of Troeltsch's second period.

On the other hand, researchers hardly differ in their judgment as to the *terminus ad quem* of this period./9/ Troeltsch's move in 1915 from the chair in systematic theology at Heidelberg to a chair in philosophy at Berlin certainly denotes a significant change in his development, though this professional shift/10/ should not be taken as a symbolic event of the collapse of his theology. Troeltsch accepted the call from Berlin on 30 July 1914 and was officially appointed to professor in the philosophical faculty at the University of Berlin on 25 August 1914. (His actual move to Berlin took place early in the next spring.) Hence we take his resignation from the professorship of systematic theology at Heidelberg in the year 1914 as the *terminus ad quem* of the second period. The second period thus covers approximately a dozen years from the year 1903 till the end of his Heidelberg period. The second period is the most prolific and fruitful time in Troeltsch's entire career. Most of his major works (except the third volume of his collected writings) were produced during this period. He worked intensely not only in the field of theology proper but also in the philosophy of religion, ethics, the sociology of religion, and the history of ideas and culture. His later preoccupation with the philosophy of history too was already foreshadowed in the works of this period./11/ Hence arises what we have called "the Troeltsch problem." The treatment of Troeltsch's thought as a whole is a highly technical task. At the first glimpse, the attempt to comprehend the full spectrum of his thought in a unified way seems almost hopeless. This problem that confronts every student of Troeltsch inevitably leads to a question as to his scientific program. Did Troeltsch have any scientific program by which his diversified academic activities could be systematized into a coherent whole? Or, should his academic activities be rather taken as a succession of contradictory or incoherent concerns? It is true that Troeltsch was preoccupied with specific problems at particular stages of his development. For example, one might hold that Troeltsch's preoccupation was: first, the problem of theology on the basis of the history of religions (1894–1902); second, concern with the question of the validity of religious knowledge (1903–1906); third, interest in the history of Protestantism and the sociology of religion (1906–1913); fourth, involvement in contemporary politics (1914–1921); and finally, the problem of *Historismus* (1916–1923). Seen in this manner, Troeltsch is more often than not regarded as the inconsistent or distracted thinker who is easily influenced by other great thinkers. But is this really the case? We adamantly deny this rather common view. In my judgment, the dominant concerns that preoccupied Troeltsch's mind at particular stages of his development cannot be arranged in chronological sequence but rather run parallel to one another from the beginning to the end. For example, his early, supposedly theological writings bore the stamp of his deep concern with the philosophy of history./12/ The period during which, under the influence of Max Weber, he was deeply engaged in the sociological study of Christian history nearly coincides with the time during which he wrote dogmatic articles for *Die Religion in Geschichte und Gegenwart.*/13/ His programmatic essay on the *religionsgeschichtliche* theology,/14/ which is generally taken as the central concern of his first period, first appeared shortly before he resigned from the professorship of systematic theology at Heidelberg. Troeltsch showed great interest in the philosophy of religion even during the period of his concentration on the philosophy of history. His great ambition was to bring his philosophy of religion to a conclusion after completing his material philosophy of history./15/ These instances suffice for our thesis that the fields of study in which Troeltsch plowed stand not in a row but rather side by side.

How, then, are such diverse fields as theology, the philosophy of religion, the sociology of religion, the history of ideas and culture, ethics, and the philosophy of history related to one another within the whole of Troeltsch's scientific program, if at all? Troeltsch conceived his scientific program along the lines Schleiermacher sketched out in his philosophical ethics and his *Brief Outline.*/16/ As early as 1898 Troeltsch took recourse to the allegedly authentic Schleiermacher who, at least in theory, "constructed his theology on the basis of his ethics and [who] through his analysis of religion and its historical development pioneered the way first to the understanding and then to the justification of Christianity."/17/ To Troeltsch's regret, however, Schleiermacher actually carried out this theological program neither in his dogmatics nor in his theological ethics. Hence Troeltsch's criticism of his mentor:

> The basic ideas of his [Schleiermacher's] general ethics are thwarted by the theological scheme of grounding Christian ethics in the [miracle of] redemption. . . . Thus, the basic thought which originally grew out of the relationship with the general scientific movement, namely, the thought of understanding religion from the viewpoint of ethics and of introducing Christian-religious ethics into its general framework, is abandoned./18/

Referring to Richard Rothe, who "attempted to carry out Schleiermacher's great and bold plan in relation not to Schleiermacher's theological ethics but to his philosophical ethics,"/19/ Troeltsch then asserted in 1902: "Ethics is the basis on which the understanding of the essence of Christianity is to be sought, and the framework within which alone the essence of Christianity can be delineated scientifically."/20/ Thus, he proposed "to excavate the older paths of

Schleiermacher and the like again and to continue them independently by eliminating Hengstenberg-mediating theology-Ritschl's
interregnum."/21/ In 1909 Troeltsch had resort to "our great master"/22/ once again. Troeltsch found "the really main basic problem"
of theology in his time in "the juxtaposition of a purely scientific
historical theology and a practical mediating dogmatics."/23/ His
proposed solution of the problem was to provide a common stem or
root from which both branches could sprout. "Remedy and clarity
are," he says, "only possible if both branches of work going their
separate ways are given a common stem and so too a common
presupposition."/24/ A philosophy of religion which tackles the
problem of the validity of Christianity in a scientific way from the
perspective of a general science of religion and the philosophy of
history is thus required by both sides as such a common stem.
Troeltsch realized at this point that the demand for such a discipline
had already been made by Schleiermacher. According to Troeltsch,
Schleiermacher presupposed a common root, namely, philosophical
theology, when he separated scientific historical work (historical
theology) from the practical mediating discipline (practical theology)./25/ Hence Troeltsch promoted the resumption of his mentor's program.

> The program has never been carried out in Schleiermacher's
> own sense. It remains to be realized, and it is the task of
> scientific theology today to take it up in complete freedom
> and with the broadest scientific education. . . . Scarcely
> one stone of Schleiermacher's own teaching can remain
> upon another, but his program remains the greatest pro-
> gram of all scientific theology. His program needs to be
> worked out, not replaced by new inventions./26/

In 1913 Troeltsch was still true to his previous agenda. He reaffirms:

> His [Schleiermacher's] program simply needs to be carried
> out consistently. Hardly any change is necessary. It need
> only be noted that since Schleiermacher's time the methods
> and results of historical science have become more radical
> and have attained to more far-reaching conclusions./27/

Troeltsch's constant reference to Schleiermacher's theological
program, such as we have just seen, is positive evidence that he
basically conceived his own scientific program along the lines his
great predecessor sketched out in his philosophical ethics and *Brief
Outline*. In view of this reference, we can understand not only that
each of the fields Troeltsch plowed is organically related to the

others, but also that all of them have theological implications. That is to say, in each of these fields Troeltsch's interest was always focused on a single goal: a new shaping and a reformulation of Christianity. Thereby historical research (inclusive of the sociology of religion and the history of ideas and culture) was, as demonstrated in the preceding chapter, intended only to serve this systematic task. Concerning the interrelationship of all systematic disciplines, Troeltsch wrote as follows:

> We must only attempt to give a new foundation to the Christian world of life and to reformulate it. For us the central field of study then shifts to the philosophy of religion, which defines the essence and meaning of Christianity from the viewpoint of philosophy of history, and to general ethics, which elaborates the ultimate goal of humanity, an end which can be comprehended only from a religious perspective. Dogmatics and moral theology thus become branches of practical theology in the narrow sense. In any event, this is how the total plan of my work is to be understood, and because its main points have already been sketched by our [German] idealist philosophy, I generally refer to it. I resume the problem that was at issue before Hengstenberg and the Restoration./28/

Thus, for Troeltsch what is of decisive importance for the intellectual and spiritual situation of the present day and therefore for the future was the philosophy of religion and general ethics, which, in turn, are grounded in the philosophy of history. In contrast, dogmatics and Christian ethics, which should be developed on the basis of philosophy of religion and general ethics, were regarded as belonging to practical theology./29/ The interrelationship among these systematic disciplines will be discussed in greater detail in the following sections. In any event, we can maintain with certainty that all the systematic disciplines were closely and organically interconnected within Troeltsch's total scientific plan (see the diagram of Troeltsch's theological program on page 82). Given this interconnection, it should be no longer permissible to speak of Troeltsch's "thoroughgoing distraction" (*Zerstreutheit*)./30/ Such a view would only reflect the critic's own parochial view of theology. To do justice to the multiplex aspects of this "complex" thinker, we are rather required to broaden our own perspective so that we might cope with the immense variety of perspectives and dimensions in his thought. At this point suffice it to say, however, that recognition of Troeltsch's scientific program and its theological origin is the key to the proper understanding of the full spectrum of his thought.

The Philosophy of History and General Ethics as the Foundation of Theology

According to Troeltsch, the most distinctive characteristic of theology is its "practical starting point and practical interests."/31/ That is to say, "every theology is determined by the concrete starting point of the nature of a church that serves particular religious communities."/32/ Theology presupposes as a matter of course "the validity of the religious idea" of the specific religious community which it serves. Proceeding from such a basic presupposition, theology then considers "the further development of this idea as normative truth" to be its most fundamental goal. The main task of theology is thus "to confirm the normative validity of its own religious community."/33/ It lacks therefore the comparative perspective of the full spectrum of religious life. In Troeltsch's opinion,

> theology is a satisfactory solution as long as the general consciousness remains within the circle of a specific religious community taken as a matter of course. Only when this confidence in the religious community taken as a self-evident fact disappears, does the task arise of seeking clarity on the meaning and significance of religion not only from the standpoint of a specific religious community but also from the perspective of the entire living religious phenomena./34/

The Enlightenment of the eighteenth century and the immense progress made thereafter in the fields of forklore, comparative linguistics, and ethnology, which greatly promoted the birth of the general science of religion and of the general history of religions, however, shattered in fact the hitherto self-evident conception of Christianity as normative truth. Thus, the philosophy of religion took its rise among scientifically oriented theological circles. Troeltsch states:

> With the introduction of relativism, philosophical thinking stretches out beyond the circle of its own community, emancipates itself from the given, and directs the perspective to the whole. Thus, it leads to the philosophy of religion./35/

ERNST TROELTSCH'S THEOLOGICAL PROGRAM

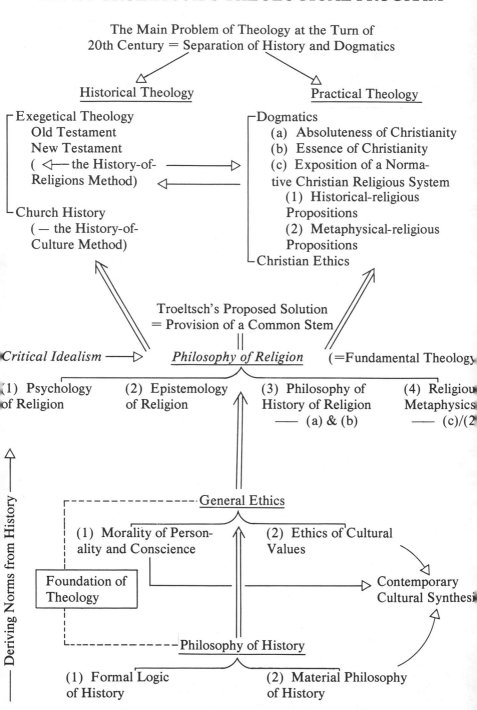

The Main Problem of Theology at the Turn of
20th Century = Separation of History and Dogmatics

Historical Theology   Practical Theology

Exegetical Theology
Old Testament
New Testament
(◁— the History-of- ———▷
Religions Method) ◁————

Church History
(— the History-of-
Culture Method)

Dogmatics
(a) Absoluteness of Christianity
(b) Essence of Christianity
(c) Exposition of a Normative Christian Religious System
(1) Historical-religious
Propositions
(2) Metaphysical-religious
Propositions
Christian Ethics

Troeltsch's Proposed Solution
= Provision of a Common Stem

Critical Idealism ——▷   *Philosophy of Religion*   (=Fundamental Theology)

(1) Psychology
of Religion

(2) Epistemology
of Religion

(3) Philosophy of
History of Religion
— (a) & (b)

(4) Religious
Metaphysics
— (c)/(2)

Deriving Norms from History

General Ethics

(1) Morality of Person-
ality and Conscience

(2) Ethics of Cultural
Values

Foundation of
Theology

Contemporary
Cultural Synthesis

Philosophy of History

(1) Formal Logic
of History

(2) Material Philosophy
of History

For Troeltsch the philosophy of religion or the science of religion/36/ is not a surrogate for theology but "the scientific foundation for theology" *(die wissenschaftliche Unterlage für die Theologie)*./37/ The task of delineating Christian religious faith for ecclesiastical communities remains the specific business of theology. In contrast, the real and specific business of the philosophy of religion is to develop a structure of support for the normative validity of Christian religion. The philosophy of religion as such, Troeltsch holds, assumes the role of theology—if it does this at all—only for the world of scientifically educated people who have turned their back on the ecclesiastical, supernaturalistic form of Christianity./38/ Since a more detailed discussion of the philosophy of religion is planned for the next section, suffice it to say that with Troeltsch the philosophy of religion is intended to perform a foundational function for theology.

Like Schleiermacher, Troeltsch considered the philosophy of religion to be a discipline subordinate to ethics./39/ Ethics as "the study of the ultimate goals and purposes of human existence"/40/ is, in his view, *"the supreme and most fundamental discipline,"* within the framework of which the science of religion fits."/41/ It is "the basis on which the understanding of the essence of Christianity can be delineated scientifically."/42/ Thus, Troeltsch gave unreserved sanction to the priority of ethics over dogmatics as a result of a specifically modern development. In pre-modern times, "ethics still belonged to the realm of the subjective and of practical application, while religion belonged to the only objective realm, that of authoritative revelation."/43/ Modern times, however, have reversed this relationship. Ethics, independent of dogmatic constraints, attained fame as a valid and indispensable discipline concerned with the practical themes of human life, while dogmatics, discredited by denominational antagonism and narrowness, almost lost its independent scientific status. Religious problems were now approached through the channel of ethics. Hence the priority of ethics over dogmatics. Kant represented this revolution and determined the path to be taken by all the generations that followed him. With their attempts "to reconstruct a badly shaken dogmatics on the basis of ethics,"/44/ even dogmatic theologians, such as Schleiermacher, Ritschl, and Herrmann, in fact followed the way prescribed by Kant and other modern ethicists. No doubt Troeltsch was in conscious alliance with these moderns/45/ when he regarded ethics as "the fundamental field of study that includes dogmatics in itself."/46/ Ethics was from the outset of critical importance for Troeltsch. The main theme of Troeltsch's lifework took its rise out of a deep and vital realization of "the clash between historical reflection and the determination of standards of truth and value."/47/ This problem, which, according to him, "presented itself to me at a very early age," was "a vital problem of the modern world that was prevalent to the present stage of human development."/48/ It was the problem concerning the relation between history and norms, the solution of which was first of all the specific business of ethics and the philosophy of history and yet also pivotal for theology. Troeltsch spells this out as follows:

> Though this problem [of deriving norms from history] confronts all of contemporary thought, it is most serious for theology, since theology stands or falls with the possibility of the attainment of universal norms and standards of value. The more legitimate the reliance on the historical approach is for theological understanding, the more of a burden it becomes to theology to tackle the problem of the relation of history to the attainment of norms. For this reason theology will be able to claim the distinction of being the battleground on which the decisive battle is being fought; the outcome of this battle will in turn affect every sphere of life. Unless a religious position can be regained and strengthened, it will be impossible to establish norms in these other areas. One's religious outlook ultimately determines whether norms will be accepted and obeyed./49/

Thus, Troeltsch's later preoccupation with ethics and the philosophy of history is quite understandable in view of this consideration.

The basic conception that characterized Troeltsch's ethical standpoint throughout his life is his division of ethics into the "morality of personality" *(Persönlichkeitsmoral)* and the "ethics of cultural values" *(Ethik der Kulturwerte)*. Troeltsch emphasized, contra the Kantian *a priori* ethic, the duality of the moral conscience. According to him, human moral experience knows not only the duties that proceed purely from the relations of the self to itself and to other selves—courage, prudence, truthfulness, etc., on the one hand, and good will, justice, piety, etc., on the other—but also the obligations toward objective values such as family, state, society, science, art, and religion. These values, though affected by natural inclinations, do contain something obligatory, not just eudaemonistic. That is to say, in these historical and cultural constructs lies something that must be sought after with the greatest sacrifice, something for which one is obliged to struggle, and which can be realized only through constant self-discipline and self-conquest. Accordingly, they are also to be recognized as the means by which personality is formed and therefore as the object of ethical reflection. Thus, Troeltsch maintains the following:

> Ethics rests upon an *a priori* idea that permeates experience, but ethics cannot work with that idea alone. Ethics must turn to experience to collect and classify the moral opinions that proceed from the ethical idea. Whenever possible, ethics must bring these opinions into a system with its appropriate graduation of what is more nearly right, the criterion being their contribution to the depth and strength of the formation of personality. But in this case ethics will make a distinction between subjective and objective morality and must thereby analyze and classify philosophico-historically *(geschichtsphilosophisch)* the purposes that proceed from objective morality./50/

Hence Troeltsch's thesis: Ethics is divided into "the formal autonomous ethics of conviction" and "the objective teleological ethics of value." Troeltsch held it necessary and justifiable to supplement the Kantian ethics by means of Schleiermacher's critique of it, and he presented his own standpoint as "the conjoining of Kant's subjective ethic with Schleiermacher's objective ethic."/51/ He asserts:

> What is important is to remain with Kant's starting point for the analysis, to derive the structure of the formal command from the idea of an autonomous rational purpose, and then further to draw out the objective values empirically from history, where they have developed and where they are constantly worked out according to their own necessity./52/

The main point involved here is that next to the principle of an autonomous subjective ethics Troeltsch introduced "a second principle, one which is far more important for the understanding of religious ethics, i.e., the principle of objective values."/53/ These objective values, however, develop in the reality of history. Accordingly, the second principle "directs us to history, from which alone we can derive these values."/54/ Thus the question of the elaboration of a concretely structured system of values became for Troeltsch the most crucial question. He spells this out with the following words:

> Therefore the primary questions of ethics do not lie in the realm of subjective ethics . . . but in the realm of objective

ethics. . . . Objective ethics requires a comprehensive, philosophico-historical vision, insight into the movement and
the growth of culture and into the formation of moral values
out of mere culture. It asks the question of the formation of
every single purpose in itself and especially the question of
the conceptualization of the relationship of these values to
one another./55/

When ethics is conceived in this way, the close ties between ethics
and the philosophy of history are obvious. Such close ties are also
attested by the fact that Troeltsch's material philosophy of history,
the completion of which was to be the task of the pre-announced but
never produced second volume of *Der Historismus*, was simultaneously intended to provide a sketch of his ethics./56/ In view of
these observations it becomes clear why Troeltsch became more and
more preoccupied with the philosophy of history. It also becomes
clear what was to be the central theme for Troeltsch's philosophy of
history. Since a full discussion of Troeltsch's philosophy of history is
planned for Chapter IV, we should like to explicate here only the
basic ideas of Troeltsch's philosophy of history set forth in his early
essay, "Modern Philosophy of History" (1903). This explication will
show that Troeltsch had already conceived in this essay the main
ideas which he spelled out in *Der Historismus* two decades later.

According to Troeltsch, the task of bringing history into relation
with a system of values is specific to the philosophy of history. This
task can be carried out only on the basic of an understanding of the
method and nature of empirical historical science, which, however,
can be clarified only through comparison with and distinction from
the natural sciences. As far as the relationship between history and
the attainment of norms is concerned, two major theories dominated
the theological circles of the time: exclusive supernaturalism and
idealist evolutionary theory. But neither of these was any longer of
use for Troeltsch. It is true that Lotze, Dilthey, Wundt, etc., offered
hints at a new solution of the problem. But the psychologism represented by Dilthey and Wundt was destined to result in an "anarchy
of values."/57/ Troeltsch's task was thus the attempt to affirm the
characteristics of the historical world in contradistinction to the
world of nature and at the same time not to surrender the former to
an anarchy of values. Exactly on this point, Rickert's logic of history
attracted Troeltsch's attention. Proceeding from the basically Kantian presupposition that "the standpoint of the strictest immanence

of consciousness is the only possible starting point of fundamental thinking,"/58/ Rickert, in alliance with his teacher Windelband, asserted that "the starting point for the logic of history cannot be the psychological subject and psychology but only the epistemological subject and the logical *a priori* involved therein."/59/ This assertion implied his critique of Dilthey, who also maintained, against a monistic view of science, dichotomy between natural sciences *(Naturwissenschaften)* and human sciences *(Geisteswissenschaften)*. According to Rickert, Diltheyan psychologism, first, cannot work out a distinction between mind and material world in the manner that provides a sufficient basis for a specific logic of history; and, second, it cannot comprehend the real contents of history as what they want to be, namely, as normative values./60/ Proceeding instead from the analysis of the epistemological subject, Rickert developed his philosophy of science based upon the dichotomy between nomothetic generalizing sciences (natural sciences) and idiographic individualizing sciences (cultural sciences). It is no wonder that Troeltsch found in Windelband-Rickert's theory "salvation and liberation"/61/ from the predicament in which theology found itself. Nevertheless, Troeltsch's acceptance of Rickert's logic of history was from the outset not without fundamental criticisms. His criticisms were primarily directed to Rickert's attribution of the dichotomy between the nomothetic and the idiographic sciences to "the antithesis of the modes of viewing,"/62/ or the different "logical attitude toward reality."/63/ Troeltsch held that this dichotomy should not be ascribed to "two different kinds of modes of viewing the same object" but to the "differentiations within the object." "The differences of the form of knowledge indicate the substantial differences of the objects."/64/ Hence Troeltsch insisted, contra Windelband and Rickert, on the necessity of tracing the differences back to the metaphysical sphere./65/ Closely related to this criticism was Troeltsch's emphasis on the 'objectivity' of history. He held that there must be objectivity for history, an objectivity analogous to that of natural sciences, if epistemological deduction should lead not only to empirical descriptive history but also through this to the construction of normative values from the perspective of philosophy of history./66/ As instances of the historical concepts that suggest such an objectivity of history, Troeltsch called attention to what Ranke called the 'idea' in the empirical sense. Such empirical ideas

are the "tendencies," the "analogies," or the "types,"/67/ which do
not receive, in Troeltsch's judgment, sufficient treatment in Rickert's
considerations.

> The specific character of historical conceptualization and
> abstraction lies not only in the uniqueness and individuality
> of the value unit that is described and combined together,
> but also in the concepts of what is common, those concepts
> which are expressed as analogies, tendencies, and types,
> signifying the common nature of cultural life that is found in
> all particularity./68/

In Troeltsch's judgment, this question concerning the similarity and
common nature of historical constructs cannot be solved within the
framework of the Rickertian pure logic. In any case, these criticisms
of Rickert by Troeltsch suggest the latter's distance from the former
even during the second period, during which Troeltsch is generally
considered to have been under the spell of Windelband and Rickert.

Now, what was Troeltsch's own solution of the problem concerning the relationship between history and the attainment of
norms? His proposed solution, as I see it, had two basic presuppositions. In the first place, he presumed that there must really exist the
ultimate value or the final end that is universally valid and ought to
be realized as such. This is Troeltsch's religious or metaphysical
presupposition./69/ In the second place, he presupposed that the
epistemological subject was endowed *a priori* with a capacity to
synthesize actual historical values somehow into a value system. He
took this epistemological premise as "the most intimate secret of the
urge to know history."/70/ Proceeding from these presuppositions of
the idealist outlook, Troeltsch tried to attain norms through the
elaboration of a concretely structured system of values based on the
reality of history. According to him, such a value system can be
worked out only by a creative synthesis of historical value constructs
and the present ideal of value. Here Troeltsch speaks of a reciprocal
relationship between these two. On the one hand, since we are
inclined to become narrow and to isolate and absolutize that which is
given, we must turn to the broadest possible context of history for "a
constant corrective for our own value constructs."/71/ We must
thereby impartially comprehend, survey, and compare the historical
value constructs of the past and proceed to arrange them in a
graduated series. The system of values that ought to be recognized
as valid will thus arise from the horizon of history. On the other

hand, however, such a graduation of the historical value constructs of the past is only possible in view of a system of values that claims universal validity. "What ought to be is the key to what is, and recognition of an absolute end of existence is the *a priori* of science."/72/ Thus, there is a circular movement *(Zirkel)* between the historical graduation of value constructs and the attainment of norms. Nevertheless, there is, according to Troeltsch, no ultimate theoretical solution to the question of how one can get out of this vicious circle. For such is "the circle between the epistemological subject and the psychological subject." It is "the primordial riddle of all reality and all human being,"/73/ in which all the antinomies find their ultimate basis. Hence Troeltsch asserts:

> The synthesis of the epistemological and psychological subject always ensues from an individual act of conviction *(eine individuelle Ueberzeugungstat)*, and exactly its individual character belongs to its ethical values./74/

For all scholarly circumspection and reflection, and for all knowledge of the broad scope of the development of history, Troeltsch therefore considered the attainment of norms or the elaboration of a system of values to be "an individual act." For the objective necessity of such an attainment or elaboration lies, in the last analysis, only in the subjective certainty that upon a careful weighing of all circumstances, any other judgment than this is contrary to one's conscience. It is true, as Troeltsch observes, that the broadest basis on which judgments are made, the continuity with past achievements, and decisions on the basis of well-considered comparisons give such an assessment its 'scientific' character, but this scientific character does not eliminate the individual character of the decision. "Every historical remains, in spite of all references to absolute values, irrational and individual. This is the destiny and dignity of human being."/75/ Hence the conclusion of Troeltsch's observations was that there is no ultimate theoretical solution of historical problems; the solely possible solution is a proximate practical solution through an individual act. After all, Troeltsch's solution was "a relatively creative act"/76/ that constantly strives for a new synthesis of historical factuality and rational validity. He would, in due course of time, venture such a creative act on the grand scale in his third period. At this point, however, suffice it to say that ethics and the philosophy of history occupy a decisive place in Troeltsch's total scientific program, and that for him both of them are the basis for the philosophy of religion and therefore serve as the foundation for theology.

The Philosophy of Religion as Fundamental Theology

In the preceding sections we have pointed out that for Troeltsch the philosophy of religion was the scientific foundation of theology and that it was intended to serve as a common stem for the two other branches of theology (historical theology and dogmatics) which had long gone their separate ways. That Troeltsch understood under the philosophy of religion or the science of religion "not . . . a general theory that floats over the multiplicity of religions, but a study that establishes normative religious thoughts"/77/ is also perceived from the fact that he sometimes called the philosophy of religion "fundamental theology" *(prinzipielle Theologie)*./78/ Accordingly, there is no doubt that Troeltsch's philosophy of religion had a Christian theological function. But the question is what kind of Christianity he represented. Troeltsch's letter to Bousset in the year 1904 is revealing on this point. He wrote:

> My great concern at present is to delineate my religious-philosophical thought and to combine with it the outline of my doctrine of faith *(Glaubenslehre)*. The question is, in the last analysis, always something positive for which one works, and despite all the difficulties, I feel the necessity to work out something positive of this kind. This positive thing is then no doubt a Christian faith. But I do not conceal that it is a Christianity which is different from all the previous forms of ecclesiastical Christianity and which cannot be developed out of ecclesiastical dogmatics as its real kernel and intention in the manner of liberal theology. It is exactly that kind of Christianity which people today seek and find in dependence on the Christian community and in reliance on the God of Christ. The main thing is that such a Christianity is not a sophisticated doctrine but rather something obtained in life./79/

The Christian character of his doctrine thus seems indisputable, though the Christianity he represented is not of the ecclesiastical stamp. Nevertheless, one may point out that such a Christianity belonged, to use the words of Troeltsch's own coinage, to "the secret religion of the modern educated person"/80/ and decide for this very reason that Troeltsch's doctrine, whether it be called theology or philosophy of religion, is no longer authentically Christian. In fact

Troeltsch was often accused with this charge./81/ Yet he on his part was rather indifferent to the question concerning his own Christian authenticity, for he was quite certain about it. He regarded himself as a Christian in his own right./82/ It is true that he identified his theology as "spiritualistic,"/83/ but, according to him, "modern philosophy of religion and theology stand in the scientific construction of thought in much closer relation to spiritualism than they do to Luther's objective authoritative theology of the word and the natural religion of the Enlightenment."/84/ Whether or not this is actually the case, Troeltsch's personal piety certainly bore "the stamp of the Christian mystic tradition."/85/ This Christian mystic, spiritualistic background is often the key to the proper understanding of Troeltsch's thought. In particular, his constant emphasis on metaphysics, which was always his last resort, becomes understandable from this perspective.

Now let us outline the specific tasks of the philosophy of religion as Troeltsch described them in his essay on "The Essence of Religion and of the Science of Religion."/86/ According to Troeltsch, there are four main types of modern scientific views on religion. In the first place stands the philosophy of religion of *critical idealism*. This idealism, abandoning every metaphysical attempt to deduce a double realm of reality from a fundamental reality conceived in the mind, limits itself to the epistemological analysis of the subjective human reason. By drawing from the *de facto* psychological content the autonomous laws of validity, this idealism seeks to present religion as the expression of a generally valid necessary reason. Kant, Fries, and Schleiermacher represent this position. In the second place, the *speculative* theory of Hegelianism represents the other wing of the idealist theory of religion. This theory of religion identifies religious consciousness with the desire for metaphysical knowledge and reduces the former to the latter. For this theory, religion is finite reason's consciousness of its own necessary emergence from infinite cosmic reason and therefore its regaining of unity with the infinite in consciousness. The substance of this consciousness, which in religion is expressed only in an imaginative form, is then translated and transformed into conceptual knowledge. A stark contrast to these idealist types is offered by the third major type, which is at present the strongest and most influential. The *positivist* theory of religion stemming mainly from the school of Comte represents this type. Proceeding from the presupposition that the only really firm element of thought is a continuum of physical reality governed by laws or at least regularities, this theory in fact reduces religion to an illusion. The major role which religion has played is seen in the function of the pre-scientific explanation of the world and of pre-scientific social ethics. Finally, the *ecclesiastical* doctrine of revelation in the modern form presents itself as the fourth major type. For this type the only concern is with the presentation of Christian religion as the final revealed truth. The non-Christian religions are, in contrast, treated at most as preparatory grace. Instead of appealing to the inspirational character of the Bible or to the miracles of salvation history, this theory validates the concept of revelation by means of the psychological analysis of the Christian religious experience of salvation. But its main ideas remain the same as those of the old exclusive supernaturalism.

According to Troeltsch, there is no way of reconciling these conflicting theories into a common basis for the science of religion. Every philosophy of religion must therefore make a decision among them for its necessary methodological presupposition. Troeltsch adopted the Kantian and Schleiermacherian standpoint as "the only possible methodological presupposition"/87/ for his own philosophy of religion. Proceeding from the general outlook of this critical idealism, Troeltsch then divided the specific tasks of the philosophy of religion into four branches: psychology of religion, epistemology of religion, history of religion, and metaphysics of religion./88/

The psychology of religion is regarded as the basis and the starting point of every scientific understanding of religion. In fact, psychological reflection of religion formed, as demonstrated in Chapter I, the basis of Troeltsch's *religionsgeschichtliche* theology. He insists that "the phenomenon should be seen in its factuality and in its objective individuality before we can ask about its validity." Thus the specific business of the psychological study of religion is said to be "to grasp the phenomenon as far as possible in its naivety, to obtain from it the experience or outlook as yet uninfluenced by scientific interpretation."/89/ The critical question to be answered by the psychology of religion is then the question of whether religious phenomena are merely mixed or derivative forms of other primary mental activities, or whether they, like logical thinking, moral judgment and aesthetic intuition, have their own autonomous character for themselves./90/ On this point, Troeltsch held William James's psychological study of religion in the highest esteem. James, as he understood him, succeeded in showing that the essential moment in the varieties of religious experience is a sense of the presence of the 'divine' in human consciousness. Nevertheless, Troeltsch criticized James as follows:

> Consequently nothing whatever is said about the content of truth or of the reality of these phenomena. This, by the very principle of such a psychology, is impossible. It analyzes, produces types and categories, and points out comparatively constant connections and interactions. At this point, however, lie the limitations of such a psychology that can never give information about the validity and the content of truth by itself, no matter how infinitely it be enlarged in its descriptions. But this [psychology] cannot be the last word for the science of religion./91/

He continues to contend:

> It is impossible to stop at a merely empirical psychology. The question is not merely of given facts, but of the content of the knowledge of these given facts. But pure empiricism will no longer succeed in answering this question. The question of the content of truth is always a question of validity. The question of validity can, however, be decided only by logical and by general, conceptual investigations./92/

Thus, the psychology of religion inevitably leads, at its most crucial point, to "the last and the most important question, namely, the question of *the epistemological value or the content of truth of religion*,"/93/ in which only epistemology has a voice.

The epistemology of religion is concerned with the validity or truth-value of the religious phenomena which must be first analyzed in their naivety by the psychology of religion. Troeltsch found the most difficult problem of the philosophy of religion in this "transition from the psychological analysis to the recognition of a real content."/94/ Dilthey, Wundt, or James were of no help on this point. Since the question was now the "synthesis of the rational and irrational, of the psychological and epistemolotical," which was, in Troeltsch's view, "the main problem raised by the teaching of Kant,"/95/ Troeltsch took recourse to Kant and neo-Kantianism. He was of the opinion that Kantian thought is in principle still valid and must be maintained as a whole, though a simple return to Kant is impossible. This recourse to Kant does not mean, however, that Troeltsch, like "the theology of value judgments that appealed to

Kant," stresses only the practical necessity of the values claimed by religion on the basis of the separation of theoretical and practical reason. Quite the contrary. Troeltsch took Kant's emphasis upon the practical character of religion as referring simply to its separation from the exact sciences or metaphysical speculation. "For Kant," he says, "the validity of religious truth rested on the rational, that is, the *a priori* transcendental truth-content of religion."/96/ Kant "constantly stressed the necessity of an *a priori* religious reason and of the object given with this"/97/ and therefore struggled to combine the rationally necessary element with the empirically psychological element of concrete religious ideas and feelings. Whether or not Troeltsch's interpretation of Kant is justified, the most important point is that he introduced a theory of the religious *a priori* into the religious-philosophical discussion. But what he really intended to convey with this subtle notion is still unsettled among researchers. Precise elucidation of this theory is too technical a task to be undertaken here. For the present, suffice it to say that the concept of the religious *a priori* was coined mainly for the purpose of "protecting against the dissolution of the religious into the flux of psychological boulders."/98/ Troeltsch's intention was then to defend the proper right of religion against positivists and psychologists by showing with this concept of the religious *a priori* that the formation of religious ideas is grounded in the structure of human reason as such. But did Troeltsch really succeed in demonstrating "the necessity of the formation of religious ideas in reason"?/99/ In response to P. Spieß's critique to the effect that nothing is demonstrated by this concept for the truth and validity of religious consciousness, Troeltsch contended: not only the validity of the religious but also the validity of the ethical and the aesthetic, and probably even that of the logical, cannot be demonstrated; this is the case because their validity cannot be derived from something superior or more certain; the religious can only validate, clarify, and purify itself in its execution. But if this evasive answer is his final word on the subject, Troeltsch obviously failed in the enterprise which he once proposed. For he had once asserted that the main task of the epistemology of religion was "to show an *a priori* law of the formation of religious ideas existing in the nature of reason and standing in an organic relationship to the other *a priori* principles of reason."/100/ In any case, the most difficult problem for the philosophy of religion in general lies in the sphere of epistemology, and Troeltsch's philosophy of religion is a good illustration of this difficulty. The specific tasks of the philosophy of religion are not exhausted by these psychological and epistemological investigations of religion. Along with them, there must be, in Troeltsch's opinion, "a logically well-considered philosophy of history of religion which pays careful attention to the modern history of religions, but which can grade the value of religions only through philosophical treatment."/101/ The task of such a "philosophico-historical theory of the development of the history of religions"/102/ is "to comprehend this variety as one which arises out of an inner unity and which in its successive phases strives toward a normative goal."/103/ The solution of this task would not be so difficult if Hegel's deductive metaphysics of the absolute were tenable. But in reality this 'finest solution' by Hegel was in the course of time entirely refuted by actual history. Hence arose a difficulty that confronted every idealist thinker after Hegel, the difficulty of maintaining Hegel's goal and yet reaching it by other logical and methodological paths. Troeltsch sought, as remarked earlier, a solution in the direction of "a metaphysics of history" as promoted by Schleiermacher, Claß, and Eucken. Such was "a metaphysics of *a posteriori* conclusions from the facts." In any event, Troeltsch's investigations move here on to "the questions in principle of the philosophy of history, which has to decide about the nature and meaning of the concept of development."/104/ The specific problem arising for the science of religion is then "the question about the goal of religious development," which culminates in the final question of "the meaning and the future of Christianity and its relationship to the religions of the East."/105/ Thus, the philosophy of history of religion is an intermediate field of study between the philosophy of history proper, whose central themes are the concepts of individuality and development, and (the prolegomena to) dogmatics, in which the question concerning the absoluteness and the essence of Christianity must be settled before the exposition of the content of Christian religious truth is performed.

Finally, if "religion indicates the reality from which these [logical, ethical and aesthetic] norms flow and in which they have their intrinsic nature,"/106/ and if "actual religion understands the relation to the transcendent as a real expereince, as a real relation to the divine which is not merely thought but is really accomplished in a moment,"/107/ then the question of the reality asserted in religion and that of its relationship to our other knowledge and experience of the world cannot be evaded. Thus, the idea of God, an object of faith asserted to be real in religion, must be taken into consideration by the philosophy of religion. Troeltsch states:

> The idea of God is admittedly not directly accessible in any other way than by religious belief. Yet it asserts a substantial content which must stand in harmony with the other forms of scientific knowledge and be in some way indicated by these, if indeed human reason represents an inner unity. Thus we arrive at *the philosophical treatment of the idea of God.*/108/

This treatment of the idea of God is, however, not possible without the help of a metaphysics. For Troeltsch, who rejected a Hegelian deductive metaphysics, there remained only a metaphysics which, proceeding *from below,* attempted to synthesize experiential facts in final terms. According to him, such a metaphysics does not contradict the outlook of critical idealism. Rather, "a strictly epistemologically directed philosophy, if it does not want to get stranded in psychologism and skepticism, [must] also contain the initial points of such a metaphysics in its concepts of validity and 'reason as such.'"/109/ Hence he boldly asserted that in the background of Kantian thought stood "an energetic theism," a modified monadology stemming from Leibniz. This modified monadology, however, was also Troeltsch's own metaphysical stance. He says:

> The unconditionality of all that is *a priori* and the continuity and logical succession of the historical forms of reason seem to me to point to an active presence of the absolute spirit in finite spirits, to an activity of the universe, as Schleiermacher says, in individual souls./110/

We will presently see what a crucial role this monadological doctrine played in his later philosophy of history. Nevertheless, Troeltsch never clearly set forth his own metaphysics. His hesitation in explicating his own metaphysical theory,/111/ to be sure, is understandable, for such an inductive metaphysics, in his opinion, must first arise out of empirical studies of history and religion. Yet it is indisputable that this hesitation has left Troeltsch's entire position unclear and dubious not only in the philosophy of religion but also in theology and the philosophy of history.

A Dogmatics on the Basis of the History of Religions

Troeltsch is generally regarded as the systematic theologian of the 'religionsgeschichtliche Schule.'/112/ Whether or not such a school really existed, there is no doubt that Troeltsch considered himself "the systematic theologian" (der Systematiker)./113/ Accordingly, one may well expect a dogmatics from him. In reality, however, his works concerned with dogmatic themes proper form merely a tiny island in an ocean of his entire work. His positive dogmatic views are conveyed only in the posthumous Glaubenslehre and the dogmatic articles written for the RGG. Given this state of affairs, critics have good reason to judge that Troeltsch was a poor theologian./114/ No objection could be made to this judgment if the criterion of theological stature were, as Barth asserts, "whether or not theologians can think dogmatically."/115/ However, such a criterion cannot do justice to Troeltsch's real achievements and easily misses his significance for theology. For Troeltsch no longer considered systematic theology to be "a simple task of handing down tradition and apologetics." He rather took it to be "a task of orienting the tradition in view of the intellectual and religious life of the present day" with a view to "a new shaping" of the Christian world of life and ideas./116/ Therefore, we should do better to follow R. S. Sleigh in thinking that Troeltsch's concern was with "the preliminary questions of theology" because it was just here that all the difficulties lay, and that "his intention was not to produce a 'new' theology, but rather to find a new basis and justification for all the essential matters of the old."/117/ I believe that our observations thus far have made this point clear.

On the other hand, however, the poverty of Troeltsch's dogmatic achievements is closely related to his peculiar conception of dogmatics. Dogmatics, as Troeltsch understands it, is "a sort of necessary evil."/118/ According to him, every living religion—including Christianity—stands, at its primordial phase, in distant relation to the scientific thought. In the case of Christianity, "its content of thought was fiery and dynamic like fresh lava spouting from a volcano"/119/ in its initial period. Dogma and dogmatics did not exist. They took their rise only as the original fervor cooled off and as there then arose the apologetic need to relate Christian truth positively to culture. Thus understood, dogmatics is "a petrification of religion" or "the herbarium of its dried imaginations,"/120/ and yet a necessary task for the church coping with cultured and sophisticated people. This understanding of dogmatics involves two important theses: doctrine or dogmatics itself is of secondary importance for religion (more important is religious cultic *life*); second, the real significance of dogmatics lies in its apologetic function. Troeltsch's seemingly small esteem of dogmatics and almost exclusive emphasis on scientific theology (historical theology and the philosophy of religion) can be explained from this viewpoint. Since the so-called dogmatics based on the old-fashioned dogmatic method of exclusive supernaturalism was, in his judgment, incapable of performing such apologetic functions in the entirely changed intellectual climate of the modern world, the philosophy of religion should take over the function of demonstrating the normativeness or prime validity of Christianity. As we have seen, Troeltsch was strongly convinced that "the philosophy of religion leads to Christianity as the supreme revelation of religious consciousness."/121/

As the result of this shift of primary accent to the philosophy of religion, dogmatics was now regarded as belonging to practical theology. Dogmatics "presupposes scientific conclusions and methods; it is itself, however, not a science; it is rather a confession of faith and a systematic exposition of this confession for the guidance of preaching and of religious instruction."/122/ This categorization of dogmatics, however, does not necessarily imply Troeltsch's devaluation of it. For he says, for instance, the following:

> I have at all times fulfilled the practical educational tasks assigned to the theological faculty with personal love for my students. I considered dogmatics a practical concern in which lack of clarity and the insecurity of human knowledge play an essentially important role but which nevertheless permits the main value of practical religion to be communicated to the hearts of the students as a burning and propulsive power./123/

Nevertheless, this categorization does reveal not only Troeltsch's verbal difference but also his material deviation from his great mentor Schleiermacher. For the latter categorized dogmatics under the heading of 'historical knowledge of the present condition of Christianity' among 'historical theology'/124/ and considered practical theology "the crown of theological studies" (*die Krone des theologischen Studiums*)./125/ Even if Troeltsch deviated from his master on this point, this deviation, however, would not be a discredit to him. For Schleiermacher's categorization of dogmatics into historical theology itself was very problematic. No German theologian, except Richard Rothe, had adopted his inclusion of dogmatics under historical theology. Schleiermacher's *Glaubenslehre* obviously has, as Troeltsch held, a practical mediating character. His treatment of Jesus shows that this revolutionary mind in modern theology was, at the most critical point, really "an unhistorical thinker."/126/ Faced with Schleiermacher's accommodations to the ecclesiastical tradition in the treatment of Christological issues, Troeltsch insisted on carrying through with the historical method in full seriousness. Troeltsch's characterization of dogmatics as a practical discipline is therefore to be taken as one of his critical modifications of Schleiermacher's otherwise excellent dogmatics. How, then, is dogmatics possible when the historical method is employed in full seriousness? Troeltsch's own posthumous *Glaubenslehre* is a good example of a dogmatics based on a full recognition of historical method.

When the historical method is applied with utter and uncompromising consistency, theology must become, in Troeltsch's opinion, a *religionsgeschichtliche* theology. This idea of a theology based on the history of religions, according to Troeltsch, was envisaged first by the Deists and then, in various forms, by Lessing, Kant, Herder, Schleiermacher, de Wette, Hegel, and finally by Baur and Lagarde./127/ Hence, Troeltsch warned that the *religionsgeschichtliche* dogmatics should not be taken as a dogmatics of a specific school called the *"religionsgeschichtliche Schule."* Rather, it simply meant a dogmatics working with the presuppositions and ideals of the *religionsgeschichtliche* method./128/ Given the diverse directions and interests concerned with the *religionsgeschichtliche* method and attitude, such a "school" was absolutely impossible for him.

The *religionsgeschichtliche* dogmatics, that is, a dogmatics proceeding on the basis of the history of religions, has three main tasks. The first task "consists in establishing, on the basis of a historical and philosophical comparison of religions, the fundamental and universal supremacy of Christianity for our own culture and civilization."/129/ This is the topic which preoccupied Troeltsch's mind throughout his life and found its first clear formulation in *The Absoluteness of Christianity and the History of Religions*. We have examined his basic ideas on this topic in Chapter I. With the passage of time, however, Troeltsch then realized that this task was concerned with the more general question of the relationship between history and the attainment of norms, the settlement of which belonged to the specific business of ethics and the philosophy of history. Hence his central concern gradually shifted to ethics and the philosophy of history. But insights attained in ethics and the philosophy of history were afterwards to be joined through the philosophy of religion (especially the philosophy of history of religion) to theology.

The second task of a *religionsgeschichtliche* dogmatics is to give a definite answer to the question about what Christianity really is./130/ This is the task of defining *the essence of Christianity*. As we have seen in Chapter I, Troeltsch attained theoretical clarity about the methodological questions involved in the definition of the essence of Christianity in his very significant essay, "What Does 'Essence of Christianity' Mean?" (1903). There he explicated the concept of "essence" using three principles: "criticism," "a developmental concept," and "an ideal concept." Troeltsch then elaborated his theology of *Gestaltung* and the program of a free Christianity on the basis of this explication of the notion of the essence. But such an elaboration of the new essence of Christianity (the proposal of a free Christianity) was certainly no longer just the second task of a *religionsgeschichtliche* dogmatics but became an independent theological task. The definition of the essence of Christianity as the second task of a *religionsgeschichtliche* dogmatics was more moderate business of formulating the totality of the historical manifestations of Christianity into one central formula, which would characterize both the fundamental driving force of the development of Christianity and the basic religious ideas underlying the total phenomena of Christianity. Troeltsch called such a central formula "the Christian principle."/131/ Consequently, the second task is, in a word, the formulation of the Christian principle. Troeltsch stated the Christian principle in several ways, but the following formulation in his posthumous *Glaubenslehre* best conveys his understanding of this principle (the essence of Christianity).

> In general, Christianity is the decisive turn in principle to a religion of personality over against all naturalistic and anti-personalistic understanding of God. This general historical character of Christianity presents itself in its present Protes-

tant version and in its probable future development as the idea of the human soul redeemed and saved through communion with the living God, elevated to God and bound with God in a kingdom which flows from God and is governed by God, around which personalities are inseparably united in religious love. This elevation consummates in the religious knowledge of God and the hearty devotion of the will to God. God is the one who establishes the ideal of personality. We meet this God in the history of revelation from the prophets to Jesus and from there down to the present. Jesus is in this the center of the redemptive and self-revelatory act of God. In a word, one can designate the Christian principle as the principle of religious rebirth or higher birth to a kingdom of God-filled spirit./132/

A more compact version of his formulation of the Christian principle reads as follows:

Christian religious faith is faith in the rebirth and higher birth of the creature that is alienated from God in the world—a rebirth and higher birth effected through the knowledge of God in Christ. The consequence of this rebirth and higher birth is union with God and social fellowship so as to constitute the kingdom of God./133/

In any case, Troeltsch's main point is that Christianity represents a personalistic religion of rebirth or higher birth in superlative terms./134/

While the tasks of establishing the supremacy or prime validity of Christianity and of determining the essence of Christianity (the Christian principle) are concerned mainly with the preliminary questions of dogmatics and therefore belong to the prolegomena to dogmatics, the third task belongs to the real and specific business of dogmatics in the strict sense. This task is the exposition of the essence of Christianity or the explication of the Christian principle./135/ According to Troeltsch, "the principle or essence of Christianity, as seen in the light of its total historical development up to the present day in which a theologian is writing, is the substance and basis of dogmatics *(Glaubenslehre)*." Thereby "the *basis of the subdivision*" of dogmatics "must also lie in the religious principle."/136/

Thus understood, a *religionsgeschichtliche* dogmatics is no longer "dogmatics" in the traditional sense, namely, a deductive, biblical science which sets forth permanent and unchangeable truths. Since Troeltsch knew no dogmas that could be set forth as an unchangeable fixed truth, he, following Schleiermacher, preferred to substitute for the term dogmatics the expression "doctrine of faith" *(Glaubenslehre)./*137/ In any case, dogmatics, if we use the term in the latter sense, is thus thoroughly historicized and made into a discipline which is concerned with the explication of the essence of Christianity (the Christian principle) as identified by historical theology on the basis of a survey of the totality of Christian history. Dogmatics is now shaped by the totality of Christian history, no longer by the Bible and the Creeds of the Church alone. Troeltsch repeatedly asserted that Christian revelation is to be found not in the Bible alone but in "the totality of Christianity's historical manifestations."/138/ At this point he introduced "the concept of a progressive revelation." In his posthumous *Glaubenslehre* Troeltsch remarks:

> . . . the Bible, or perhaps the history attested by it, is the fundamental and central revelation, the ecclesiastical-historical tradition and the modern world of religious feeling are the ongoing revelation, and the present-day religious experience is the present-day revelation. Revelation has therefore its stages and its history down to the present and never comes to an end./139/

The implication of this eminently modern and idealistic concept of revelation is enormous for dogmatics. For not only does Christian history as conceived in its totality now enter into the dogmatic task, but also the Gospel of Jesus ceases to be "the sole norm and source" of dogmatics, even though it is still regarded as "the authentically classical source of Christian faith."/140/ Instead, the Bible, the "tradition" conceived as "a body of material to be worked through in freedom" *(ein frei durchzuarbeitender Stoff),*/141/ and "the present-day religious experience"/142/ are considered to be the sources of dogmatics. And Troeltsch even asserts that present-day religious experience is "the really decisive source and authority."/143/ It hardly needs to be said that such a dogmatics represents a considerable break with the old Protestant dogmatics. Troeltsch's posthumous *Glaubenslehre* was thus consciously a manifesto of "Neo-Protestantism."/144/

This consciously modern dogmatics is, however, not only deeply rooted in the history of Christianity as a whole but also determined by the religious-historical *(religionsgeschichtlich)* perspective. According to Troeltsch, every higher religion involves a practical fundamental relationship of God, the world, and human being, in which human being, by the relationship it seeks to win with the divine in its religion, is in some sense overcoming the world. And always associated with this fundamental relationship are a religious community and the hope for a final consummation./145/ Thus God, the world, human being, redemption, religious community, and final consummation are the common categories discovered by the history of religions in every higher religion. Like every other higher religious principle, the Christian principle involves these six concepts. The actual ordering of the Christian principle (the essence of Christianity) into a dogmatic system must therefore employ these common categories. A *religionsgeschichtliche* dogmatics thus expounds the Christian principle under the six headings: God, the world, human being, redemption (spiritual elevation), religious community (the kingdom of God), and final consummation./146/ Troeltsch thereby asserted that dogmatics must explicate the conception implied in the Christian principle in complete independence, "without any intermingling of historical elements" *(ohne jede Einmischung historischer Elemente)*./147/ Why did he assert this? Because Troeltsch, following the example of Schleiermacher, wanted to construct his dogmatics *(Glaubenslehre)* upon the "present-day consciousness of the religious community"/148/ and yet tried to straighten out Schleiermacher's illegitimate amalgamation of the religious idea with history, which had been severely attacked by Strauss. Thus, Troeltsch asserted that dogmatics must "set forth our faith in God as something existing in the present experience and renewing itself with each individual in the experience of redemption,"/149/ so that it may contain only "purely present-day religious statements."/150/ The most significant implication of this exclusion of historical elements from dogmatic statements is that the object of faith is restricted to the God of Jesus alone. Jesus himself, in contrast, is transformed into the historical mediator and revealer. Troeltsch's own spiritualistic religious position, as we have observed in the preceding chapter, is clearly also at work in this bold assertion./151/

However, Troeltsch was not so single-track a thinker as to place one-sided emphasis on the spiritualistic conception of Christianity. He was from the outset well aware of Biedermann's error in separating "the Christian principle" from "the person of Jesus."/152/ Contra such a Biedermannian separation of the person and the principle, he affirmed an inner relationship between both: "Not a new [Christian] religious principle created faith in the person of Jesus but, on the contrary, this faith created the new principle."/153/ How, then, did the Christian principle arise from the person of Jesus? Troeltsch answered this question by introducing a social-psychological consideration. According to him, the "law of social psychology" shows that every group or community (including a religious one) needs a concrete focal point or center. "In the religions of spirit it is the prophets and founder personalities who serve as archetypes, authorities, sources of power, and rallying points."/154/ In Christianity, the historical figure of Jesus, which is transmitted through the Christ cult to the present-day believer, serves as the source of power and rallying point. Thus, Troeltsch mediated the person of historical Jesus and the Christian principle through the cultic image of Christ. He argues: "The Christian idea . . . will never become a powerful reality without community and cult"; "a cult illuminated by the Christian idea must therefore always center on gathering the congregation around its head, nourishing and strengthening it by immersion in the revelation of God contained in the image of Christ . . ."; "as long as Christianity survives in any form it will always be connected with the central position of Christ in the cult."/155/ Whether or not Troeltsch's mediation of the person of Jesus and the Christian principle through such a cultic Christ is persuasive—his account is, in my judgment, social-psychologically relevant but theologically insufficient—, he is right in maintaining that the present religious experience needs its point of anchorage in the historical person and work of Jesus. As Troeltsch rightly asserted, "this present-day religious experience receives its power, its vitality, and its definiteness, and especially its capacity to take social organization" from its historical background, "particularly from the prophets and Jesus." Without these "sources of power" and "centers of concentration," the personal piety of the present-day believer "would be impoverished and crippled, and the religious community would possess no center."/156/ As the result of this social-psychological consideration Troeltsch maintained that a religious interpretation of the historical background of the Christian principle must also be involved in the task of dogmatics.

Is not this inclusion of the historical background of the Christian principle into the dogmatic system yet another phase of what we have characterized as Troeltsch's dilemma? For Troeltsch was basically of the opinion that dogmatics should contain only purely

present-day religious statements. Such a suspicion may well be
aroused but cannot be justified on closer examination. For the
Christian principle, as Troeltsch understands it, is not an autonomous, timeless principle hovering above history but a dynamic
creative principle operating within the reality of history. Furthermore, knowledge of God is, in his opinion, not simply the result of
reflection on the basic data of consciousness but rather "something
acquired historically" (ein Erwerb der Geschichte). It "comes to the
individual only through history by the medium of Christian community."/157/ This primacy of historical givenness over autonomous
rationality, of the collective spirit over the atomistic individual, is in
fact one of the points which Troeltsch persistently stressed. For
example, he remarks:

> Nowhere does autonomy produce the contents of our mod-
> ern thought and life. Everywhere they rest, for the most
> part, on tradition and authorities . . . In religious thought
> this is simply the case to a greater degree./158/

However, for Troeltsch the connection of redemption with history
was paradoxical:

> Christian redemption does not spring from religious auton-
> omy. We have received it from history. . . . [However] the
> death of Jesus is the overcoming of what was merely time-
> bound in his person. It is the great liberation of his spirit
> through suffering and death, . . . Hence redemption, in
> trust toward Jesus, is not directed backwards. It acquires its
> connection with history only because the community which
> is imbued with the spirit of Christ and which mediates
> redeeming faith to the individual soul has its origin in the
> historical figure of Jesus and inwardly regulates and
> strengthens itself from there./159/

For this very reason, the historical background of present-day Christian religious experience, especially the historical figure of Jesus, is
indeed intrinsic to a dogmatic system but does not constitute its
main body, which treats the purely present-day religious propositions.

Thus the specific and real business of dogmatics in the narrower
sense now splits into two great divisions: "historical-religious statements" and "metaphysical-religious statements." In the historical-
religious part, the task of dogmatics is to "set forth the religious
significance of the historical foundations—of the prophets, of Jesus,

of the development of the Christian spirit in history."/160/ In particular, the delineation of the significance of the person of Jesus for
the Christian piety is a central task here. In the metaphysical-
religious part, on the other hand, explication of the Christian conception of God, the world, human being, redemption, religious
fellowship, and consummation is the main task.

To sum up the above considerations, a Troeltschian dogmatics is
divided into three parts: (I) prolegomena (in which the preliminary
questions, above all, those of the absoluteness and the essence of
Christianity, must be settled); (II) a historical-religious part (in
which the religious significance of historical reality, especially of the
historical personality of Jesus is discussed); and (III) a metaphysical-
religious part (in which the specifically Christian idea are worked
out with reference to God, the world, human being, redemption,
religious fellowship and consummation; the subdivision of this systematic part is thus: (1) the doctrine of God, (2) the doctrine of the
world [creation], (3) anthropology, (4) soteriology, (5) ecclesiology,
and (6) eschatology). In fact, Troeltsch's posthumous *Glaubenslehre*
fits this structure perfectly.

Since our concern in this study is not with a material exposition
of Troeltsch's dogmatics but with a formal analysis of its salient
features, we cannot go into the details of its content here. For such a
material exposition of Troeltsch's posthumous *Glaubenslehre*, I
should like only to call the reader's attention to two recent Ph.D.
dissertations by American students as well as to B. A. Gerrish's
brief, but superb, essay./161/

In conclusion, a *religionsgeschichtliche* dogmatics, as Troeltsch
outlined in the essay "The Dogmatics of the '*Religionsgeschichtliche
Schule*'" and exemplified in his posthumous *Glaubenslehre*, is a
highly self-consistent, thoroughly historicized theology. It not only
perfectly fits Troeltsch's entire scientific framework but also conveys
the heart of his powerful thought. True, it is vulnerable to criticism
at many points. In particular, it is theologically (though not sociologically and psychologically) weak and unsatisfactory in its
Christology. But such weakness is more or less common to all
modern theologies, especially to idealistically oriented theologies.
Even Barth's strongly Christologically oriented theology is not without serious difficulties when it is viewed from a different angle.
Given the drastic impact of modern historical thinking on human
understanding, Christology in the traditional form is no longer a

foregone conclusion. One must therefore settle the problem of *Historismus* before he/she employs Christology as the controlling and organizing principle of theology. This taken into consideration, Troeltsch's serious struggle with the problem of *Historismus* is by no means theologically irrelevant. Rather, his *religionsgeschichtliche* theology, despite all the difficulties it involves, will be the force for theology in the future. For it best represents, in my judgment, a possibility of theology in a historically conscious age.

NOTES

/1/ E. Lessing, in view of Troeltsch's philosophy of history, and G. v. Schlippe, in the light of the question of the absoluteness of Christianity, hold that roughly the year 1900 marks the end of Troeltsch's early activity (E. Lessing, *Die Geschichtsphilosophie Ernst Troeltschs* [Hamburg: Herbert Reich Evang. Verlag, 1965], p. 16; G. v. Schlippe, *Die Absolutheit des Christentums bei Ernst Troeltsch auf dem Hintergrund der Denkfeld der 19. Jahrhundert* [Neustadt an der Aisch: Verlag Degener & Co., 1966], pp. 51–54). J. Wendland, H. R. Niebuhr, and K. Kondo are all at one in regarding the year 1903 as the beginning of the second period, but the bases of their arguments are slightly different. Wendland takes notice of the change of Troeltsch's philosophical position. According to Wendland, Troeltsch's initial philosophical position was "a metaphysics based on the independence of spiritual life." Though "Troeltsch did not abandon this metaphysics" in the works from 1903 onward he allied himself with "the transcendental philosophy advocated by Windelband and Rickert. Thus the starting point of his philosophy changed strongly" (J. Wendland, "Philosophie und Christentum bei Ernst Troeltsch im Zusammenhang mid der Philosophie und Theologie des letzten Jahrhunderts," *ZThK* 24 [1914]:142). For Niebuhr the decisive factor is the shift in Troeltsch's central concern. He argues:

"As the first period was marked by attention to the problem of theology on the basis of history of religions, so the second was marked by concern with the question of the validity of religious knowledge. The watch word of the first period was 'the Absoluteness of Christianity,' of the second, 'the religious apriori'" (H. R. Niebuhr, "Ernst Troeltsch's Philosophy of Religion," p. 66).

Kondo identifies the beginning of the second period with the formation of the *Gestaltungslehre* as elaborated by Troeltsch first in his essay on the essence of Christianity (1903) (see K. Kondo, "Theologie der Gestaltung bei Ernst Troeltsch," pp. 24, 39, 238–239 n. 1).

Contra these views, R. Röhricht regards the year 1904, in which Troeltsch's study of Kant first appeared, as the beginning of the second period and discusses Troeltsch's thought of this period under the heading of "the attempt of transcendentalism" (R. Röhricht, "Zwischen Historismus und Existenzdenken: Die Geschichtsphilosophie Ernst Troeltsch's," Phil. Diss., Tübingen, 1954). Finally, H.-G. Drescher holds that Troeltsch's work on *The Absoluteness of Christianity* (1902) marks the transition from the first to the second period. He characterizes this transition as a "transition from a more Hegelian position to the neo-Kantianism of Windelband and Rickert" (H.-G. Drescher, "Troeltsch's Intellectual Development," pp. 13, 16).

/2/ Troeltsch, G.S. II. p. 227 n. 11.

/3/ Ibid., p. 716.

/4/ Ibid., p. 450 n. 32.

/5/ The official date of the first edition of this book is 1902. In reality, however, it was already in circulation in late December of 1901. For this reason the editors of *Ernst Troeltsch Bibliographie* (Tübingen: J. C. B. Mohr, 1982) list it among the publications of 1901.

/6/ E. Troeltsch, "Moderne Geschichtsphilosophie," *Theologische Rundschau* 6 (1903):106. This paragraph is revised in the essay now contained in Troeltsch's collected writings. Cf. G.S. II, p. 716.

/7/ In the *Theologische Literaturzeitung* (June, 1899), Troeltsch reviewed Rickert's *Kulturwissenschaft und Naturwissenschaft* (Freiburg: J. C. B. Mohr, 1898) along with G. v. Below's essay on "Die neue historische Methode." There he expressed high appreciation for the clarity, thoughtfulness, and enlightenedness with which Rickert worked out the program of *Kulturwissenschaft*. Nevertheless, he drew a line of demarcation between Rickert and himself. He remarks:

> Of course, I, on my part, cannot share the purely imma-
> nent, antimetaphysical starting point of this entire argu-
> ment and therefore cannot consider the ordinary division of
> natural sciences and *Geisteswissenschaften* (despite suspi-
> cion of the latter term) as wrong as Rickert does" (E.
> Troeltsch, review of "Die neue historische Methode," by
> Georg von Below; *Kulturwissenschaft und Natur-
> wissenschaft*, by Heinrich Rickert, in *ThLZ* 24 [1899]:377).

/8/ See especially Troeltsch, *Absolutheit*, pp. 27–29.

/9/ Contra the common view, H. R. Niebuhr assigns the beginning of the third period, which, in his opinion, is "the philosophy of history period," to the year 1913. But this periodization, as he himself admits, is "an arbitrary division." H. R. Niebuhr, "Ernst Troeltsch's Philosophy of Religion," p. 76.

/10/ For a fuller account see Chapter IV.

/11/ K. Mannheim marvels that Troeltsch had already set forth the basic ideas which he later developed in *Der Historismus* as early as 1903 in an essay on the "Modern Philosophy of History." See K. Mannheim, "Historismus," in *Wissenssoziologie: Auswahl aus dem Werk*, ed. and with an Introduction by K. H. Wolff (Berlin and Neuwied: Hermann Luchterhand Verlag, 1964), p. 276.

/12/ In fact, Troeltsch was from the outset philosophico-historically oriented. In 1920 Troeltsch wrote the following retrospect of his student days in Göttingen (1886–1888): "For my part I was already devoting my time to philosophy very much at that time, searching out a conception of the development of mind in which I could range the Christian world. That search was also one of the germs of all my later works, for indeed such germs must arise during youth" (Troeltsch, "Die 'kleine Göttinger Fakultät' von 1890," p. 282). Troeltsch's deep concern with the philosophy of history can also be perceived in his letter to Bousset of 11 September 1889, according to which his academic endeavor in that year centered on the attempt "to find a framework for the theological system . . . through the widest possible knowledge of history." He considered both the specification of the essence of Christianity through purely historical critique and the supplementation of the absolute foundation of the Gospel by means of the philosophy of history ("*eine . . . geschichtsphilosophische Ergänzung*") to be "the only possible task of a theological system" (Troeltsch to Bousset, 11 September 1889, "Brief an Bousset," p. 23 n. 6).

/13/ See the bibliography.

/14/ E. Troeltsch, "The Dogmatics of The 'Religionsgeschichtliche Schule'," *The American Journal of Theology* 17 (1913):1–21 (hereafter cited as "The Dogmatics"); also id., G.S. II, pp. 500–524.

/15/ Id., G.S. IV, pp. 14–15.

/16/ F. Schleiermacher, *Kurze Darstellung des theologischen Studiums zum Behuf einleitender Vorlesungen* (critical edition of Henrich Scholz, Leipzig: Deichert'schen Verlagsbuchhandlung Nachf., 1910; reprint ed., Darmstadt: Wissenschaftliche Buchgesellschaft, 1977). Eng. tr.: id., *Brief Outline on the Study of Theology*, trans. Terrence N. Tice (Atlanta: John Knox Press, 1977).

/17/ Troeltsch, "Metaphysik," p. 28; cf. ibid., pp. 27, 55.

/18/ E. Troeltsch, "Grundprobleme der Ethik," *ZThK* 12 (1902):59–60. Words in bracket are supplements from the year 1913; cf. G.S. II, p. 568.

/19/ Ibid., p. 60.

/20/ Ibid., p. 61.

/21/ Troeltsch to Bousset, 8 March 1902 [1904], "Briefe an Bousset," p. 42.

/22/ E. Troeltsch, "Rückblick auf ein halbes Jahrhundert der theologischen Wissenschaft," *Zeitschrift für Wissenschaftliche Theologie* 51 (1909):134.

/23/   Ibid., p. 129.

/24/   Ibid., p. 130.

/25/   Ibid., p. 133.

/26/   Ibid., p. 134.

/27/   Id., "The Dogmatics," p. 17 n 1.

/28/   Id., G.S. II, p. 767.

/29/   Ibid., p. vii; id., *Briefe*, p. 93.

/30/   Barth regards Troeltsch as a "distracted" theologian. He says: "We must compare Schleiermacher's attitude with the thoroughgoing distraction with which Troeltsch was a theologian a hundred years later." K. Barth, *Die protestantische Theologie im 19. Jahrhundert. Ihre Vorgeschichte und Geschichte* (Zurich: Theologischer Verlag Zürich, 1946), p. 384.

/31/   Troeltsch, "Religionsphilosophie," p. 446.

/32/   E. Troeltsch, "Vorlesung über Religionsphilosophie," copy of the stenographic transcript by Gertrud von le Fort of the lectures delivered at the University of Heidelberg, 1912, University Library Heidelberg, Heid. Hs. 3653, p. 1.

/33/   Id., "Religionsphilosophie," pp. 446–447.

/34/   Id., "Vorlesung über Religionsphilosophie," p. 1.

/35/   Ibid.

/36/   Troeltsch, more often than not, uses the term "philosophy of religion" *(Religionsphilosophie)* and "science of religion" *(Religionswissenschaft)* without making a clear distinction between the two. "Philosophy of religion" in the broad sense is, in most cases, interchangeable with "science of religion." Nevertheless, the difference is clear. The "philosophy of religion" in the strict and narrow sense means the philosophical treatment of the knowledge and truth-content of religion and is therefore one department of philosophy, while the "science of religion" is an independent field of study concerned with the religious phenomena of humankind in general. The "science of religion," thus understood, involves, as will be discussed, psychological, epistemological, philosophico-historical, and metaphysical reflection of religion.

/37/   Troeltsch, G.S. II, p. 462.

/38/   Id., "Religionsphilosophie," p. 485.

/39/   See F. Schleiermacher, *Der christliche Glaube*, ed. M. Redeker (Berlin: Walter de Gruyter, 1960), §2. 2; id., *Kurze Darstellung*, §23.

/40/   Troeltsch, G.S. II, p. 552.

/41/   Ibid., p. 553 (emphasis original).

/42/   Ibid., p. 570.

/43/   Ibid., p. 560.

/44/   Ibid., p. 564.

/45/   However, it is wrong to conclude from this alliance that Troeltsch represented so-called "Culture-Protestantism." Troeltsch was very critical of "the identification of the Christian ethical ideal with the formal Kantian ethics of conviction" which was characteristic of the Ritschlians (cf. Troeltsch, G.S. II, pp. 626–639). He also criticized Schleiermacher for perceiving "no problem in the relationship between extra-mundane and intra-mundane values, no tension between Christianity and culture" (ibid., p. 567). What prevented Troeltsch, in spite of his deep concerns with culture, from falling victim to Culture-Protestantism was his thoroughly eschatological understanding of Jesus' message. According to Pannenberg, Troeltsch was "the only systematic theologian of his time" to establish the basic significance of the coming Kingdom of God in Jesus' message in its systematic relevance for ethics (W. Pannenberg, "Die Bedeutung der Ethik bei Ernst Troeltsch," in *Ethik und Ekklesiologie* [Göttingen: Vandenhoeck & Ruprecht, 1977], p. 79). Nevertheless, Christianity, as Troeltsch pictured it toward the end of his life, was almost completely captured within the domain of European culture. Though such a cultural captivity of Christianity in the last phase of Troeltsch's thought must be distinguished from "Culture-Protestantism," critics have good reason to criticize it (cf. Chapters IV and V). Concerning Culture-Protestantism and Troeltsch's stand on it, see G. Rupp, *Culture-Protestantism: German Liberal Theology at the Turn of the Twentieth Century*, AAR Studies in Religion 15 (Missoula, Montana: Scholars Press, 1977).

/46/   Troeltsch, G.S. II, p. 564.

/47/   Id., *Überwindung*, p. 63; cf. *Christian Thought*, p. 4.

/48/   Ibid., pp. 63–64; cf. *Christian Thought*, pp. 4–6.

/49/   Id., G.S. II, pp. 676–677.

/50/   Ibid., pp. 622–623.

/51/   Ibid., p. 623.

/52/   Ibid.

/53/   Ibid., p. 624 n. 54.

/54/   Ibid.

/55/   Ibid., pp. 624–625.

/56/   In his letter to F. von Hügel of 24 October 1922, Troeltsch wrote: "Of course it will take still a couple of years to complete the second volume [of

Der Historismus]. It will give an outline of my view of the European universal history, and to this outline it will join my solution of the task of philosophy of history. Therefore, it will fundamentally delineate my ethics" (Troeltsch, *Briefe*, p. 138).

/57/   Troeltsch, G.S. II, p. 678 (an interpolation from 1913); cf. id., G.S. III, p. 125.

/58/   Id., G.S. II, p. 683.

/59/   Ibid., p. 687.

/60/   Ibid., pp. 686–687.

/61/   Ibid., p. 717.

/62/   Ibid., p. 719.

/63/   Ibid., p. 682.

/64/   Ibid., p. 720 (an interpolation from 1913).

/65/   Troeltsch was always persistent in this emphasis on the necessity of metaphysics. From the beginning he was more concerned with the *object* rather than the subject of knowledge. Even in the second period, during which Troeltsch is generally considered to have been under the spell of the Neo-Kantianism of the Windelband-Rickert school, he did not abandon the metaphysical standpoint which he had espoused in the first period. Given this consistency in the emphasis on metaphysics, it is problematic to place stress upon the influence of these Neo-Kantian philosophers on Troeltsch in the second period.

/66/   Troeltsch, G.S. II, p. 696.

/67/   Ibid., pp. 721–723. In the original essay of the year 1903, Troeltsch mentioned only Jellinek in reference to the concept of "types." In the revised form of the essay, now contained in the collected writings, he has added reference to Max Weber and Burckhardt in this context. It is understandable that Troeltsch did not refer to Weber's "ideal type" in his original essay because Weber first elaborated that celebrated notion the following year. In any event, it is impermissible to attribute Troeltsch's concept of "types" exclusively to Weber's notion of "ideal type" in view of his initial reference to Jellinek.

/68/   Ibid., p. 724.

/69/   Ibid., p. 708. Recognition of the metaphysical and religious moment in Troeltsch's thinking, which was to play a very important role in his program of a cultural synthesis, is crucial for a proper understanding of his entire work. Cf. id., G.S. III, p. 175.

/70/   Troeltsch, G.S. II, p. 700.

/71/   Ibid., p. 701.

/72/ Ibid., p. 707.

/73/ Ibid., p. 709.

/74/ Ibid., p. 712.

/75/ Ibid.

/76/ Ibid., p. 727.

/77/ Ibid., p. 817.

/78/ E. Troeltsch, *Glaubenslehre. Nach Heidelberger Vorlesungen aus den Jahren 1911 und 1912*, with a Foreword by Marta Troeltsch, ed. Gertrud von le Fort (Munich and Leipzig: Verlag von Duncker & Humblot, 1925; reprint ed., with an Introduction by Jacob Klapwijk, Aalen: Scientia Verlag, 1981), p. 1; cf. id., G.S. II, p. 504 (hereafter cited as *Glaubenslehre*).

/79/ Id., "Briefe an Bousset," pp. 43–44.

/80/ Id., *Die Bedeutung der Geschichtlichkeit Jesu für den Glauben* (Bern: Verlag von A. Francke, 1911), p. 5 (hereafter cited as *Geschichtlichkeit*).

/81/ In fact, Theodore Kaftan leveled such an accusation at Troeltsch in his 'exemplary polemical treatise.' According to Kaftan, Troeltsch is by no means a theologian and scarcely a Christian, but is rather "a philosopher of religion of the Christian world of culture" or at best "a Christian philosopher of religion." See T. Kaftan, *Ernst Tröltsch. Eine Kritische Zeitstudie* (Schleswig: Druck und Verlag von Julius Bergas, 1912), esp. pp. 60–62.

/82/ Troeltsch defended himself against Kaftan's accusation with the following statement:
"... I contend that matters are not settled by the charge of a deviation from church doctrine. ... I am pleased, therefore, with the designation 'Christian Neoplatonist' which Kaftan has bestowed on me, the more so as one can invert it to Neoplatonic Christian. This put me in the goodly company of the most highly educated church fathers, who of course had to face a similar charge. Also, I comfort myself with the thought that God is not the General Superintendent of the universe and therefore continue unperturbedly to regard myself as a Christian" (Troeltsch, *Absolutheit* 2d ed., p. 109 n. 1).
When Troeltsch confessed that theology had become "something disgusting" for him (see W. Köhler, *Ernst Troeltsch*, p. 331), his aversion to theology was obviously related largely to such ecclesiastical censorship or "the assessment of Christian identity" *(die Abwägungen des Noch-Christentums oder Nichtmehr-Christentums)* (id., G.S. II, p. 825) characteristic of the theological faculties. "To forbid anyone collaboration for the reason that the person concerned has stepped out of Christianity, as if Christianity were a club that no longer needs to endure the member who no longer agrees to

regulations," is, in Troeltsch's view, "trumps of theologians" (ibid., pp. 825–826).

/83/ Id., G.S. I, p. 926 n. 504a. Troeltsch admits that his thought, in the long run, "comes close to Neo-Platonism, Meister Eckhardt, and a mysticism which includes a real developmental process and a real personality" (id. G.S. II, p. 832).

/84/ E. Troeltsch, "Zur Religionsphilosophie," *Kantstudien* 23 (1918):75.

/85/ Apfelbacher, *Frömmigkeit und Wissenschaft*, p. 44.

/86/ E. Troeltsch, "Wesen der Religion und der Religionswissenschaft," G.S. II, pp. 452–499. This is a third, revised edition of the essay which appeared, under the same title, first in 1906 and then in 1909. Cf. E. Troeltsch, "Wesen der Religion und der Religionswissenschaft," in *Die Kultur der Gegenwart*, ed. Paul Hinneberg (Berlin and Leipzig: B. G. Teubner, 1906), I (IV/2): *Die christliche Religion mit Einschluss der israelitisch-jüdischen Religion*, vol. 2: *Systematische christliche Theologie*, pp. 461–491; 2d rev. ed., in *Die Kultur der Gegenwart*, ed. Paul Hinneberg (Berlin and Leipzig: B. G. Teubner, 1909), I (IV/2): *Systematische christliche Religion*, pp. 1–36.

/87/ Id., G.S. II, p. 488.

/88/ Troeltsch was, however, not always consistent in his division of the tasks of the philosophy of religion. It is true that he divided the specific tasks of the philosophy of religion into four distinctive branches in the essay under question. But at other places he divided them into three branches: psychology of religion, epistemology of religion, and the philosophy of history of religion (cf. E. Troeltsch, *Briefe*, p. 62; "Die theologische Lage der Gegenwart," *Deutsche Monatschrift für das gesamte Leben der Gegenwart* 4 [1903]:396; "Zur Religionsphilosophie," p. 66). The difference between these two kinds of classification concerns the inclusion of a religious metaphysics among the specific tasks of the philosophy of religion.

/89/ Troeltsch, G.S. II, p. 492.

/90/ Id., "Religionsphilosophie," p. 474.

/91/ E. Troeltsch, *Psychologie und Erkenntnistheorie in der Religionswissenschaft* (Tübingen: J. C. B. Mohr, 1905), p. 17.

/92/ Ibid., p. 18.

/93/ Id., "Religionsphilosophie," p. 475 (emphasis original).

/94/ E. Troeltsch, review of *Die Grundlagen der Religionsphilosophie Ernst Troeltsch's*, by W. Günther, in *ZThK* 41 (1916):449. [Göttingen: Vandenhoeck & Ruprecht, 1904], p. 26). See A. Schüler, /138/ Ibid., s.v. "Dogmatik," by E. Troeltsch, 2:108.

/95/ Id., *Psychologie und Erkenntnistheorie*, p. 24.

/96/   Ibid., p. 27.

/97/   Ibid., p. 28.

/98/   Id., G.S. II, p. 761.

/99/   Ibid., p. 494.

/100/   Ibid.

/101/   Id., "Religionsphilosophie," p. 483.

/102/   Id., "Zur Religionsphilosophie," p. 66.

/103/   Id., G.S. II, p. 495.

/104/   Ibid.

/105/   Ibid., p. 496.

/106/   Id., "Religionsphilosophie," p. 477.

/107/   Ibid., p. 478.

/108/   Id., G.S. II, p. 496 (emphasis original).

/109/   Ibid.

/110/   Ibid., p. 764.

/111/   Id., review of *Die Grundlage der Religionsphilosophie Ernst Troeltsch's*, by W. Günther, pp. 449–450.

/112/   See F. W. Graf, "Der 'Systematiker' der 'Kleinen Göttinger Fakultät,'" in *Troeltsch-Studien*, pp. 235–290; cf. Troeltsch, G.S. II, p. 500. However, clarity has not yet been attained on the "religionsgeschichtliche Schule" itself. Given this state of affairs, it is impermissible to speak of the "religionsgeschichtliche Schule" as an established, well-defined entity, as Rubanowice does. Cf. Rubanowice, *Crisis in Consciousness*, pp. 14, 31, 33, 40–49, 52, 55, 62.

/113/   Troeltsch, *Absolutheit*, p. vi. Here Troeltsch presents himself as "a systematic theologian" *(Systematiker)* in contrast to Adolf von Harnack as "a church historian" *(Kirchenhistoriker)*, though he admits that they are both at one in their emphasis upon the importance of the history of religions for theology.

/114/   Needless to say, Karl Barth held this view. According to Barth, "the dogmatics of Troeltsch is formally the nadir of the Neo-Protestant development" (K. Barth, *Dir kirchliche Dogmatik*, III/3, 3d ed. [Zurich: Theologischer Verlag Zürich, 1979], p. 475). Immediately after designating Troeltsch as the "last great systematic exponent" of Neo-Protestantism, Barth remarks in the same breath that "it was with him [Troeltsch] that a crisis came on Neo-Protestantism as a whole" (ibid., IV/1, p. 423); cf. H.

Diem, *Dogmatics*, trans. Harold Knight (Edinburgh and London: Oliver and Boyd, 1959). Here Diem speaks of "the end of dogmatics in the work of Ernst Troeltsch."

/115/ K. Barth, *Die protestantische Theologie im 19. Jahrhundert: Ihre Vorgeschichte und Geschichte* (Zollikon/Zurich: Evangelisher Verlag, 1952), p. 384.

/116/ Troeltsch, G.S. II, p. 227 n. 11.

/117/ R. S. Sleigh, *The Sufficiency of Christianity: An Enquiry Concerning the Nature and the Modern Possibilities of the Christian Religion, with Special Reference to the Religious Philosophy of Dr. Ernst Troeltsch* (London: James Clarke & Co., 1923), p. 169.

/118/ Troeltsch, *Vernunft und Offenbarung*, p. 3; "Selbständigkeit," 5:420.

/119/ Id., *Lage*, p. 13.

/120/ Id., "Selbständigkeit," 5:418.

/121/ Id., "Religionsphilosophie," p. 484.

/122/ Id., G.S. II, p. 514; cf. id., "The Dogmatics," p. 16.

/123/ Id., G.S. IV, pp. 12–13.

/124/ Schleiermacher, *Kurze Darstellung*, §97–98; §195–231.

/125/ This phrase appeared in the first edition of *Kurze Darstellung*. See the third edition, ed. by H. Scholz (Darmstadt: Wissenschaftliche Buchgesellschaft, 1961), p. 10 n. 2.

/126/ A. Schweitzer, *Geschichte der Leben-Jesu-Forschung* (Tübingen: J. C. B. Mohr, 1913), p. 63. On this point, Wilhelm Pauck's argument is instructive. See W. Pauck, "Schleiermacher's Conception of History and Church History," in *Schleiermacher as Contemporary*, Journal for Theology and the Church, vol. 7, ed. Robert W. Funk (New York: Herder & Herder, 1970), pp. 41–56.

/127/ Troeltsch, G.S. II, p. 738. In Troeltsch's judgment, among the thinkers of the eighteenth century, especially "a number of Herder's works contain the modern program of a *religionsgeschichtliche* theology" (id., "Religionswissenschaft und Theologie des 18. Jahrhunderts," pp. 55–56).

/128/ As far as Troeltsch is concerned, it is false to deem the *religionsgeschichtliche* method a special method of historical investigation. For him the *religionsgeschichtliche* method signified at bottom nothing other than general critical-historical method applied to the study of religion in general and Christianity in particular (see Troeltsch, "Ueber historische und dogmatische Methode in der Theologie," G.S. II, pp. 729–753). Accordingly, Rubanowice is completely wrong in thinking that the *re-*

ligionsgeschichtliche method is a method peculiar to the *religionsgeschichtliche Schule*. He holds that Troeltsch's *Soziallehren* is "the best available illustration . . . of the application of the dogmatics of the *religionsgeschichtliche Schule*" (Rubanowice, *Crisis in Consciousness*, p. 43) and that its methodology is "that of the *religionsgeschichtliche Schule*" (ibid., p. 44). Rubanowice is wrong in three ways. First, he takes the existence of the *religionsgeschichtliche Schule* as a matter of course, whereas it is still an open question. Second, he considers the *religionsgeschichtliche* method to be "the method of the *religionsgeschichtliche Schule*" (ibid., p. 62). Third, he does not distinguish between the *religionsgeschichtliche* method as Troeltsch's theological method and the *kulturgeschichtliche* method which Troeltsch employed in writing *Die Soziallehren*. Though there is a close connection between the two, they must be clearly distinguished.

/129/ Troeltsch, G.S. II, p. 509; cf. "The Dogmatics," p. 10.

/130/ Ibid.; cf. "The Dogmatics," p. 11.

/131/ Troeltsch's reference to the Christian principle dates back to his first extensive essay, "The Christian World-view and the Scientific Counter-currents" (1893/94) (see *ZThK* 3 [1893]:494; 4 [1894]:206, 207, 230). In the following, even longer essay on "The Independence of Religion" (1895/96) he spoke of "the formative principle" (*das gestaltende Prinzip*). According to him, "the task of understanding a specific religion in its inner unity," namely, the task of grasping "what is the organizing spirit, the spiritual driving force," or "the formative principle" of a specific religion is one of "the most difficult and most profound problems of the science of religion" (*ZThK* 5 [1895]:429). The definition of the "principle" which he gave in his essay on "History and Metaphysics" (1898) is worthy of note. He states:

"The following should be designated by the 'principle': that which gives an immense complex of historical phenomena the inner unity which covers individual moments; that which involves in itself a driving and developmental force which exerts its influence in accommodation and logical consequence; the mystery of spiritual life, in which it is grounded that the great historical nexus of a sphere of life can be regarded, despite all its diversity, as an innerly coherent unity and as controlled by a germinal force which drives forward that sphere of life" (*ZThK* 8 [1898]:56).

Otherwise, see *Die Religion in der Geschichte und Gegenwart*, 1st ed., s.v. "Prinzip, religiöses," by E. Troeltsch.

/132/ Troeltsch, *Glaubenslehre*. pp. 71–72.

/133/ Id., G.S. II, p. 512.

/134/ The reader of Troeltsch's works will notice that Troeltsch placed more and more emphasis upon the personalistic aspect of Christianity as time went on. Troeltsch defined Christianity as "the religion of personalism in the highest sense" (E. Troeltsch, *Politische Ethik und Christentum* [Götingen: Vandenhoeck & Ruprecht, 1904], p. 26). See A. Schüler, "Christlicher Personalismus: Gedanken zu Ernst Troeltschs Werk," in *Der Mensch vor Gott: Beiträge zum Verständnis der menschlichen Gottesbegegnung*, eds. P. Weindel and R. Hofmann (Düsseldorf: Patmos-Verlag, 1948), pp. 264–277.

/135/ Troeltsch, G.S. II, p. 512; "The Dogmatics," p. 13.

/136/ *RGG*, 1st ed., s.v. "Prinzip, religiöses," by E. Troeltsch, 4:1846 (emphasis original).

/137/ Ibid., s.v. "Dogmatik," by E. Troeltsch, 2:109; id., G.S. II, p. 516; cf. "The Dogmatics," p. 17.

/138/ Ibid., s.v. "Dogmatik," by E. Troeltsch, 2:108.

/139/ Troeltsch, *Glaubenslehre*, p. 40. Troeltsch states that *Glaubenslehre* has "three sources," namely, "the Bible, tradition, and personal [religious] experience" (ibid., p. 24). In consideration of the high rank which he gives to modern life and though, however his *Glaubenslehre* may be said to have actually *four* theological norms.

/140/ Ibid., pp. 20–21.

/141/ Ibid., p. 21.

/142/ Ibid., p. 24.

/143/ Ibid.

/144/ Ibid., p. 14: "It [Neo-Protestantism] is the foundation of our *Glaubenslehre.*"

/145/ *RGG*, 1st ed., s.v. "Prinzip, religiöses," by E. Troeltsch, 4:1846; cf. id., "Selbständigkeit," 6 (1896):186–200; *Absolutheit*, pp. 79–80. It is disputable, however, that every higher religion embodies these six categories. Troeltsch's argument here seems to be based on Judeo-Christian premises.

/146/ Ibid.; id., G.S. II, p. 512; *Glaubenslehre*, p. 73.

/147/ Id., G.S. II, p. 513.

/148/ Id., *Glaubenslehre*, p. 14; cf. ibid., p. 132. Troeltsch remarks: "No theologian of the present keeps so close to the method and intent of Schleiermacher, or feels himself in such inward agreement with him [as I do]" (ibid., p. 130).

/149/ Id., G.S. II, p. 513.

/150/ Ibid.

/151/ According to Troeltsch, the basic assumption of spiritualism is that Christianity is "a living faith in God that is new in every moment" (id.,

Geschichtlichkeit, p. 3). He summarizes the spiritualistic conception of Christianity as follows:

> "Redemption is not something achieved once for all in the work of Christ and then appropriated by individuals. It is something always new which takes place through knowledge of God in the operation of God upon the Soul. No historical work of salvation is then necessary . . . ; no historical Christ is necessary . . . ; there is no inner necessity for the appeal to a historical fact. The historical personality of Jesus and his saving work are not absolutely necessary" (ibid., p. 4).

Troeltsch certainly shares this spiritualistic conception of Christianity in his own most intimate personal piety.

/152/   In his early essay on "The Independence of Religion," Troeltsch criticized Biedermann as follows:

> "Biedermann methodically separates the Christian principle from the person of the founder and recognizes in the former the source of the *Glaubenslehre* as well as the unified agent in the development of Christianity. But it should always be noticed that the question here at stake is a specifically *religious principle*, not merely an idea in general; that the revelatory basis of the principle is therefore inseparable from this principle; and that for this reason the person of the founder too necessarily has abiding religious significance. . . . Only as long as the development remains in relation to this basis and retains its relation to such an authority and revelation, does it remain *religion* and *this* religion. Biedermann failed to see this relation and therefore defined both the Christian principle and its relation to the person in such a way that it has little resemblance to a positive religion and especially to Christianity. . . . Accordingly, my presentation will not replace the person with the principle in Biedermann's manner" (Troeltsch, "Selbständigkeit," 6 [1896]:206).

In short, contra Biedermann's separation of the person of Jesus from the Christian principle, Troeltsch emphasized an inner relationship between the two by asserting that "not a new religious principle created faith in the person of Jesus," but that the Christian principle entered human history in and with the personality of Jesus (see "Metaphysik," p. 60).

/153/   Troeltsch, "Metaphysik," p. 60.

/154/   Id., *Geschichtlichkeit*, pp. 15–16.

/155/   Ibid., p. 16. Troeltsch's emphasis on the cult and community is generally regarded as the result of his sociological studies of religion done under the influence of Max Weber, which resulted in his monumental work, *Die Soziallehren*. But this emphasis cannot be simply ascribed to the result of his religious-sociological studies of this period. His attention to the cult as a very important moment of religion is traceable back to his early writings. As early as 1895, Troeltsch already spelled out the importance of the cult as follows:

> "In particular, the central point of a common cult is indispensable for all religions which do not intend to slumber in a dim consciousness or go wild owing to their fantasies, but to draw new life constantly out of the source of their spiritual strength" (Troeltsch, "Religion und Kirche," *Preußische Jahrbücher* 81 [1895]:239).

Thus, the cult was considered to "form the most important phenomenon of religion" (id., "Selbständigkeit," 5:424). "Faith and cult are," he says, "the souls of religion" (ibid., 5:427). In short, "a religion without cult is not a real living religion" (id., G.S. II, p. 41) but "only half a religion" (id., *Neuzeit* 2d ed., p. 706).

/156/ Troeltsch, G.S. II, p. 513.

/157/ Id., *Glaubenslehre*, p. 339.

/158/ *RGG*, 1st ed., s.v. "Glaube und Geschichte," by E. Troeltsch, 2:1452; cf. id., "Autonomie und Rationalismus in der modernen Welt," *Internationale Wochenschrift für Wissenschaft, Kunst und Technik* 1 (18 May 1907):199–210.

/159/ Id., *Glaubenslehre*, pp. 360–361.

/160/ Ibid.

/161/ B. A. Gerrish, "Ernst Troeltsch and the Possibility of a Historical Theology," in *Ernst Troeltsch and the Future of Theology*, pp. 100–135; W. E. Wyman, Jr., *The Concept of Glaubenslehre: Ernst Troeltsch and the Theological Heritage of Schleiermacher* (Chico, California: Scholars Press, 1983); D. D. Perkins, Jr., "Explicating Christian Faith in a Historically Conscious Age: The Method of Ernst Troeltsch's *Glaubenslehre*" (Ph.D. dissertation, Vanderbilt University, 1981).

CHAPTER IV

THE BROADENING OF THE HORIZON TOWARD UNIVERSAL HISTORY: A PROJECT OF A CONTEMPORARY CULTURAL SYNTHESIS

Troeltsch's Professional Shift from Theology to Philosophy

In the early spring of 1914 the call to the philosophical faculty at the University of Berlin was extended to Troeltsch. After deliberation he accepted the call on 30 July 1914, avowing that "he is thoroughly determined to draw consequences from the new position and to fit himself to the interests of the philosophical faculty without qualification." The philosophical faculty of Berlin then officially appointed him to the chair of philosophy of culture and history on 27 August. Troeltsch moved to Berlin towards Easter of the next year. Thus the Heidelberg period, during which Troeltsch worked intensely in the capacity of a systematic theologian, ended, and his third period as a professional philosopher began.

The question involved in this career change is what significance the professional shift of the year 1914/15 had for Troeltsch. Did it signify a renunciation of theology, to which he had dedicated himself for over two decades up to this point? Or, did it take place without any radical break with his previous theological activities?

Karl Barth, for example, ascribes programmatic importance to Troeltsch's move from the theological faculty to the philosophical faculty. He sees in this professional change a symptomatic and symbolic event of the *eclipse* of 19th-century liberal theology, implying also the collapse of Troeltsch's theology. Barth writes:

> The actual end of the 19th century as the "good old days" came for theology as for everything else with the fateful year of 1914. Accidentally or not, a significant event took place during that very year. Ernst Troeltsch, the well-known professor of systematic theology and the leader of the then most modern school, gave up his chair in theology for one in philosophy. /2/

Tactically enough, Barth goes on immediately to talk about "a black day in early August 1914" when he was horrified by the proclamation of ninety-three German intellects in support of Wilhelm II's war policy, thus involving Troeltsch in guilt by association—though Troeltsch did not endorse the proclamation. Since Barth had long before dismissed Troeltsch as a theologian,/3/ it is clear why he would tend to overplay the importance of Troeltsch's professional shift, namely, to make a case for his own radical break with a liberal Protestant theology with which he had affiliated himself up to that point. In any event, Barth never paid serious attention to Troeltsch as a theological power./4/ Accordingly, Barth's judgment on Troeltsch's career shift is more than disputable.

Gotthold Müller, in an essay entitled "The Self-Dissolution of Dogmatics in Ernst Troeltsch," regards Troeltsch's exchange of the theological chair for the chair in the philosophical faculty as the consequence of Troeltsch's 'dogmatic' position, which, according to him, "was no longer theological but [represented] a more and more deep gliding into philosophy."/5/ Viewed in this way, Troeltsch's development toward a philosophy of history is detrimental, though not discontinuous. Walter Bodenstein holds a similar view. He regards Troeltsch's later development as a "broadening of the horizon of his thought." That is to say, "Troeltsch's philosophy of culture is nothing other than a secularized form of the theology of his preceding epoch."/6/ Bodenstein's intention is, however, not to affirm Troeltsch's consistency as a theologian but rather to assert that "Troeltsch is a wrecked theologian."/7/ Benjamin A. Reist endorses Bodenstein's view. Although Reist holds that "there is a conclusive case for the view that Troeltsch never considered himself as having abandoned finally the basic concerns of theology,"/8/ his study of Troeltsch, like Bodenstein's, results in the demonstration of "the collapse of Troeltsch's theology."/9/

Whether these critics assert Troeltsch's renunciation of theology or the detrimental development of his theology, they are all in one in their negative judgment on a Troeltschian conception of theological tasks. However, to suspect the problematic nature of Troeltsch's theology is one thing, and to grasp the real cause of his professional shift is another. The critics have often confused these two different issues.

Troeltsch's move to the philosophical faculty of Berlin, as I understand it, involved both internal and external reasons.

Externally, his professional shift from theology to philosophy involved somewhat complicated factors. The call of Troeltsch to the philosophical faculty of Berlin has "an interesting pre-history," as Ulrich Pretzel disclosed./10/ The first attempt to gain Troeltsch for the philosophical faculty there was made shortly after the death of Friedrich Paulsen in the winter of 1908/09. But this initial attempt did not come to fruition because opponents of the call of Troeltsch successfully emphasized the possible pernicious effect of his basic theological mentality or faith-motif upon the scientific demand of philosophy—though proponents maintained that Troeltsch's "high philosophical talent might be developed much more freely and more completely in free scientific circumstances," pointing out that his thought "had long been no longer specifically theological."/11/ Interesting and significant for our study is the fact that some held that Troeltsch's general outlook was "very untheological" and "smelled little of the theological faculty" (Eric Marcks's estimation),/12/ whereas others had "serious doubt" whether "the decided theological orientation" evident in Troeltsch's hitherto scientific work "will allow him to accomplish the professorship of philosophy in the manner that corresponds to the nature of the philosophical faculty."/13/ To suffer from such antithetic judgments was the destiny of a scholar who was engaged in two conflicting professions—theology and philosophy—at the same time.

The next opportunity for Troeltsch to move to Berlin presented itself in the year 1914. This time the call of Troeltsch to a philosophical chair achieved reality. But the situation was not as simple as it is usually assumed to have been. If what Walther Köhler reported about Troeltsch's move to Berlin is correct, Troeltsch originally wanted to enter the theological faculty there./14/ Harnack, who had been fighting a lonely battle for liberal lines at Berlin, urgently requested Troeltsch to join the theological faculty and stand by him. However, Reinhold Seeberg, who had great power over the faculty, strongly opposed Troeltsch's entry into the theological faculty, and Adolf Deissmann, Troeltsch's one-time colleague at Heidelberg and then professor in New Testament at Berlin, stood against Troeltsch. Thus, Troeltsch's wish to join the theological faculty was hindered./15/ On the other hand, the academic atmosphere of Heidelberg, in which Troeltsch had occupied the chair in systematic theology for two decades, had become less attractive and less stimulating for him. For his old friends Johannes Weiss and Georg Jellinek were dead, his relationship to Max Weber was about to enter a cooling-off period,/16/ and Hans von Schubert, who too had been Troeltsch's colleague and friend, was considering leaving Heidelberg for Leipzig. Furthermore, as Köhler remarks, "the entire framework within which Troeltsch had to act was strongly determined by theological-ecclesiastical interests, and yet his scientific thinking was utterly untheological! Theology had become, as he confessed, 'something disgusting' for him."/17/ Thus, "things became," so writes Troeltsch, "too narrow for me in Heidelberg."/18/

Given this state of affairs, the call to the philosophical faculty of Berlin, with a commission being given him to teach the philosophy of culture and history, the philosophy of religion, and the history of Christian religion, might well be pleasing to Troeltsch in all respects. But for him the decision for the acceptance of that call was not easy. Georg Wünsch, one of Troeltsch's devoted pupils at Heidelberg, remarks: "He [Troeltsch] did not easily make up his mind to accept the call, for he loved romantic and picturesque Heidelberg . . . ; in essence, however, things had become too narrow for him."/19/ Troeltsch wrote the following to his most intimate friend Wilhelm Bousset in his letter of 27 July 1914:

> Alas! Since the beginning of May I have been deliberating over it [the call to the philosophical faculty of Berlin] and have gradually become quite exhausted and nervous because of contradictory feelings. The thing has become terribly hard for me./20/

Nevertheless, Troeltsch eventually decided to accept the call for the following reason:

> In the present ecclesiastical and political situation I have little faith in theology and perceive the conflict of my theology with all contemporary theology so sharply that there is only little to hope for here. I shall come to a full truthfulness with myself only when I get rid of these considerations./21/

Gertrud von le Fort, the Catholic novelist and most devoted pupil of Troeltsch, provides vivid testimony to the real intention behind Troeltsch's career exchange as well as to the reaction of his students at Heidelberg to the teacher's proposed move to Berlin.

> . . . the call to the philosophical faculty of Berlin was extended to Professor Troeltsch. In his lecture course I witnessed the most passionate demonstration by the students

who were seeking to retain him in the theological faculty at Heidelberg. He showed his gratitude to them without expressing a decision. But after the lecture, as he escorted me home, he told me that he was determined to accept the Berlin call and to exchange the theological faculty for the philosophical. As he saw the future of the former, he believed he would have more possibilities in the philosophical faculty to address the human spiritual and religious consciousness than in theology./22/

In view of these considerations, it is safe to say that the main reasons for Troeltsch's professional shift in the year 1914/15, seen from the external viewpoint, were, first, his deep-seated disgust with the narrow-mindedness and pseudoscientific nature of the ecclesiastically biased theology of the theological faculty; second, his ardent desire for free research and pursuit of scientific nature; and, third, the situation directly wrought by church politics. Our observations in the preceding chapters show, however, that Troeltsch's move to the philosophical faculty of Berlin was not a mere accident. It also involved, in my opinion, the moment of an inner necessity. Troeltsch's intellectual development up to this point required of him a more earnest dedication to the philosophy of history proper from all the sides. First of all, the *religionsgeschichtliche* theology, in Troeltsch's view, must establish, first, the supremacy or prime validity of Christianity on the basis of a historical and philosophical comparison of religion (the first task of a *religionsgeschichtliche* dogmatics); and, then, it must define the essence of Christianity (or formulate the Christian principle) through philosophico-historical analysis of Christian history (the second task). These tasks, however, belonged to the specific business of the philosophy of history in general. Second, the philosophy of religion, as Troeltsch conceived it, involved as its third task the comprehension of religions as arising out of an inner unity and striving in their succession toward a normative goal. Troeltsch designated this as the task of the philosophy of history of religion *(Geschichtsphilosophie der Religion)*. The solution of this task was, however, possible only through the study of the nature and meaning of the concept of development, which belonged in principle to the philosophy of history. Third, submergence in the philosophy of history was also required from his ethical viewpoint. As we have seen, Troeltsch divided ethics into "the formal autonomous ethics of conviction" and "the objective teleological ethics of value." Thereby the elaboration of a concretely

structured system of values became the most crucial question for
him. However, since the objective values develop in the reality of
history, Troeltsch's ethics culminated in the task of bringing history
into relation with a system of value. This task was a specific business
of the philosophy of history.

Thus, Troeltsch's theology, philosophy of religion, and ethics all
converged on the philosophy of history. H.-J. Gabriel is therefore
certainly right in saying that "Troeltsch's entry into the philosophical
faculty took place . . . without a break *(bruchlos)* and organically
fitted in his course of development."/23/ Apart from his dubious
value-judgment of Troeltsch's theology, Bodenstein too is not far
from the truth in considering Troeltsch's transition from systematic
theology to the philosophy of history and culture to be the "broadening of the horizon" *(Horizonterweiterung)*./24/ For Troeltsch himself said that with the passage of time he "broadened the horizon
(Gesichtskreis), emancipated the general comprehension more and
more from theological thought, and approached a universal-historical mode of thinking."/25/ In the conclusion of the first chapter of
Der Historismus, Troeltsch remarks:

> If one knows the norms for shaping life *(Lebensgestaltung)*
> no longer in church dogma or in its descendant, rationalistic
> dogma, then there remains only history as the source and
> the philosophy of history as the solution./26/

Hence we propose to view Troeltsch's intellectual development toward the philosophy of history in terms of the broadening of the
horizon toward universal history. Thus the relevant questions are of
the following sort: To what extent did Troeltsch's theological interests
remain continuous despite his change of career? What theological
implications did his philosophy of history involve? What transformation did his former theology undergo?

The Problems of Historismus and Troeltsch's Philosophy of History

As the title of his massive work *Der Historismus und seine
Probleme* suggests, Troeltsch's deep absorption in the philosophy of
history arose from his full realization of the seriousness of the
problems posed by so-called *Historismus*./27/ Troeltsch, to be sure,
had been quite aware, from the very beginning, of its devastating
effects on human normative thinking as well as on Christian
faith./28/ But, accelerated by the outbreak of World War I, the

theme of *Historismus* now became the most urgent issue for him. Troeltsch was always insistent that the word *Historismus* "is to be completely disconnected from the bad secondary meaning and to be understood in the sense of *the fundamental historicizing of all our thinking about human being, its culture, and its values.*"/29/ His own concise characterization reads as follows:

> The word "Historismus" . . . signifies the historicizing of our entire knowledge and experience of the spiritual world, as it has taken place in the course of the nineteenth century. Here we see everything in the stream of becoming, in endless and always new individualization, in determination by the past towards an unrecognizable future. The state, law, morality, religion, and art are dissolved in the flow of historical becoming and are comprehensible only as ingredients of historical development./30/

Accordingly, *Historismus* in Troeltsch's proper sense denotes, to use Calvin G. Rand's expression, "a *specific* historical way of thinking," and that rather as "a *Weltanschauung*" than as "a methodology."/31/

What problems, then, did *Historismus*, so characterized, involve? In diagnosing the problems, Troeltsch, in accordance with the general principle of *Historismus*, treated them genetically. As the historical horizon became very much wider both in space and in time, and as human knowledge of the past became much more differentiated, more exact, and more objective, the immense variety and movement in the gigantic body of material for historical comparisons at first profoundly interested and broadened human minds. However, such was only the case as long as all the variety and movement could be easily arranged in a series of an evolutionary progress and as long as the position of the observer of historical dramas, as the summit of this progress, remained unquestioned. But the more difficult the construction of such an evolutionary series became by virtue of the increasing exactitude of research, and the more the observer's own confident present revealed alarming cleavages and gaps, the more difficult the attainment of firmly fixed standards for the living present became. For example, the idea of a humane European order, expressing itself in the organization of the states and the societies appertaining to it, was dissolved by criticism and gave way to all sorts of plans for distant future, to pessimism, or to purely materialist apprehension of interests which can only be realized by violence./32/ Thus, the entire domain of the ethical standard was drawn into the flow of historical changes and came to be considered mainly in its historical conditionality and complexity, while historical scholarship itself, owing to the increase of specialist research, the abandonment of the philosophy of history of any sort, and the demand for a detachment from the observable objects, surrendered itself more and more to aesthetic indulgence in pure detail and ongoing historical specialization. The results were, from both sides, skepticism or a historical relativism that weakened human moral vigor. Thus "what had been a liberation and an elevation became a burden and a [source of] confusion."/33/ Above all, the problem that burdened Troeltsch heavily and required of him an urgent solution was the "shaking of the ethical system of values both in its foundation and in its substantial content."/34/

Troeltsch's approach to the problems of *Historismus* was paradoxical. For him history was not only the source of the problems but also the source of their solutions. Although a modern historical way of thinking was responsible for the modern crisis in values, Troeltsch believed that a fundamental philosophical mastery of history, that is, a carefully considered philosophy of history, could provide the solution to that crisis. This is exactly what Troeltsch's famous motto, "to overcome history with history" *(Geschichte durch Geschichte überwinden)*, meant./35/ Fundamental to his position was his conviction that "an unlimited relativism, a playful occupation with the historical materials, and a paralysis of the will to live one's own life" have nothing to do with an authentic *Historismus*. He was emphatic in his assertion that an authentic historical way of thinking should be clearly distinguished from a "base *Historismus*"/36/ which ends in such pernicious results. The authentic *Historismus* Troeltsch advocated was something eminently practical, ethical, and constructive. For "the purely contemplative view of history,"/37/ or "a *Historismus* that makes merely passive observations, indulges in witty comparisons, and finally learns dull lessons,"/38/ in his opinion, inevitably leads to the base *Historismus* which he repudiated.

Troeltsch began his philosophy of history with a diagnosis of the contemporary crisis of *Historismus* and its modern backdrop in order to find a remedy for its present disease, which his proposed philosophy of history intended to prescribe. As a result of the diagnosis, he proposed to make a clear distinction between "two paths" of the philosophy of history: "the formal logic of history" *(die formale Geschichtslogik)* and "the material philosophy of history" (*die materiale Geschichtsphilosophie*)./39/ "Both should indeed be carefully separated," he says, "even if naturally they must eventually flow together." "It was an error of the older philosophy of history," he continues to say, "that it, in most cases, mixed both up and neglected to construct the logical foundation from the viewpoint of empirical history."/40/ Hence Troeltsch intended to make *Der Historismus* a two-volume work, "of which the first furnishes," he says, "the conceptual foundation and the second the material exposition of what I can discern as the philosophy of history"/41/—though the second volume never saw the light of day owing to his premature death. Concerning the relationship between the formal logic of history and the material philosophy of history, Troeltsch wrote as follows:

> The logic of history without the construction of the universal process is a torso, merely a logical theory of empirical history. The construction without logically secured empirical data is a house without the foundation, merely an ideal construct outlined by the dreaming mind or sovereign caprice. Both are actually and psychologically most closely connected with each other. If however this is so, then, in a scientific and logical sense, the material philosophy of history must grow out of the formal./42/

In view of this statement, Troeltsch's philosophy of history, which lacks the material construction of the historical process, remains a torso, no matter how impressive his treatment of 'the logical problem of the philosophy of history' may be. Nevertheless, the first volume of *Der Historismus* was packed full of hints about his unfinished material philosophy of history. (In fact, the fourth chapter of this work presents the outline of his proposed second volume.) Moreover, Troeltsch's posthumous work *Der Historismus und seine Überwindung* (1924)/43/ contains, according to his own remarks, part of his own material philosophy of history./44/ Furthermore, some essays now contained in another posthumous work, *Deutscher Geist und Westeuropa* (1925), also convey Troeltsch's basic material ideas./45/ Consequently, we are in a position to be capable of discussing not only Troeltsch's formal logic of history but also, to some extent, his material philosophy of history, although we, at the same time, always have to bear in mind that Troeltsch's philosophy of history remains unfinished.

Troeltsch's basic thesis in elaborating the *specific* logic of history was that "the logic of the concrete fields of scholarship (*Real-*

wissenschaften) grows instinctively out of intimate contact with the subject matter and is basically determined by the objects." From this basic premise he upheld "a plurality of fundamental methods."/46/ Thus he rejected the imposition of any elementary logic or metalogic upon history on one hand and fought for the autonomy of the logic of history in adamant resistance to the "monism of method" *(Methodenmonismus)*/47/ of the natural sciences on the other. This twofold combat for the formal logic of history partly accounts for Troeltsch's double dedication of *Der Historismus,* namely, to Wilhelm Dilthey and Wilhelm Windelband./48/ Troeltsch was a decided pupil of the Neo-Kantianism of the Windelband-Rickert school in that he strongly asserted the distinction between the *Naturwissenschaften* and the *Geisteswissenschaften,* which, stated in its sharpest form, is the distinction between "pure natural science as mathematical, mechanical, physical, and chemical theory on one hand and pure history as investigation and presentation of the spiritual *(seelischen)* movements, creations, and contexts of humanity on the other."/49/ But he rejected the Windelband-Rickert view that the logic of history is based ultimately upon the deductive analysis of the transcendental rules and concepts./50/ In this respect he instead allied himself with Dilthey in his assertion that the logic of history must be worked out of the empirical data of the actual processes of history. In the long run, however, Troeltsch did not content himself with Dilthey's life-philosophical position. He states:

> Without question, this [Diltheyan intuitive] method hit the real nerve of the historical better than any of the others hitherto described. Especially with its immunity from theories did it perceive the flow of history which can be grasped solely intuitively. . . . But is this [immunity from theories] really possible? Does this understanding, illustrating, and comprehending really ensue without logical categories, without transformation and modification of the materials through principles of selection, formation, and combination? . . . Can there be a philosophy of life at all which comprehends life through life, not through thought?/51/

That is to say, for Troeltsch the logic of history needed to be deeply rooted in *historical reality* itself, and yet it had to be the *formal logic* of history. Hence he proposed to *work out* the formal logic of history by proceeding "from what the historian actually practices" *(aus der Praxis der Historiker heraus)./52/*

What, then, was characteristic of Troeltsch's own elaboration of the formal logic of history? In his view,

> The logic of history consists in certain logical presupposi-
> tions, principles of selection, formation, and combination,
> which, in comprehending the reality of experience estab-
> lished through criticism or through spontaneous intuition,
> we practice, to begin with, utterly unconsciously. They
> become more and more conspicuous in intimate contact
> with the object or in dedication to the subject matter and
> finally require logical formulation./53/

According to Troeltsch's formulation, the categories or concepts with which the historian actually works in historical investigations are: (1) "individual totality," (2) "originality and uniqueness," (3) "narrow selection," (4) "representation," (5) "unity of value or meaning," (6) "tension between the common spirit and individual spirits," (7) "the unconscious," (8) "the creative," (9) "freedom in the sense of choice," (10) "accident," and (11) "development."/54/ Out of these eleven basic historical categories those of "individual totality" *(individuelle Totalität)* and "development" *(Entwicklung)* are fundamental and pivotal, and the rest are corollary. Troeltsch's subsequent discussion in *Der Historismus* centers on these two "basic concepts" *(Grundbegriffe)*./55/

It should be noted that Troeltsch deliberately coined the term "individual totality" to replace the commonly used term "individuality." "Individual totality" clearly has the advantage of expressing not merely an individual person but also a collective entity. Accordingly, the category of the individual or the concept of historical individuality in Troeltsch's usage includes "family, race, class, nation, circumstances of the time, total spiritual situation, and finally, the association of humanity." Thus "the proper subjects of scientific history," in Troeltsch's opinion, are less "single biographical individuals" than "collective individualities" *(Kollektiv-Individualitäten)*, that is, "people, states, classes, social ranks, cultural tendencies, religious communities, and complex occurrences of all kinds such as wars, revolutions, and so forth."/56/ In Troeltsch's writings, therefore, collective entities, such as Antiquity, Christianity, the Middle Ages, or the German nation, were treated as the "historical individuals."

Thus understood, the concept of individual totality, however, already implies the second basic concept of "development." For no

historical individual totality is *static*. Movement and dynamics are
certainly the essence of the individual totality. Historical entities
"are a part of an uninterrupted flow of becoming and must be set
into this flow."/57/ Hence arises the concept of development as a no
less fundamental category of historical investigations. According to
Troeltsch, the concept of development has its ultimate root in the
essence and *capability* of the human spirit. Human being is essentially disposed to integration and is capable of giving a unified
interpretation to a multiple complex of historical events. The historian or the thinker conceives historical development by creating
from the multiple diversity of historical phenomena a logically com-
prehensible succession of events which gives the impression of a
movement with an inner consistency./58/ This human essence and
capability, in Troeltsch's view, is also the matrix of the impulse
toward universal history.

Universal History and the Idea of a Contemporary Cultural Synthesis

Troeltsch's painstaking labor in *Der Historismus* culminates in
the discussion of the two pivotal ideas of "universal history" (*Universalgeschichte*) and "contemporary cultural synthesis" (*die gegenwärtige Kultursynthese*).

As Troeltsch maintained, universal history is certainly "the natural completion and crown of history, the comprehensive achievement of the concept of development."/59/ In the time of Troeltsch,
however, the impulse toward universal history had dried up. The
general reason for this "drying-up of universal history," as Troeltsch
understood them, were: (1) the "immense increase of demands for
the proof and specialist study by means of textual criticism," (2) "the
weariness of the universal and humane spirit in general," (3) "the
after-effect of the old spirit of Organology and its opposition to
Hegelian speculation," (4) "the shaking of the idea of value, [that is,]
the idea of a general religious or ethical goal, and the complete
disintegration of the idea of European humanity."/60/ But the more
specific and intrinsic reason for the dissolution of the conception of
universal history was the devastating effect of the concept of individuality. Troeltsch remarks:

> In its permanent effect it [the idea of individuality] has been
> altogether disastrous to the conception of universal history.

It dissolved and disintegrated that conception; it enslaved it to notions of 'relativity'; it transmuted it either into specialization, buttressed by 'method,' or pure national introspection./61/

In the face of such a detrimental development of historiography as well as the general intellectual climate of the day, Troeltsch felt an urgent need for "a return to a way of thinking, and a way of feeling about life, which was not merely 'historical,' but 'universal-historical.' "/62/ Troeltsch boldly asserts:

> But if you want universal history, you must have some notion of the future and its goal (Zukunfts- und Zielgedanken); for only in the light of such a notion can the record of man be drawn together into a unity. How far that is possible, is one of the great burning questions of the day. The attitude towards history which is merely specialist, or for that matter merely contemplative, has to be transcended: the image of Clio has to be made to face, once more, towards the great and universal problems of the future. The rigour, the width of equipment, and the devotion of research into what has happened (Gewesenes), must be combined with the will that acts and shapes the future (dem handelnden und zukunftsgestaltenden Willen); . . ./63/

The paragraph cited here adequately epitomizes the salient feature of Troeltsch's proposed material philosophy of history. The prominent traits of his philosophy of history, as we shall now discuss them, are its (1) universal-historical, (2) activist, and (3) future orientations. These are all combined in his idea of a contemporary cultural synthesis.

A thrust toward universal history did inform Troeltsch's thought from the very beginning. In his philosophy of history of the Berlin period, however, universal history as such first became the central theme for philosophical reflection and received a comprehensive treatment./64/ We have just seen how keenly Troeltsch perceived a need for a universal history. Nevertheless, the task was not so easy. The actual writing of universal history involved difficult philosophical problems. Troeltsch spells out the main reasons for the difficulties as follows:

> It seems necessary that universal history purport, in the nature of things, to be a history of humankind as a whole both in the width of space and in the immensity of time, and that it regard the nexus not only as a real causal one but also as a one executed in a unified development. However, this

whole, as far as it has already come into existence, cannot be
surveyed spatially and temporally. Also the existing principal major groups—apart from individual contacts—actually constitute neither a real causal nexus nor the uniformity
of a cultural sense. Above all, however, the future is unknown, of course. Because of the great variety of its real
possibilities the future cannot be drawn into the unity of a
meaning which is derived from the survey of the whole./65/
To paraphrase this statement, the reason why Troeltsch had to
renounce the actual writing of universal history in the unimpaired
sense was threefold. First of all, Troeltsch could never overcome
Kantian epistemology, according to which the total meaning of
humanity was beyond our grasp. He was of the opinion that the
feeble human intellect was simply too weak to grasp it./66/ In the
second place, "the unity and correlation of meaning *(Sinneinheit
und Sinnbeziehung),*" in Troeltsch's opinion, "is indispensable for
the universal-historical development."/67/ For "there is a historical
object only as far as it is combined by a knowable unity of meaning
and culture, and a development only as far as a common meaning
and cultural spirit underlies it."/68/ In the time of Troeltsch, however, "humankind as a whole [had] no spiritual unity and therefore
no unified development."/69/ Since humanity as a unified totality
had no historical reality, a universal history of humankind was
impossible for Troeltsch. In the third place, the openness of history
to the future made any decisive construction of universal history
problematic. Neglect of the open future was admittedly one of
Hegel's fatal mistakes. Troeltsch had learned too many significant
lessons from Hegel's failure to construct another grand theory of
universal history.

Thus Troeltsch was confronted by the practical impossibility of
universal history, though he felt an urgent need for it. He found
himself in a dilemma. To abandon universal history signified surrender to historical relativism, but to construct it was an impracticable enterprise. Troeltsch's proposed way out of this quandary was to
narrow down the scope of universal history to a manageable scale by
imposing restrictions on it while preserving its larger significance.
The idea proposed for the solution of that dilemma was his queer
notion of "a universal history of Europeanism" *(Universalgeschichte
des Europäismus)*./70/ According to Troeltsch,

> A unity of meaning of continuous development can be con-
> structed only from the standpoint of the observer, that is to

say, only for the sphere of a cultural circle which comprises
the observer and is composed of an actual sequence of
events and their effects. In our case, therefore, only such a
construction of the process of the Occidental cultural circle
is possible./71/

"In truth we know," he says, "only ourselves and understand only
our own being and for that reason only our own development."/72/
"One must have the courage," he continues to say, "to confess one's
own historical destiny as a whole because we cannot get out of our
historical skin."/73/ Thus he concluded that "for us [Europeans]
there is only a universal history of Europeanism (*eine Weltgeschichte
des Europäertums*). The old idea of universal history must assume
new and more modest form."/74/ Here we should not take this
espousal of a universal history of Europeanism by Troeltsch as the
expression of "European arrogance"(*Europäerhochmut*)./75/ Quite
the contrary. Since "Europeanism is intended by Troeltsch to be a
criticism of the 'self-absolutizing' . . . of the European standpoint,"/76/ the universal history of Europeanism is rather the expression of his humility as a European thinker. The term itself,
however, does indicate Troeltsch's dilemma: the practical impossibility of universal history on one hand and the importance of an
impulse toward universal history on the other. The question is
therefore how the universal history of the Europeanism is possible at
all. How can the history of European-American cultural circle,
which is itself a particular cultural circle, represent the total picture
of world culture, and for that matter universal history? This is the
question which touches the heart of the metaphysical dimension of
Troeltsch's philosophy of history.

Troeltsch adopted "a Leibnizian doctrine of monads and a Mal-
ebranchean doctrine of participation"/77/ for the solution of the
difficult problems confronting him. Concerning the problem of historical knowledge in general, Troeltsch writes:

> Not Spinoza's identity of thought and being, or of nature
> and spirit, but the substantial and individual identity of
> finite minds with the infinite mind, and precisely thereby
> the intuitive participation in its concrete content and active
> unity of life, this is the key to the solution of our prob-
> lem./78/

Troeltsch took recourse to the same doctrines for the solution of the
problem with which we are now concerned. Combining Leibniz's
monadology, Malebranche's doctrine of participation, Ranke's doc-

trine of epochs, and others, he conceived a sort of historical-meta-physical monadology, though he never clearly spelled it out. According to this historically modified monadology, the individual historical entity, understood in terms of a monad, participates in the All-Life *(Alleben)* or All-Spirit *(Allgeist)* and represents through this participation a realization of the common ground of life in its peculiar historical situation./79/ Accordingly, any historical individual totality, in spite of its individuality, historical conditionality, and spatio-temporal limitation, carries in itself the universality and the metaphysical perfection of the goal of history. Thus understood, the history of European culture and civilization as an individual totality, despite its historical and geographical particularities, does bear the significance of universal history./80/ This being the case, however, a universal history of the Islamic world or, perhaps, that of Chinese culture would, in principle, also be possible. Troeltsch certainly did not deny the possibility of constructing such a universal history./81/ But he believed that he could present a very strong case for his espousal of a universal history of Europeanism owing to "an un-precedented uniqueness" *(eine unerhörte Einzigartigkeit)*/82/ of the European-American cultural circle. This uniqueness, in his view, was ultimately rooted in "the synthesis of two most peculiar and . . . most singular cultural stages: the North-European culture and the Mediterranean-ancient culture" as well as the decisive role played by the Christian Church in creating and maintaining this synthesis./83/ Whether or not Troeltsch's argument is persuasive enough to justify his claim about the *universal* history of Europeanism, European-American culture, in my judgment, certainly involves universal moments, such as science, law, morality, the idea of personality, humanity, and so forth. Therefore, even without the help of the historical monadology, Troeltsch's claim to the universality of European culture is to some extent empirically justifiable. In any case, Troeltsch's philosophy of history now turned its attention from the epistemological problem of universal history to the ethical problem of the cultural synthesis of Europeanism.

In the face of the crisis in values of European culture and civilization as well as in view of the practical impossibility of constructing universal history, Troeltsch focused his labor on the revitalization of European culture and spirit. That was his celebrated idea of a contemporary cultural synthesis. Abandoning the teleological construction of universal history as a process moving toward the realization of the goal in gradual successions,/84/ Troeltsch turned his material philosophy of history to the urgent ethical task of solving the contemporary crisis of cultural values in Europe. He formulated the task as follows:

> But what remains then as the task of the material philosophy of history? Primarily nothing other than the production of a standard, an ideal, an idea of the actual present—seen on the whole as a total situation and a result of thousands of years—for creating a new unity of culture./85/

In other words, "a cultural synthesis which is bound to shape the present and future out of a disciplined historical illustration of the past"/86/ was the central major task of Troeltsch's material philosophy of history. This task became all the more urgent for Troeltsch because of the catastrophes of the European society caused by World War I and the Russian Revolution, not to mention pernicious effects of historical relativism. Thus he spells out:

> A task that cannot be avoided, however, is the welding together *(Zusammenarbeitung)* of these cultural values into a unified whole for the present and the future within a large given sphere of culture. Here, and here alone, is the one possibility of a solution for our problem—the problem of damming and shaping the historical stream of life *(Dämmung und Gestaltung des historischen Lebensstromes).*/87/

In the long run, "a conceptual synthesis on a large and broad scale and a penetrating correlation" between historical judgments of the past and the philosophico-historical perspective of the present and the future was "the solely possible philosophical mastery of *Historismus."*/88/

The two prominent traits of Troeltsch's philosophy of history which we have characterized as its "activist" and "future orientations" are evident in the idea of a contemporary cultural synthesis. According to Troeltsch, "there is no purely contemplative science either in nature or in history, either in motif or in result. . . . Thus there is no purely contemplative history which does not flow into the understanding of the present and the future."/89/ In contrast to historiography, which is mainly oriented toward the past, the philosophy of history is oriented toward the past, present, and future. Its main task is "the problem of the further formation *(Weiterbildung)* of historical life on the basis of a historical understanding of the present."/90/ To put the matter more philosophically, "the individual in its present formation is always at the same time a task and an oughtness, a further formation (*Weiterbildung*) of the universal moment which is comprised and actualized in all individuals." With this oughtness, however, "a purely descriptive and inquisitive study of history" stops and "active history (*die handelnde Geschichte*) or a historical life which always forms itself"/91/ begins. Thus "the philosophy of history flows into ethics" and therefore occupies "the middle position" (*Mittelstellung*) between an empirical study of history and ethics./92/

As is clear from these general observations, Troeltsch's philosophy of history bore an eminently *practical* and, in this sense, ethical tone. Since it aimed at "mastering an exuberance of historical life and knowledge by fitting it to the direction with which our shaping will (*unser gestaltender Wille*) is bound to comply," it was "the sheer opposite of any purely contemplative attitude toward history." It was, to use Troeltsch's own expression, essentially "practical, ethical, if one follows the Greeks in understanding the word 'ethic' in the broad sense, or cultural-philosophical."/93/ And for the very reason it was "naturally teleological." This, however, does not signify that Troeltsch's philosophy of history represented "the teleology of the objectively constructible course of the world, seen from the final eternal end." Rather it was teleological in the sense of "the teleology of the will which forms and shapes its past with a view to the future from the standpoint of the present moment."/94/ As illustrated by this citation, Troeltsch's philosophy of history was trained exclusively on the task of "the shaping of the future" (*Zukunftsgestaltung*). This *Zukunftsgestaltung* was undoubtedly the leitmotif of his philosophy of history./95/ Its future orientation was thus beyond question. Troeltsch's point was, however, not to speculate about the future but to shape or form it. His future orientation was thus practical and ethical in character. In this sense, his philosophy of history was also action-oriented. Because of this activist orientation he laid special emphasis on activist and volitional notions./96/ For example, such expressions as "the will that acts and shapes the future" (*der handelnde und zukunftsgestaltende Wille*), "the acting and shaping human being" (*der handelnde und gestaltende Mensch*), "the acting and forming mind" (*der handelnde und formende Geist*), all attest to Troeltsch's activist orientation./97/

Now that the general characteristics of Troeltsch's material philosophy of history have been described, it is incumbent on us next to examine its key notion, the idea of a contemporary cultural synthesis, in detail. Since his philosophy of history had a decidedly practical and ethical import, it is necessary to inspect that key notion in close relationship to his ethics.

As we have seen in the preceding chapter, Troeltsch divided his ethics into two parts: "the formal autonomous ethics of conviction" and "the objective teleological ethics of value" or, more simply, "the morality of personality and conscience" *(die Persönlichkeits- und Gewissensmoral)* and "the ethics of cultural values" *(die Ethik der Kulturwerte)*. According to Troeltsch, the morality of personality and conscience is "the one and only thread which guides us into the realm of standards beyond the reach of time or history."/98/ It "originates in the aim of achieving the dignity and unity of the personality, and is therefore purely formal." Because of this "quality of pure formality" it is "outside time or history" *(zeit- und geschichtslos)* and "can be developed into a timeless valid and comprehensive system of precepts."/99/ The ethics of cultural values, in contrast, is *zeitgebunden* (time-bound) because ethical cultural values, such as family, state, law, the economic system, science, art and religion, are "entirely historical creations" *(durch und durch historische Gebilde)* and each of them "an individual creation corresponding to the definite conditions of the period."/100/ Thus, while the morality of personality and conscience "by virtue of the formality leads us out of history into the sphere of the timelessly valid," the ethics of cultural values "conducts us back into history and development, and more particularly into the realm of the individual."/101/

When Troeltsch proposed the idea of a contemporary cultural synthesis, he was being confronted by the fact that "the entire domain of the ethical standards had itself been drawn, by modern psychology, by *Historismus*, and by evolutionism, into the flow of things," and been "undermined and washed away by this stream."/102/ Behind his proposal of that idea lay therefore "the most living problem of actual life," that is, "the question whether, and how far, a conceptually assured and clarified ethics can master and limit this historical relativism."/103/ His proposed solution to this problem of "damming and shaping the historical stream of life" *(Dämmung und Gestaltung des historischen Lebensstromes)*/104/ was an "individual and personal combination of the morality of

conscience, cultural values, and the given situation."/105/ Thereby
he designated such a combination that must constantly be worked
out   afresh   as   a   "creative   compromise"   (schöpferischer
Kompromiß)/106/ and emphasized its "metaphysical character of
individuality" as well as its "character of struggle and labour"
(Kampf- und Arbeitscharakter)./107/ At this point, however, there is
no doubt that such an individual and personal combination of the
morality of conscience and cultural values in a particular given
situation signified his idea of a contemporary cultural synthesis.

   In view of these observations, we can say that the contemporary
cultural synthesis consisted in the synthesis of the morality of conscience and personaltiy and the ethics of cultural values. Thereby
the former embodied the *a priori* element of the cultural synthesis
and the latter its *a posteriori* element. The contemporary cultural
synthesis was thus, by design, a new synthesis of the universally
valid and the historical-individual which the contemporary Europe
so urgently needed. By virtue of the creative combination of these
two moments, the cultural synthesis was deeply rooted in the reality
of history, and yet it was anchored fast to the eternal transcendent
ground of life and being which prevented it from being washed away
by the stream of relativism. Thus Troeltsch asserted:

> . . . there is in particular syntheses, when they are made
> with a wide vision and deep thought, something objective
> and   universally   valid   (etwas   Objektives   und   Allge-
> meingültiges), which is ever pressing forward, and, in its
> special individual application to place and condition, can
> rather be felt than intellectually constructed. And this feel-
> ing, joined to broad and objective considerations, estab-
> lishes sufficient security against all scepticism and all funda-
> mental relativism./108/

How, then, can a cultural synthesis be achieved? Troeltsch made
a distinction between an "unconsciously produced, fundamental,
and fateful synthesis" (unbewußt geschaffenen, grundlegenden und
schicksalsartigen Synthesen) and a "conscious and constructive synthesis" (eine bewußte und konstruktive Synthese)./109/ Needless to
say, the latter was the synthesis Troeltsch was concerned with. This
conscious and constructive synthesis, according to Troeltsch, is not
"an *a priori* construction which proceeds from the essential nature
of reason or the law of the world-process" but rather "an *a posteriori*
construction which essentially demands a knowledge of the prem-

ises, history, and destiny of the particular sphere of culture." Such a synthesis must be based on a conceptual grasp of the premises and bases of its own existence, as they have been shaped in unconsicious process: the geopraphical and biological conditions of its own sphere of life; the logical necessity of its own development; the interplay of necessity and chance, and so forth. Therefore, every synthesis is from the outset determined by and is only concerned with "the historical individuality of the particular sphere of culture and the particularity of reason as it has developed here in this given place."/110/ Once this knowledge has been attained, the system thus evolved must be refined, concentrated, liberated, and oriented in a certain direction. The essential point is to determine the direction by bringing out the central value. Determination of this central value is, in the last analysis, "a personal act of life" *(eine persönliche Lebenstat)*, which can only afterwards be expressed as a system and justify itself by its result. For this very reason "the creative act" *(die schöpferische Tat)* and "a conscience ready to assume responsibility" *(das verantwortungsbereite Gewissen)* are the decisive factors./111/

After all, for the contemporary cultural synthesis which consisted in the synthesis of the universally valid (the morality of conscience) and the historical-individual (historical cultural values) there was no *a priori* system available; the only means was "the tact and resolution of the acting and shaping mind" *([der] Takt und die Entschlußkraft des handelnden und formenden Geistes)*. Thus, the synthesis was fundamentally only possible as "a living act" *(lebendige Tat)* and "a historical achievement" *(geschichtliche Leistung)*, resting upon an understanding of the whole sweep of history leading towards us and upon the "courage to refashion and further develop it" *(Mut zu deren Um- und Weiterbildung)*./112/ Hence Troeltsch concluded:

> The task of damming and shaping [the historical stream of life] is therefore essentailly incapable of completion and essentailly unending; and yet it is always soluble and practicable in each new case. A radical and absolute solution does not exist; there are only working, partial, synthetically uniting solutions. . . . History cannot be transcended within itself and knows of no salvation except in the form of devout anticipations of the Hereafter or glorified transfigurations of partial salvations. The Kindom of God and Nirvana lie outside all history. In history itself there are only relative victories *(relative Überwindungen)*. . ./113/

The Theological Implications of Troeltsch's Philosophy of History

Now that the profile of Troeltsch's philosophy of history has been sketched out, the final question we have to deal with is that of the theological implications of his philosophy of history.

That Troeltsch never ceased to be a theologian in his innermost self was attested by Friedrich Meinecke, his colleague and friend of the Berlin period. In his obituary tribute to Troeltsch, Meinecke remarked that "the theologian in him [Troeltsch], who had by the way no theological posture, was never completely lost in the philosopher and the historian of ideas, toward whom he developed himself more and more."/114/ Martin Schmidt even asserts:

> Exactly in his [Troeltsch's] discussion of *Historismus* theological accents become surprisingly prominent at decisive points. Certainly, one can say that without theology he [Troeltsch]—in distinction to Meinecke—would never have become aware of the problem of history and of the adequacy of its treatment by *Historismus*./115/

If this is the case, what theological implications did his philosophy of history have, and what transformation did his theology have to undergo in the purgatory of the philosophy of history?

First of all, it should be noted that the metaphysical and religious moment stood at the center of Troeltsch's philosophy of history. According to him, "history goes . . . in its borders back to a mystical background of All-Life *(Alleben)*."/116/ "A metaphysical faith which elevates him [the historian] above empirical confirmations and characterizations and makes him believe in a continuity operating in the deepest ground of an event"/117/ or "a religious conviction of the unity and meaningfulness of reality"/118/ was the *sine qua non* of every cultural synthesis. Troeltsch states:

> If we seek to give them [social circles] an association and a connection and to conceive of them not as coordinated but as concentric circles, we find ourselves at once confronted with the metaphysical and religious element which alone can unite them under one common dome./119/

In other words, the contemporary cultural synthesis presupposed a metaphysical and religious world-view, according to which the content of historical life was considered to be "an expression and revelation of the divine ground of life and of the inner movement of this ground towards a total meaning of the world which is unknown to us" and the cultural ideal growing out of a particular situation to be "a representation of the unknowable absolute." Thus it was at bottom a "matter of faith in the profound and full sense of the word."/120/ To put it in another way, "the idea of God" (*Gottesgedanke*) underlay the idea of a cultural synthesis. For "without it [the idea of God] or something analogous," Troeltsch says, "a standard cannot be erected."/121/

But the question is what kind of idea of God it was that underlay Troeltsch's cultural synthesis. In the theological and religious-philosophical writings of the preceding years he had placed special emphasis on the "fundamental dualism" and "religious personalism" characteristic of the Christian religion and had conceived of God mainly in ethical terms./122/ Accordingly, there is no doubt that it was not a Spinozistic monism or pantheism but rather a prophetic-Christian personalism and religious dualism that informed Troeltsch's conception of God. Nevertheless, in his philosophy of history he found his final resort in a Leibnizian monadology, no matter how modified it might be. The "identity of finite minds with the infinite mind" and the "participation" of the former in the latter were pivotal for his solution of the central problems of the philosophy of history. Did not these notions, however, bear a tinge of impersonalism and pantheism? Or, were they simply yet another expression of Troeltsch's mystical or spiritualistic conception of the Christian God? One can only say that he did not make himself clear on this point. This unclarity involved in his conception of God, to be sure, existed with good reason. Although he presupposed in his philosophy of history a faith in the common divine ground from which all individualities spring, Troeltsch was convinced of the following:

> . . . the unity and meaning of the whole can only be sensed and felt (*nur ahnen und fühlen*); it cannot be expressed and constructed scientifically. Not from the All can we establish an individual moment, but from the establishment of the individual moment can we sense that the All is always living and working in its total meaning./123/

Thus the "common spiritual ground" and the "common goal of oughtness," in his opinion, could only be sensed and believed. The idea of God was available to the philosophy of history only as a "presentiment" (*Ahnung*) or a "hint" (*Andeutung*)./124/ But Troeltsch should have made his own concept of God clearer because the metaphysical and religious notion of All-Life or All-Spirit played

a decisive role in his philosophy of history. He is therefore vulnerable to criticism to the extent that he did not clarify his own concept
of God.

With all this vulnerability, the theological connotations of
Troeltsch's philosophy of history are undeniable. The most conspic-
uous instance is a notion of the "shaping of the future"
(Zukunftsgestaltung), the leitmotif of his philosophy of history. As
we have seen in Chapter I, Troeltsch, with the help of Rickert's
formal logic of history, first developed his doctrine of shaping *(Gestaltungslehre)* in his essay on the essence of Christianity. There he
asserted: the definition of the essence of Christianity involves not
merely an intuitive historical abstraction, a religious and ethical
critique, and an insight into its historical development, but also the
perspective toward its future (the ideal concept); the definition of
the essence is, in the last analysis, a "creative act" *(schöpferische
Tat)*; "to define the essence is to shape it afresh" *(Wesensbestimmung ist Wesensgestaltung)*; the definition of the essence is the
elucidation of the essential idea of Christianity in the manner that it
ought to be a light for the future, and simultaneously it is a living
view of the present and future world together in this light./125/
There is no doubt that the notion of *Zukunftsgestaltung* whose
crystallization was the idea of a contemporary cultural synthesis was
a variant of this *Gestaltungslehre*. While the shaping of the new
essence of *Christianity* for the future had been at stake for the
Troeltsch of the Heidelberg period, the shaping of a new *European
culture and spirit* for the future was now the question at issue. In
any case, the theological origin of the notion of *Zukunftsgestaltung*
is undeniable.

Furthermore, the question of "how the way from the historical-
relative to valid cultural values can be found," of which the idea of a
contemporary cultural synthesis was the solution, was, as Troeltsch
himself affirmed, "the old problem of the absoluteness which is
taken up in a much broader context and in view of the whole of
cultural values, not merely of the religious position."/126/ The real
problem Troeltsch tackled in *The Absoluteness of Christianity* was,
to use his own expression, the question of how one can work out "an
ever-new creative synthesis *(die immer neue schöpferische Synthese)* that will give the absolute the form *(Gestalt)* possible for it at a
particular moment" and yet remain true to its inherent limitations as
a mere approximation of true, ultimate, and universally valid

values./127/ Seen against this backdrop, the contemporary cultural synthesis was at bottom an attempt to work out a new synthesis that was to give the absolute the *Gastalt* possible for it in the contemporary European social and cultural context. This being the case, there were strong ties between Troeltsch's theology and his philosophy of history. Given these strong ties, Troeltsch's theology cannot be properly understood without reference to his later philosophy of history, and vice versa.

Finally, the theological implications of a series of Troeltsch's activist, volitional, and existentialist notions, such as "a creative act," "a personal act of life," "a living act," "a creative compromise," "the will that acts and shapes the future," "the resolution of the acting and shaping mind," "the will to responsibility and decision," "a conscience ready to assume responsibility," "risk," and so forth, should be mentioned. As Paul Tillich discriminatingly pointed out,/128/ these notions were deeply rooted in the Protestant doctrine of justification by faith. In fact, Troeltsch himself remarks:

> Without a risk *(Wagnis)*, without a mistake, and without martyrdom, there is no grasp of truths and values. At this point, too, [the doctrine of] "justification by faith" is valid. Certainly, this is the most universal meaning of this magnificent Protestant basic dogma./129/

To quote another formulation:

> . . . there is no possibility of any limitation of the historical stream of life which is finally valid. Limitation in this direction . . . remains an act of compromise, which is one with conscience. It is not for nothing that religion . . . teaches us that pure will and devotion to an ideal world is sufficient for righteousness and that life itself remains sinful—that is to say, a mixture of nature and the divine life. Justification by faith is only a specifically religious expression of this universal relation of things./130/

As is clear from these quotations, the Protestant doctrine of justification by faith had vital importance for Troeltsch's contemporary cultural synthesis. "The creative act" and "a conscience ready to assume responsibility" or "the tact and resolution of the acting and shaping mind" and "the courage to . . . refashioning and further development" were, as we have seen, the decisive factors for the cultural synthesis. These factors, however, were, in Troeltsch's view, merely different phases of one and the same doctrine of justification by faith./131/ If such is the case, then Troeltsch's philosophy of history in general and the idea of a contemporary cultural synthesis in particular could be regarded as the *application* of Christian thought to the broad canvas of human history./132/

In view of these considerations, we are in a position advantageous to the assertion of Troeltsch's consistency as a Christian theologian in his own right. Such consistency is then a strong case for the existence of a "systematic unified thought" in Troeltsch's lifework. (This issue will be presently dealt with in the concluding chapter.)

There is, however, one more question to be touched upon before we close this chapter. It is the question concerning the reflex effects of Troeltsch's philosophy of history upon his former theological position.

Troeltsch himself perceived, from the practical standpoint, no need of recanting his former theological position, yet he observed, from the theoretical viewpoint, the necessity of modification at two points. In the first place, Troeltsch came to realize, through his study of the philosophy of history, that Christianity, seen as a whole or in its several forms, is "a purely historical, individual, relative phenomenon," and that Christianity, as the European peoples find it today, could only have arisen on the territory of classical culture and among the Latin and Germanic races. The inference from this realization was that "a religion, in the several forms assumed by it, always depends upon the intellectual, social, and national conditions among which it exists." In the second place, further study of the non-Christian religions convinced Troeltsch more and more that "their naive claims to absolute validity are also genuinely such." Especially Buddhism and Brahmanism deeply impressed him as "really humane and spiritual religions, capable of appealing in precisely the same way to the inner certitude and devotion of their followers as Christianity." Thus, from both sides, Troeltsch was forced to acknowledge that the concept of individuality was not so easily reconcilable with that of supreme validity as he had formerly assumed./133/

The result of these discoveries was:

> The individual character of European civilization (*Individualität des Europäertums*), and of the Christian religion which is intimately connected with it, receives now much greater emphasis, whilst the somewhat rationalistic concept of validity, and specifically of *supreme validity*, falls considerably into the backgrounds./134/

That is to say, Christianity was now viewed by Troeltsch exclusively in its historical fate of having been indissolubly bound up with the civilization of Greece, Rome, and Northern Europe. It was regarded as "the religion of all Europe" *(die Religion des gesamten Europäertums)* which had entirely "lost its Oriental character" *(entorientalisiert)* and had been "hellenized" *(hellenisiert)* and "westernized" *(europäisiert)*. It was now said to "stand or fall with European civilization."/135/ Hence Troeltsch asserted that "the validity of Christianity consists, first of all, in the fact that only through it have we become what we are, and that only in it can we preserve the religious forces that we need." In a word, Christianity's primary claim to validity was now sought in the fact that "Christianity has grown up with us and has become a part of our very being."/136/ Accordingly, its validity was, in the first instance, only "validity *for us*." Chistianity was "God's countenance as revealed to us" *(das uns zugewandte Antlitz Gottes)*; it was "the way in which, being what we are, we receive, and react to, the revelation of God"; it was "final and unconditional for us, because we have nothing else, and because in what we have we can recognize the accents of the divine voice."/137/ Nevertheless, "a truth which, in the first instance, is *a truth for us*," Troeltsch believed, "does not cease, because of this, to be very truth and life." Behind this claim stood undoubtedly a modified Leibnizian monadology. Based upon such a metaphysical view, Troeltsch asserted that "in our earthly experience the divine life is not One, but Many. But to apprehend the One in Many constitutes the special character of love."/138/ Thus the endorsement of "polymorphous truth"/139/ or religious pluralism was Troeltsch's final position.

> . . . all historical religions tend in the same direction and . . . seem impelled by an inner force to strive upward towards some unknown final height, where alone the ultimate unity and the final objective validity can lie. And, as all religion has thus a common goal in the Unknown, the Future, perchance in the Beyond, so too it has a common ground in the Divine Spirit ever pressing the finite mind onward towards further light and fuller consciousness, a Spirit which indwells the finite spirit and whose ultimate union with it is the purpose of the whole many-sided process./140/

However, is such polymorphous truth or religious pluralism in the above sense theologically adequate? Is not the advocacy of such a polymorphous truth an indication of what critics have often branded as the failure of Troeltsch's theology?/141/ Is it possible to dam and shape the stream of historical relativism with the idea of polymorphous truth? Or, should we take that idea as a most sophisticated and most sincere response to historical relativism by a European intellectual who was facing "the sunset of Christianity"?/142/ To answer these recurrent questions is the final task we have to address in the following concluding chapter.

NOTES

/1/ U. Pretzel, "Ernst Troeltschs Berufung an die Berliner Universität," in *Studium Berolinense: Aufsätze und Beiträge zu Problemen der Wissenschaft und zur Geschichte der Friedrich-Wilhelms-Universität zu Berlin*, eds. H. Leussink, E. Neumann, and E. Kotowsky (Berlin: Walter de Bryuter & Co., 1960), p. 508.

/2/ K. Barth, "Evangelical Theology in the 19th Century," in *The Humanity of God*, trans. John Newton Thomas & Thomas Wieser (Atlanta: John Knox Press, 1960), p. 14.

/3/ K. Barth, "Autobiographische Skizzen," in *Karl Barth Gesamtausgabe*, vol. 5/1: *Karl Barth-Rudolf Bultmann Briefwechsel 1922–1966*, ed. Bernd Jaspert (Zurich: Theologischer Verlag Zürich, 1971), p. 305: "The name of Troeltsch, which stood in the center of our discussion at that time [around the year 1909], designated the limits this side of which I thought I must refuse to follow the then dominant theology."

/4/ Barth's grand neglect of Troeltsch is striking in comparison to his serious struggle with Schleiermacher. With a conservative family background and a basic theological training under Wilhelm Herrmann, the great antipode to Troeltsch, Barth seems to have been unable to reckon with Troeltsch as a theological power. To this extent Pannenberg is right when he says that Barth did not really overcome the problem of Troeltsch's 'historical relativism' but escaped it ("A Theological Conversation with Wolfhart Pannenberg," *Dialog* 2 [1972]:294). Cf. T. W. Ogletree, *Christian Faith and History: A Critical Comparison of Ernst Troeltsch and Karl Barth* (New York and Nashville: Abingdon Press, 1965). Concerning the dialectical theologians' relation to Troeltsch, see Robert Morgan's instructive essay, "Ernst Troeltsch and the Dialectical Theology," in *Ernst Troeltsch and the Future of Theology*, pp. 33–77. Wilfreid Groll's condensed study on the tangential relation between Troeltsch and Barth also deserves note in this connection, though it has little to say for our present study. Cf. W. Groll, *Ernst Troeltsch und Karl Barth—Kontinuität im Widerspruch* (Munich: Chr. Kaiser Verlag, 1976).

/5/ G. Müller, "Die Selbstauflösung der Dogmatik bei Ernst Troeltsch," *Theologische Zeitschrift* 22 (1966):346.

/6/ W. Bodenstein, *Neige des Historismus: Ernst Troeltschs Entwicklungsgang* (Gütersloh: Gütersloher Verlagshaus Gerd Mohn, 1959), p. 187.

/7/ Ibid., p. 207.

/8/ Reist, *Toward a Theology of Involvement*, p. 243 n. 1.

/9/ Ibid., Chapter Six. "The Collapse of Troeltsch's Theology" is the heading of this chapter. Here Reist also speaks of "the failure" and "the ruins" of Troeltsch's theology.

/10/ See Pretzel, "Ernst Troeltschs Berufung an die Berliner Universität."

/11/ Ibid., p. 511.

/12/ Ibid., p. 514. Nevertheless, E. Marcks does affirm that "the core of his [Troeltsch's] personality is religious." In this sense he remarks: "In the innermost heart he [Troeltsch] will feel himself a theologian, if I am not wrong" (ibid.).

/13/ Ibid., 513.

/14/ Köhler reports: "One did not dare to place him [Troeltsch] in the theological faculty, though he wished it" (Köhler, *Ernst Troeltsch*, p. 5); "The Church hindered him [Troeltsch] from entering the theological faculty at Berlin" (ibid., p. 46).

/15/ Ernst Troeltsch to Wilhelm Bousset, 27 July 1914, "Briefe an Bousset," p. 48. According to H.-J. Gabriel, "that he [Troeltsch] was not called to the theological faculty, obviously occurred out of regard for the church authorities, who, in view of their presuppositions, were unable to accept Troeltsch as a theological teacher" (H.-J. Gabriel, *Christlichkeit der Gesellschaft?: Eine kritische Darstellung der Kulturphilosophie von Ernst Troeltsch* [Berlin: Union Verlag Berlin, 1975], p. 20).

/16/ Concerning the unhappy end of the friendship between Troeltsch and Weber, see Wilhelm Pauck, *Harnack and Troeltsch: Two Historical Theologians* (New York: Oxford University Press, 1968), pp. 73–74. Cf. Eduard Baumgarten, *Max Weber: Werk und Person* (Tübingen: J. C. B. Mohr, 1964), p. 624.

/17/ Köhler, *Ernst Troeltsch*, p. 331. This remark by Köhler should be understood in the context of Troeltsch's view of the nature of both theology and the theological faculty. Troeltsch wrote the following:

> "It [the contemporary theology of the theological faculties] is determined by the general situation of politics as well as by the relation of the thrones and the Cabinets to the parliamentary parties and to the parties working behind the scenes. The theological faculties are an element in the state's political game for power. Here one can therefore seek the pure expression of the intellectual situation and its

demands only in a very limited way. The theological faculties must satisfy very diverse demands which have little to
do with the intellectual and scientific situation. They can
never be measured simply according to the latter's claims.
Consequently, the call of their members is also executed, in
most cases, neither from scientific nor from religious viewpoints, but from political-ecclesiastical viewpoints. The me-
diocrity of their scholarly achievements is determined by
this procedure" (Troeltsch, G.S. II, p. 828).
For Troeltsch, what was "disgusting" about theology was the intervention of
such political and ecclesiastical interests in it. He regrets that "the systematic theology of today is much too closely allied with large ecclesiastical
corporations, political forces, and the instincts of the masses. . . ." (ibid., p.
755). Otherwise, Troeltsch loved his job as a teacher of Christian theology.
Retrospectively he says: "I have at all times fulfilled the practical educa-
tional tasks assigned to the theological faculty with warmest respect for the
great subject and with personal love for my students" (id., G.S. IV, p. 12).

/18/   Ernst Troeltsch to Walther Köhler in the spring of 1915; quoted in
Köhler, *Ernst Troeltsch*, p. 331.

/19/   G. Wünsch, "Ernst Troeltsch," in *Lebensbilder aus dem Bayerischen
Schwaben*, vol. 9, ed. Wolfgang Zorn (Munich: Verlag Max Heuber, 1966),
p. 388.

/20/   Troeltsch to Bousset, 27 July 1914, "Briefe an Bousset," pp. 47–48.

/21/   Ibid., p. 48. Another letter of Troeltsch to Bousset on 27 November
1915 convinces us that one of the main causes which propelled Troeltsch to
resign the theological chair was his long-standing disgust with the narrowness of the theological faculty caused by its ecclesiastical interests. He
writes: "Farewell . . . to theology was at first very difficult for me. Now I
completely consent to it. I have freedom and no longer need to demonstrate
whether or not my results are useful to the Church" (ibid., p. 51). Tillich
holds that Troeltsch's professional shift "had its ultimate reason in the
situation of theology" at that time (Tillich, *Gesammelte Werke*, vol. 12, p.
176).

/22/   G. v. le Fort, *Hälfte des Lebens: Erinnerungen* (Munich: Ehrenwirth
Verlag, 1965), pp. 122–123.

/23/   Gabriel, *Christlichkeit der Gesellschaft?*, p. 21.

/24/   Bodenstein, *Neige des Historismus*, p. 187. D. D. Perkins views
Troeltsch's professional shift in the same way. He contends that "it is best to
regard Troeltsch as not abandoning theology with his occupation of a philosophical chair, but rather broadening his intellectual domain and yet maintaining intact the religious impulse which guided his life" (D. D. Perkins,
"Explicating Christian Faith in a Historically Conscious Age: The Method of
Ernst Troeltsch's *Glaubenslehre*" [Ph.D. dissertation, Vanderbilt University, 1981], p. 24).

/25/ E. Troeltsch, *Die Sozialphilosophie des Christentums* (Zurich: Verlag Seldwyla, 1922), p. 25 n. 1. Here Troeltsch refers to his intellectual development after the publication of *Die Soziallehren* (1912). According to Helmut Thielicke, however, such a broadening of the horizon had already taken place during the decade between the first and the second edition of *Die Absolutheit des Christentums* (1st ed., 1902; 2d ed., 1912). He states that in the decade following the initial publication of *Die Absolutheit*, Troeltsch's "historical horizon *(Gesichtskreis)* was incomparably broadened." See H. Thielicke, *Glauben und Denken in der Neuzeit* (Tübingen: J. C. B. Mohr, 1983), p. 572.

/26/ Troeltsch, G.S. III, p. 110.

/27/ *Historismus* in Troeltsch's proper sense is difficult to translate. The English counterpart "historicism" is certainly misleading. *Historicism*, as Karl Popper, for example, understands it, is an "approach to the social sciences" aiming at "historical prediction" through the evolutionary and recurrent laws of history. Thus understood, historicism is "a method which does not bear any fruit," and its "logic—often so subtle, so compelling and so deceptive— . . . suffers from an inherent and irreparable weakness" (K. Popper, *The Poverty of Historicism* [Boston: Beacon Press, 1957], pp. 3, ix, xi). Such historicism as an attempt to introduce law and prediction into history, however, is diametrically opposed to what Troeltsch understood under *Historismus*. "The Historical Standpoint," as Friedrich von Hügel translates the term (in his Introduction to *Christian Thought: Its History and Application*, p. xiii), is admittedly "too neutral." But Reist's "historical relativism," which was borrowed from H. A. Hodges's study of Dilthey, is also too paraphrastic (see Reist, *Toward a Theology of Involvement*, esp. p. 228 n. 3). For "relativism," in Troeltsch's opinion, is not "Historismus" as such but its inevitable concomitant. H. R. Niebuhr, in turn, proposes to render *Historismus* as "Historism" (Niebuhr, "Ernst Troeltsch's Philosophy of Religion," p. 33 n. 1). W. Pauck seems to follow Niebuhr basically, though he also uses the term "historicism" (Pauck, *Harnack and Troeltsch*, pp. 86, 88). Professor Peter C. Hodgson suggested to me that *Historismus* be translated "historicality," remarking that what Troeltsch means by the term is essentially similar to Heidegger's *Geschichtlichkeit*. Whether or not this is the case, "radical historicality" in the title should be understood in the sense of a Troeltschian *Historismus*. Otherwise, I use the original German word throughout this study, following Dean Jack Forstman's suggestion that "Historismus" be best left untranslated.

/28/ For example, in his essay of 1895 Troeltsch considered "the historicizing observation" *(die historisierende Betrachtung)* of religion to be the main cause for the present difficulty in maintaining Christianity's claim to the absoluteness (Troeltsch, "Selbständigkeit," 5:372). Three years later he discussed the impact of *Historismus* on human understanding, morality, and religion and spoke of "a latent theology of *Historismus*" (id., "Metaphysik," pp. 68–69).

/29/ Troeltsch, G.S. III, p. 102 (emphasis mine).

/30/ Id., "Die Krisis des Historismus," *Die Neue Rundschau* 33 (1922):573.

/31/ C. G. Rand, "Two Meanings of Historicism on the Writings of Dilthey, Troeltsch, and Meinecke," *Journal of the History of Ideas* 25 (1964):503–518 (italics original). But the distinction between "historicism as a methodology" and "historicism as a *Weltanschauung*," as Rand introduces it, is not clear in Troeltsch's usage of the term *Historismus*. Troeltsch, for example, speaks of "the method as a world-view" in the context in which "*Historismus* as a whole," "the relativism which can be rectified and balanced only from the total viewpoint," and "an exuberance of stimulus springing from the immense historical intuition" are also mentioned (Troeltsch, G.S. III, p. 530). Hence Otto Hintze, who first asserted the necessity of making a distinction between *Historismus* as a "concept of a methodical direction of thinking in the sense of a logical conceptual structure of the mind" *(Begriff einer methodischen Denkrichtung im Sinne einer logischen Kategorialstruktur des Geistes)* and *Historismus* as a concept of "a general world- and life-view" *(einer allgemeine Welt- und Lebensanschauung)*, criticizes Troeltsch's usage of the term *Historismus* for the lack of clarity about this distinction. See O. Hintze, "Troeltsch und die Probleme des Historismus," in Otto Hintze, *Gesammelte Abhandlungen*, vol. 2: *Soziologie und Geschichte: Gesammelte Abhandlungen zur Soziologie, Politik und Theorie der Geschichte*, ed. G. Östreich (Göttingen: Vandenhoeck & Ruprecht, 1964), p. 325.

/32/ Cf. Troeltsch, *Überwindung*, pp. 2–3; cf. *Christian Thought*, pp. 41–42.

/33/ Id., G.S. III, p. 10. Troeltsch was well aware of the pernicious dangers of *Historismus* at a fairly early age. In an essay of 1898, Troeltsch, for instance, wrote the following:

> "Playful relativism, for which everything is something becoming and passing, conditional and relative, the iridescent change and renunciation of every personal conviction, the asphyxiation of all productiveness and robust strength of simple faith in generally valid standards, the disintegration of scholarship in the creation of endless duplications of what has already formerly passed, the habituation to the destitute routine of historical specialization, these are the oppressive defects of *Historismus*, which are now and then so strident that they can make one apprehensive about the continuation of our civilization" (Troeltsch, "Metaphysik," p. 68–69).

/34/ Id., "Die Krisis des Historismus," p. 582.

/35/ Ibid., p. 772; cf. "Überwindung des Historismus durch Historismus" (ibid., p. 649); "die Überwindung der Historie durch die Historie" (id.,

G.S. II, p. 205). Troeltsch holds that the solution to the modern crisis of *Historismus* "can only be found in a fundamental philosophical mastery of the essence of history and of the question of its spiritual aims and contents" (id., G.S. III, p. 10).

/36/ Ibid., p. 68. In Troeltsch's opinion, a "base *Historismus*" came into existence mainly because of "a misunderstood assimilation of history to the specific elements, universal laws, successive formations, and necessities of the natural sciences" (ibid., p. 67).

/37/ Ibid., p. 67.

/38/ Ibid., p. 724.

/39/ Ibid., p. 26.

/40/ Ibid.

/41/ Ibid., p. vii. The first volume of *Der Historismus* is subtitled "The Logical Problem of the Philosophy of History." The second volume which never came into existence was, according to Troeltsch's design, to "give my outline of the European universal history" and to "connect with that my solution to the task of a philosophy of history." "Therefore," he says, it was to "present at bottom my ethics" (Troeltsch, *Briefe*, p. 138).

/42/ Id., G.S. III, p. 70.

/43/ This work was originally written as the lectures to be delivered in England during March 1923. For this reason, the English translation, *Christian Thought: Its History and Application*, trans. by various hands and edited with an Introduction and Index by Friedrich von Hügel (London: University of London Press, 1923), appeared a few months earlier than the German original. The title of neither of the editions was determined by Troeltsch himself.

/44/ In his letter to Friedrich von Hügel on 11 January 1923, Troeltsch wrote that "these three lectures for delivery in London [the lectures on "Ethics and the Philosophy of History"] contain part of the basic ideas of my forthcoming second volume of *Der Historismus*" (Troeltsch, *Briefe*, p. 148).

/45/ Troeltsch referred to "Humanismus und Nationalismus in unserem Bildungswesen" and "Deutsche Bildung" as such. See E. Troeltsch, *Die Bedeutung der Geschichte für die Weltanschauung* (Berlin: Verlag bei Ernst Siegfried Mittler und Sohn, 1918), p. 43.

/46/ Troeltsch, G. S. III, p. 27.

/47/ Ibid., p. 24.

/48/ In a sense, *Der Historismus*, which was "dedicated to the memory of Wilhelm Dilthey and Wilhelm Windelband," is a monumental document of the attempt to reconcile the "antithesis of the formal thinker and the philosopher of life" (ibid., p. 283) or the "strife of those who look at life

(Lebens-Anschauer) and those who think in terms of form *(Form-Denker)*"
(ibid., p. 673).

/49/ Ibid., p. 29. It would be unfair, however, to view Troeltsch's emphasis
on this distinction solely from the perspective of his alliance with the Neo-
Kantianism of the Windelband-Rickert school. For Dilthey too advocated
the dichotomy between the *Naturwissenschaften* and *Geisteswissenschaften*. The truth is rather that Dilthey was the initiator of such a distinction, as far as the term "Geisteswissenschaften" is concerned. Accordingly,
it would be more precise to say that Troeltsch was a pupil of both Dilthey
and the Baden school in this respect.

/50/ In spite of his high esteem for Rickert's achievements in the elaboration of the formal logic of history, Troeltsch severely criticized Rickert for
fleeing from the Heraclitean flux of history for the stability of a "Parmeni-
dian principle" (ibid., p. 563). In Troeltsch's judgment, Rickert's standard
for judging historical things was, in the final analysis, "no standard growing
out of history itself, but an extraneous one, floating above it, produced by
pure reason" (ibid., p. 156).

/51/ Ibid., p. 531.

/52/ Ibid., p. 31; cf. ibid., p. 669.

/53/ Ibid., p. 29.

/54/ Ibid., pp. 32–56.

/55/ Ibid., p. 54.

/56/ Ibid., p. 33.

/57/ Ibid., p. 54.

/58/ After the exhaustive survey of modern notions of development,
Troeltsch remarks:

> "It [the historical concept of development] is founded,
> firstly, in the essence of the human spirit *(in dem Wesen des
> menschlichen Geistes)*, which produces inner consistencies
> of germinal ideas or tendencies and works them out in a
> logically comprehensible succession in constant confronta-
> tion with geographical and biological presuppositions and
> with various contingent factors. It is founded, secondly, in
> the capability of this same spirit *(in der Fähigkeit desselben
> Geistes)* to accept certain . . . natural, social, or historical
> conditions and adopt, in adaptation to them, the course
> which gives the impression of a logically coherent progress"
> (ibid., p. 657).

/59/ Ibid., p. 689.

/60/ Ibid., p. 654; cf. ibid., p. 652.

/61/   E. Troeltsch, "Naturrecht und Humanität in der Weltpolitik: Vortrag in der deutschen Hochschule für Politik" (1922), in *Deutscher Geist und Westeuropa*, p. 22. The English translation is borrowed from E. Troeltsch, "The Ideas of Natural Law and Humanity in World Politics," compiled as an Appendix to Otto Gierke, *Natural Law and the Theory of Society, 1500–1800* (Cambridge: Cambridge University Press, 1934), pp. 22; here p. 217.

/62/   Ibid.; "The Ideas of Natural Law and Humanity," p. 218.

/63/   Ibid.

/64/   "Universal history" *(Universalgeschichte)* is a highly elusive concept. Martin J. Buss, for instance, asserts that the term "universal history" involves at least three different meanings: (1) "the study of all of history—the whole West or both East and West"; (2) "the elementary pattern of historical development"; (3) "the totality of history seen as a meaningful whole" (M. J. Buss, "The Meaning of History," in *Theology as History*, eds. James M. Robinson and John B. Cobb, Jr. [New York: Harper & Row, 1967], p. 136). In Troeltsch's usage the term certainly involves all these three meanings. However, a somewhat different formulation would be necessary for the clarification of his usage. "Universal history," as Troeltsch is using the term, is often interchangeable with "world history" *(Weltgeschichte)* in the sense of a history of humankind. Sometimes it means a developmental or process or evolutionary view of history that does not radically separate world history (secular history) and Christian history (salvation history). In this sense a universal-historical view of history is the antipode to a salvation-historical *(heilsgeschichtliche)* view of history. Furthermore, it denotes the most comprehensive hermeneutical frame of reference for meaning.

By the way, in Troeltsch's usage the German term meaning "universal history" is not always *Universalgeschichte*. He sometimes used the term *Universalhistorie* (e.g., "Naturrecht und Humanität," p. 22). These two terms and their respective adjective forms, "universalgeschichtlich" and "universalhistorisch," are, in most cases, interchangeable, though basically the former refers more to the ontic aspect of universal history and the latter more to the noetic one.

/65/   Troeltsch, G.S. III, p. 689.

/66/   Troeltsch, for example, says the following:
> "Survey of the whole amount of the historical can be fun only for the gifted epicure or a quietist skepticism or a pantheistic feeling of the Universe. In reality, and fortunately for human health, such surveyes are, however, entirely impossible with our epistemological and conceptual means. Something like that is possible only for God" (ibid., pp. 708–709).

For Troeltsch description of the development of humankind appeared to be "a monstrous enterprise" and a "superhuman achievement which exceeds every possibility of knowledge" *(übermenschliche, jede Wissensmöglichkeit überschreitende Leistung)* (ibid., p. 74).

/67/   Ibid., p. 692.

/68/   Ibid., p. 707. Cf. Ibid., p. 705: "The historical object can be held together only through a . . . unified or convergent content of meaning. This content of meaning must be accessible to common experience and understanding."

/69/   Ibid., p. 706. Troeltsch considered the philosophically constructed development of humanity to be "speculative soap bubbles and castles in the air" (ibid., p. 703) and humankind as a whole to be "works of fiction, which tell metaphysical fairy tales about something that does not exist at all" (ibid., 707).

/70/   E.g., ibid., p. 725. Troeltsch employed several expressions to designate the same notion: "Weltgeschichte des Europäertums" (p. 708); "Universalgeschichte der europäischen Kultur" (p. 710); "Universalgeschichte des Europäertums" (p. 727), and so forth. As far as I understand his usage, there is a slight difference in meaning between "Europäismus" and "Europäertum." Both terms refer to European culture and civilization as a whole, but sometimes the former more to its superstructure and the latter more to its spatial expanse as a realistic complex. (In Troeltsch's usage of the term, *Europäismus* or *Europäertum* includes both American and Russian cultural spheres.)These terms are both translated as "Europeanism" in this study.

/71/   Ibid., p. 75.

/72/   Ibid., p. 709.

/73/   Ibid., p. 710.

/74/   Ibid., p. 708; cf. ibid., p. 710.

/75/   Ibid., p. 707.

/76/   T. Rendtorff, "Europäismus als geschichtlicher Kontext der Theologie: Bemerkungen zur heutigen Kritik an 'europäischer' Theologie im Licht von Ernst Troeltsch," in *Europäische Theologie: Versuche einer Ortsbestimmung*, ed. Trutz Rendtorff (Gütersloh: Gütersloher Verlagshaus Gerd Mohn, 1980), p. 173. Cf. Troeltsch, G.S. III, p. 716.

/77/   Troeltsch, G.S. III, p. 684.

/78/   Ibid., p. 677.

/79/   Cf. ibid., p. 210.

/80/   Reist's study of Troeltsch has totally failed to take notice of this subtle but very important point of Troeltsch's philosophy of history. His criticism to the effect that Troeltsch's philosophy of history "is necessarily doomed to failure" because "*development* has been subsumed under *individuality*" is therefore unjustifiable. Reist, *Toward a Theology of Involvement*, p. 83; cf. pp. 77–78.

/81/   Cf. ibid., p. 727: "Hence Islam has a universal history for itself . . . , and it does not belong to the universal history of Europeanism."

/82/   Ibid., p. 719.

/83/   Ibid., pp. 716–721.

/84/   Cf. ibid., p. 111. It cannot be the task of the material philosophy of history, in Troeltsch's opinion, "to formulate ultimate, definitive, and universal goals for humankind, which could only become realized, indeed, in a perfect and universal community of the human race," or "to construct the process of universal history in such a manner that this goal springs up from it" (ibid., pp. 198–199).

/85/   Ibid., p. 112.

/86/   Ibid., p. 221.

/87/   Id., *Überwindung*, p. 37; cf. *Christian Thought*, p. 37.

/88/   Id., G.S. III, p. 113.

/89/   Ibid., p. 70.

/90/   Ibid., p. 79.

/91/   Ibid., p. 78.

/92/   Ibid., p. 79.

/93/   Ibid., p. 113.

/94/   Ibid., p. 112: "die Teleologie des seine Vergangenheit zur Zukunft aus dem Moment herausformenden und gestaltenden Willens."

/95/   Troeltsch used this term and its derivatives frequently, and that often at critical points, in *Der Historismus*. Cf. pp. 79, 83, 114, 118, 125, 132, 137, 148, 169, 178, 235, 272, 296, 337, 364, 388, 417, 487, 704, 710. This motif of *Zukunftsgestaltung* not only informs the constructive aspect of Troeltsch's philosophy of history but also sharply distinguishes it from Spengler's pessimist and defeatist *The Decline of the West*. See E. Troeltsch, review of *Der Untergang des Abendlandes*, by Oswald Spengler, G.S. IV, pp. 677–691.

/96/   Such were "to act" (*handeln*), "to shape" (*gestalten*), "to form" (*formen*), "to create" (*schaffen*), "act" (*Tat; Akt*), "will or volition" (*Wille; Wollen*), "decision" (*Entscheidung*), "resolution" (*Entschluß; Entschließen*), "bold venture or risk" (*Wagnis*), "responsibility" (*Verantwortung*), and so forth. The reader of Troeltsch's writings will be deeply impressed not only by his frequent use of these terms but also by their critical importance for his thought.

/97/   Troeltsch, *Deutscher Geist und Westeuropa*, p. 22; id., G.S. III, p. 157; id., *Überwindung*, p. 40. Rubanowice suggests Paul de Lagarde's influence on Troeltsch's activist orientation. He also holds the latter's "action-oriented concern" to be partly "attributable to wartime and immediate post-war German problems that desperately needed solutions." Such might have been the case. But I am of the opinion that Troeltsch's emphasis on activism was more deeply rooted in his own theory of *Gestaltung*, which had been elaborated independently of Lagarde in the pre-war time. Cf. Rubanowice, *Crisis in Consciousness*, pp. 89, 156 n. 149.

/98/   Troeltsch, *Überwindung*, p. 21; cf. *Christian Thought*, p. 71.

/99/   Ibid., p. 27; cf. *Christian Thought*, pp. 79–80.

/100/   Ibid., pp. 27–28; cf. *Christian Thought*, p. 80.

/101/   Ibid., pp. 29–30; cf. *Christian Thought*, p. 82.

/102/   Ibid., pp. 4, 3; cf. *Christian Thought*, pp. 44, 42.

/103/   Ibid., p. 4; cf. *Christian Thought*, p. 43.

/104/   Troeltsch frequently used this metaphorical expression in his London lectures on the "Ethics and the Philosophy of History." See *Überwindung*, pp. 33, 37, 41, 44, 59, 60. Its official English translation, *Christian Thought*, has translated this phrase as "damming and controlling the historical stream of life." If one puts more value on how it sounds to the English ears, then "controlling" might be a better translation of the German word "Gestaltung" than its somewhat literal translation "shaping." But the reader who reads only the English translation will inevitably miss Troeltsch's real point, which was not merely to limit (dam) and master (control) the historical stream of life, but also to *shape* it into a certain form or *Gestalt*. For this reason I venture to translate the term as "shaping."

/105/   Troeltsch, *Überwindung*, p. 56; cf. *Christian Thought*, p. 123.

/106/   Ibid., p. 47; cf. ibid., pp. 19, 31, 43, 56, 97, 101–104. Concerning the meaning and significance of Troeltsch's notion of *Kompromiß*, see T. Yasukata, "The Concept of 'Kompromiß' in Ernst Troeltsch," *Journal of Christian Studies* 2 (1979):104–118; cf. J. R. Hanson, "Ernst Troeltsch's Concept of Compromise," *The Lutheran Quarterly* 18 (1966):351–361.

/107/   Ibid.

/108/   Ibid., p. 44; cf. *Christian Thought*, p. 106. Seen against this background, the following assertion by Troeltsch is understandable: "There can be genuine and true validity which is not timeless and eternally immutable validity, but which suits the existence of the present time being, and, for that reason only, thus has general validity" (id., G.S. III, p. 183).

/109/   Ibid., pp. 38–39; cf. *Christian Thought*, p. 95.

/110/   Ibid., p. 39; cf. *Christian Thought*, p. 96.

/111/   Ibid., pp. 39–40; cf. *Christian Thought*, pp. 96–97.

/112/   Ibid., cf. *Christian Thought*, pp. 97–98.

/113/   Ibid., pp. 59–60; cf. *Christian Thought*, pp. 128–129.

/114/   F. Meinecke, "Nachruf," *Historische Zeitschrift* 128 (1923):185–187; now contained in *Friedrich Meinecke Werke*, vol. 4: *Zur Theorie und Philosophie der Geschichte*, ed. Eberhard Kessel (Stuttgart: K. F. Koehler Verlag, 1965), pp. 364–366; here p. 365; cf. ibid., p. 369.

/115/   M. Schmidt, "Züge eines theologischen Geschichtsbegriffs bei Ernst Troeltsch," in *Reformatio und Confessio*, Festschrift für D. Wilhelm Maurer zum 65. Geburtstag am 7. Mai 1965, eds. Wilhelm Kantzenbach and Gerhard Müller (Berlin and Hamburg: Lutherisches Verlagshaus, 1965), pp. 248–249.

/116/   Troeltsch, G.S. III, p. 87.

/117/   Ibid., p. 175.

/118/   Ibid., p. 695.

/119/   Id., *Überwindung*, p. 56; cf. *Christian Thought*, p. 123.

/120/   Id., G.S. III, p. 175.

/121/   Ibid., pp. 183–184.

/122/   Troeltsch, for example, characterized Christianity as follows: "Christianity is an ethic of redemption *(Erlösungsethik)* whose world-view combines optimism and pessimism, transcendence and immanence, an abrupt polarisation of the world and God and the inward linking of these two, a dualism, in principle, which is abrogated again and again in faith and in action" (Troeltsch, G.S. II, p. 422).
He designated such a dualism as "the fundamental dualism" *(der prinzipielle Dualismus: der grundlegende Dualismus)* (ibid., pp. 843–844).
        Troeltsch's emphasis on the personalistic aspect of Christianity was no less prominent. He regarded Christianity as "the religion of personalism in the highest sense" (id., *Politische Ethik und Christentum*, p. 26; cf. G.S. II, p. 845) or "the personalistic religion of redemption" (*Absolutheit* 2d ed., pp. 92; G.S. II, pp. 356–357).

/123/   Troeltsch, G.S. III, p. 183.

/124/   Cf. ibid., p. 199. Such an opinion seems to be deeply rooted in Troeltsch's view of religion. For he once spoke of "the semi-darkness in which alone is communicated the animating power of religion, in which human being first becomes aware of its pettiness and meanness, and in which—through intuition *(Ahnung)* and faith—human being first senses its true dimensions" (id., *Absolutheit*, p. 86).

/125/   Cf. *supra*, Chapter I, the fourth section.

/126/   Troeltsch, G.S. IV, p. 14.

/127/   Id., *Absolutheit* 2d ed., p. 58.

/128/   Tillich, *Gesammelte Werke*, vol. 12, pp. 172, 209.

/129/   Troeltsch, G.S. III, p. 185.

/130/   Id., *Überwindung*, pp. 20–21; cf. *Christian Thought*, p. 67.

/131/   Ibid., pp. 40–41; cf. *Christian Thought*, pp. 97–98.

/132/   The title of the English translation of Troeltsch's last work suggests this possibility. It reads "*Christian Thought: Its History and Application.*" But this title was not set by Troeltsch himself but by Friedrich von Hügel. According to Hügel, Troeltsch "left no indication concerning a common title for these lectures, all carefully entitled by himself" (Troeltsch, *Christian Thought*, p. viii).

/133/   Troeltsch, *Überwindung*, p. 75; cf. *Christian Thought*, pp. 21–23.

/134/   Ibid., p. 76; cf. *Christian Thought*, p. 24 (emphasis the English translator's).

/135/   Ibid., pp. 76–77; cf. *Christian Thought*, p. 24.

/136/   Ibid., p. 77; cf. *Christian Thought*, p. 25.

/137/   Ibid., p. 78; cf. *Christian Thought*, p. 26.

/138/   Ibid., p. 83; cf. *Christian Thought*, pp. 34–35.

/139/   By the way, the expression "polymorphous truth," which is generally taken as the most adequate catchphrase to express Troeltsch's final position, did not originate with Troeltsch himself, although he spoke of "die vielen Wahrheiten" or "verschiedene möglicher Weise giltige Wahrheiten" (E. Troeltsch, *Trennung von Staat und Kirche* [Tübingen: J. C. B. Mohr, 1907], pp. 7–8). To my knowledge, that expression is a coinage of Friedrich von Hügel. He seems to have either summarized Troeltsch's conception of truth set forth in the above-mentioned book under this catchword or rendered those somewhat flat expressions by Troeltsch into this attractive English expression (F. v. Hügel, Introduction to *Christian Thought*, by E. Troeltsch, pp. xix–xx; id., Introduction to *Der Historismus und seine Überwindung*, by E. Troeltsch, pp. vii–viii). W. Köhler, then, cited Hügel's brief German summary of Troeltsch's conception of 'polymorphous truth' in double quotation marks as if it were a quotation from Troeltsch's own text: "Truth is always polymorph, never monomorph; it manifests itself in different forms and kinds, not in different degrees" (Köhler, *Ernst Troeltsch*, p. 1). That expression was henceforth taken as a coinage of Troeltsch's own in the English speaking countries. W. Pauck, for example, quoted the paragraph in question from Köhler's book as Troeltsch's own statement (Pauck, *Harnack and Troeltsch*, p. 90). R. J. Rubanowice seems to be in no doubt about its direct Troeltschian origin (Rubanowice, *Crisis in Consciousness*, pp. 55–59, 92, 151).

/140/   Troeltsch, *Überwindung*, p. 82; cf. *Christian Thought*, p. 32.

/141/   Reist, *Toward a Theology of Involvement*, pp. 197–201; Hughes, *Consciousness and Society*, p. 241; cf. Bodenstein, *Neige des Historismus*, p. 207; le Fort, *Hälfte des Leben*, p. 88; Tillich, *Gesammelte Werke*, vol. 12, p. 173, etc.

/142/   In the semi-autobiographical novel of Gertrud von le Fort, the guardian and professor of the heroine, whose model was Treoltsch, was deeply convinced of "the sunset of Christianity." Le Fort describes that professor's dark outlook in the following moving passages:

> ". . . I expressed my gratitude for his lectures and the in-
> ward strengthening I had derived from them.
> He replied: 'Oh, all I have been able to do for you is that I
> showed you the sunset of Christianity *(die Abendröte des
> Christentums)*. When the sun has set, it still glows for a long
> time.'
> 'Does not the sunset promise a new dawn?' I quickly asked.
> 'You too believe, don't you, that the sun will rise again?'
> 'I do not know,' he said, honestly. 'No, I really do not know
> that; but then, we do not need to know everything. What I
> do know is that it is possible to stay alive with a great
> sunset.'
> 'But can the sunset last long?' I asked" (G. v. le Fort, *Der
> Kranz der Engel*, 10th ed. [Munich: Ehrenwirth Verlag,
> 1968], p. 244; the English translation here is borrowed from
> Pauck, *Harnack and Troeltsch*, pp. 91–92 n. 62).

A little later, the conversation between the professor and the heroine about the sunset of Christianity occurs once again:

> "He replied in a friendly fashion: 'Indeed, I do know that
> you have learned a few things from me' . . . 'However, I
> have,' he continued, 'never really been able to help you, for
> of that which really helps you I possess only the echo,
> exactly the sunset glow, as we have once confirmed to each
> other. You asked me afterwards with reason: 'Can the sunset
> last long?' . . .
> 'Oh, I regret that question very much,' I cried, 'and I also
> have told you that!'
> He replied: 'But you do not need to regret at all—your
> question was posed completely justly. Indeed, it is possible
> to stay alive with a great sunset for a while, but just only for
> a while; the sunset glow itself cannot last long. That is
> impossible by its nature. When the sunset glow appears,
> the sun has already set" (ibid., p. 273).

CHAPTER V

A CRITICAL EVALUATION OF TROELTSCH'S THEOLOGY

The Systematic Unified Thought of Troeltsch's Entire Work

At the start of this study we posed the fundamental hermeneutical question of how it is possible to comprehend the full spectrum of Troeltsch's diversified thought in a unified way. We declared the aim of this study to be the identification of what Troeltsch himself described as the "systematic unified thought" *(ein systematischer Einheitsgedanke)* of his lifework, and thus the provision of the hermeneutical frame of reference by which the whole range of his thought, with its immense variety of perspectives and dimensions, is able to be understood systematically and organically. The preceding chapters, which dealt with Troeltsch's basic central thoughts at each distinctive phase of his intellectual development, were dedicated solely to this aim. Now that his major ideas have been highlighted, we must finally answer the above question on the basis of our preceding observations.

Our observations in the preceding chapters clearly show that in spite of constant changes and developments, there was a continuous thread in Troeltsch's thought as a whole. As Heinz-Horst Schrey justly asserts, "it is the peculiarity of Troeltsch's intellectual development that with him all the problems that dominate his thought until its last phase are already posed from the beginning."[1] What, then, was the central theme of Troeltsch's lifework which presented itself to him at the very beginning? According to Troeltsch's retrospective remarks which he provided toward the end of his intellectual pilgrimage, the central theme of pivotal importance for his entire career took its rise out of "a deep and vivid realization of the clash between historical reflection and the determination of standards of truth and value."[2] He states:

I was confronted, on the one hand, with the perpetual flux and overflow of the variety of historical events and the critical and distrustful attitude [of the historian] towards conventional traditions, the knowledge of the real events of the past being obtained from them only as a reward of ceaseless toil, and then only with approximate accuracy. And, on the other hand, I perceived the human impulse towards a definite practical standpoint—the devotional and trustful attitude towards life, which keeps the human mind open and obedient to the divine revelation and the divine commands. It was largely out of this conflict, which was no hypothetical one, but a fact of my own practical experience, that my entire scientific formulation of the question *(meine ganze wissenschaftliche Fragestellung)* took its rise./3/

This clash or conflict between history and norms was, however, "no mere personal and accidental experience" of Troeltsch but rather "the personal form in which a vital problem of the modern world *(Lebensproblem der modernen Welt)*, prevailing in the present stage of human development, presented itself to [him]."/4/ Thus, the *Lebensproblematik* of Troeltsch's scientific endeavor was the problem of the relationship between history (a historical way of thinking) and norms (the determination of normative values and truths). This problem, according to Troeltsch, was at bottom brought into existance by *Historismus*. The theme of *Historismus* thus permeated his entire work, even though it received a clear formulation at a later phase of his intellectual development. His well-known epigram "Everything is tottering" *(Es wackelt alles)*, as Walther Köhler has handed down the phrase along with an interesting episode related to it, bears eloquent testimony to this fact. Thereby Köhler rightly suggests that this phrase could be taken as the leitmotif of Troeltsch's theology and philosophy, if it is safeguarded against misuse and misunderstanding. That is to say, for Troeltsch "the question [was] not a 'tottering' theology and philosophy, but rather it [was] precisely to provide them with a solid foundation that would stand firm against all storms."/5/ In this sense, Friedrich Meinecke's saying "παντα ρει, δóς μοι πον στω (everything is in flux, but give me a place to stand)" applies not only to Troeltsch's *Der Historismus* but also to his entire scientific endeavor./6/ To use another expression of Meinecke, the whole of Troeltsch's academic labor could be epitomized as an "attempt to see," in the face of "the horizontal ceaseless stream of being," "the matter also *vertically* and to construct a firm bridge over the stream."/7/ For Troeltsch, who started his career as one of the last students of Ritschl, the teacher's solution of the problem seemed to be "much too weak a dam against the historical leveling of Christianity." Hence "a fundamental confrontation with the historicization of theology" became the central theme for the early Troeltsch./8/ The problem of "damming and shaping the historical stream of life" (*Dämmung und Gestaltung des historischen Lebensstromes*), which became the major task of Troeltsch's later philosophy of history, had been already keenly felt within the theological framework of the early Troeltsch.

Throughout his entire career Troeltsch was consistent in his conviction that history is not only the source of the problems but also the source of their solutions./9/ Confronted by the devastating effects of *Historismus* on Christian faith, he was nevertheless convinced that "*Historismus* itself will not let itself be shaken off again, and supernaturalism will not be called back again."/10/ He had rather the vocational sense that he would revolutionize and thus revitalize theology with the historical method. Hence he made a strong demand that the historical method be applied to theology in full seriousness and without reservations. The consequence of this demand was the advocacy of a *religionsgeschichtliche* theology, which was, by design, an actualization of "a latent theology of *Historismus*."/11/ It should be noted here, however, that a sort of metaphysical form of thought based on his idealist faith in the divine reason actively operating in history lay behind Troeltsch's idea of a *religionsgeschichtliche* theology and prevented such a thoroughly historicized theology from falling victim to historical relativism. He thus asserted the necessity of "a metaphysics of history" (*eine Metaphysik der Geschichte*)/12/ for a theology of *Historismus*.

Although Troeltsch did not completely renounce the idea of a metaphysics of history in his second period, he now considered the construction of such an inductive and experiential metaphysics to be "a relatively creative act."/13/ Thus that somewhat Hegelian notion was replaced by the activist notion of "a creative act" (*eine schöpferische Tat*)/14/ and its realted idea, a Neo-Kantian idea of the system of historical values. *The Absoluteness of Christianity* (1902) marked this 'transition' from a Hegelian standpoint blended with a Diltheyan psychological immanentism to a transcendental and critical one. In Troeltsch's time, the problem of the absoluteness of Christianity had come to a serious crisis, because in Christianity's claim to the absoluteness the historical-individual and the universally valid were combined, and yet because exactly this knot was called into question by *Historismus*. Troeltsch's proposed solution to the problem in this classic work was of exemplary significance for his subsequent academic endeavors. Declaring the impossibility of establishing the absoluteness of Christianity on the basis of a historical way of thinking or by the use of historical means, Troeltsch nevertheless did not deny the "simple normative value" of Christianity. According to him, the most important task of history is to discern in a variety of historical value-constructs a normative, universally valid goal toward which the whole is directed, thus evaluating each historical construct against this orienting goal and ideal. The criterion of evaluation is, despite a scrupulous survey of history, unprejudiced hypothetical empathy and impartial comparison, in the last analysis based on a personal, ethical, religious conviction. Thus "the final decision between the values is," in Troeltsch's opinion, "ultimately an axiomatic act."/15/

The second edition of *The Absoluteness of Christianity* (1912) has made this point much clearer. Troeltsch now spells out:

> The problem of history is not that of making an either/or choice between relativism and absolutism but that of combining the two, namely, that of discerning, in the relative, tendencies toward the absolute goal. How does one work out an ever-new creative synthesis *(die immer neue schöpferische Synthese)* that will give the absolute the form *(Gestalt)* possible for it at a particular moment and yet remain true to its inherent limitation as a mere approximation of true, ultimate, and universally valid values? That is the gist of the problem . . ./16/

Thus, elaboration of an ever-new creative synthesis of the absolute (the universally valid) and the relative (the historical-individual) was the fundamental solution that the Troeltsch of the second period and thereafter proposed with reference to the problem of the relationship between history and norms. As far as the basic manner of solving the problem is concerned, there was no essential change between the second and the third periods. The difference referred only to the focus of interest and the scope of horizon of investigation. In the first period, Troeltsch's major interest was "to derive [the] normativeness [of Christianity] from the history of religions instead of from scholastic theories of revelation or apologetics against philosophical systems."/17/ The advocacy of a *religionsgeschichtliche* theology embodied this interest. In the second period, however,

Troeltsch's central academic concerns were not merely to establish the supremacy or prime validity of Christianity through psychological and historical analysis of religion and religions but, above all, "to give the Christian world of ideas a form that will correspond to the present religious and intellectual situation" (*diejenige Gestaltung der christlichen Ideenwelt zu schaffen, die der heutigen geistigen Lage entspricht*)./18/ The new shaping (*Neugestaltung*) or new formation (*Neuformung*) of the Christian world of ideas and life occupied his thought. Focused on this central theme, his studies in this period ranged over theology, philosophy of religion, sociology of religion, the history of ideas and culture, ethics, and philosophy of history. In the third period the focus of Troeltsch's scientific interest was no longer merely the vindication of the supreme validity of Christianity or the new shaping of Christianity itself but rather new synthesis and revitalization of the European culture and civilization with which Christianity was, in his opinion, indissolubly bound up by the decrees of fate. The scope or horizon of his investigation was broadened from the religious sphere proper toward a much broader sphere enveloping the entirety of culture./19/ The question was no longer merely a new creative synthesis that would give the Christian world of ideas and life a new *Gestalt* corresponding to the present religious and intellectual situation but rather "a contemporary cultural synthesis" centered on European history and culture. Troeltsch intended to counter the present-day crisis in values with such a fresh synthesis of culture.

In view of these considerations, it is apparent that Troeltsch was thoroughly consistent, first of all, in his formulation of the question./20/ The *Problematik* of *Historismus* or, more precisely, "the tension between the absolute and the relative" (Tillich), permeated his entire work. In the second place, as far as the solution of the problem is concerned, Troeltsch was largely and basically consistent from the year 1903 onward. He was, to be sure, always consistent in his basic conviction that history can be overcome by history. However, the changes in his actual manner of overcoming historical relativism or in that of deriving norms from history between the first and the second and third periods were not minor. The strong link between the second and third periods in this respect was provided by his theory of *Gestaltung*, namely, the idea of an ever-new synthesis of antinomies through a personal creative act. The shift in central concerns between these periods was nonetheless no insig-

nificant change from the viewpoint of theology. For the broader and
the more universal-historical Troeltsch's horizon became, the more
contextual his understanding of Christianity was forced to become.
Christianity, as Troeltsch pictured it toward the end of his earthly
pilgrimage, was almost completely captured within the domain of
European culture and civilization. Such a cultural captivity of Christianity unmistakably involved serious consequences for theology.

Nevertheless, one cannot deny that a systematic unified thought
underlies the whole of Troeltsch's writings by referring to the
cultural captivity of Troeltsch's theology. For to prove the former is
one thing, and to confute the latter is another. At all events, our
observations certainly indicate that a systematic unified thought
underlies Troeltsch's entire corpus. H. Richard Niebuhr seems to
support us at this point when he remarks:

> While Troeltsch did not contemplate the possibility of pro-
> ducing a system of philosophy, he nevertheless regarded his
> thought as having systematic connections. The system he
> sought to prepare was to [be] the result of detailed empirical
> research into history and of labor in all of the separate
> disciplines of philosophy, hence also it was to be a modifi-
> able and an open system, which would constantly correct
> itself. /21/

What, then, was the systematic unified thought of Troeltsch's
lifework? In the first place, the systematic unified thought does not
mean "a closed system of basic *a priori* concepts."/22/ Troeltsch had
strong doubts about such a closed system. In this sense he had "no
real system."/23/ If he nonetheless had a 'system,' it must have been
"an open and modifiable system,"/24/ which "would always be in
growth, constantly correct itself, and preserve open places."/25/ It
was therefore "a somewhat variable system" which "cannot be deduced purely logically from certain basic apercus but must grow
with the entire study in the constant mutual correction of life and
thought."/26/ In any case, Troeltsch had no system in the ordinary
sense of the word, be it a theological or a philosophical one. His
thought was too much directed toward detailed empirical research
into history to reach completion as a system. Such was certainly his
lot as the thinker of *Historismus*. Nevertheless, Troeltsch made a
claim to be a systematic thinker by implying that a systematic
unified thought underlay his lifework./27/ Again, what, then, was
the systematic unified thought? Since it does not mean a system of

thought in the ordinary sense, it must be construed as denoting a *consistency in central basic concerns* or the *existence of a leitmotif* throughout his entire career. Taken in this sense, a systematic unified thought unmistakably underlay Troeltsch's entire work. As we have shown above, the central theme of Troeltsch's lifework was the question of how it is possible to establish solid normative values on the basis of the basic acknowledgment of "a fundamental historicizing of all our thought about human being, its culture, and its values."/28/ Troeltsch posed this fundamental question as a theologian and, after having voyaged the ocean of theology, philosophy of religion, sociology of religion, the history of ideas and culture, and ethics, he eventually found its solution in the philosophico-historical idea of a contemporary cultural synthesis. This idea of a synthesis of culture, however, was an expanded version of that "ever-new creative synthesis that will give the absolute the form *(Gestalt)* possible for it at a particular moment" which Troeltsch had proposed as the solution to the problem of the relationship between history and norms in his theological period./29/ According to him, an ever-new synthesis as an individual creative act at which his idea of *Gestaltung* aimed was the solely practicable solution of all the antinomies of our life including that of history and norms./30/ Thus, we may say that *Gestaltung* or, more precisely, *Neugestaltung* (new shaping), explicated in adamant confrontation with the stream of historical relativism as a shaping of Christianity or of European culture, was the leitmotif of Troeltsch's entire scientific endeavor.

Troeltsch's theory of *Gestaltung*, however, cannot be fully understood without reference to its religious and metaphysical dimensions. Accordingly, a few remarks on these aspects are necessary. As we have occasionally indicated, an idealist religious and metaphysical outlook lay behind Troeltsch's entire thought, especially behind his doctrine of *Gestaltung*. His doctrine of *Gestaltung* presupposed as its basic premise "an active presence of the Absolute Spirit in finite spirit" *(eine handelnde Gegenwart des absoluten Geistes im endlichen)* or "an activity of the universe . . . in individual souls."/31/ According to Troeltsch, God or the Absolute is, first of all, "the creative will," "the personal active will,"/32/ or "the will to creation and shaping which becomes, in finite spirits, a self-formation of the divine ground and impulse."/33/ God or the Absolute "must always be first grasped and, above all, first shaped" by "the acting and shaping mind" in order to become "the power of this world."/34/ Such an act of grasping and shaping, however, is only possible by virtue of inspiration from the depths of the divine ground. Thus, *Gestaltung* means not only a creative act of giving the Absolute the *Gestalt* possible for it at a particular moment but also a participation in the "life process of the Absolute."/35/

Troeltsch's theory of *Gestaltung* was thus deeply rooted in his religious and metaphysical conception of the Absolute. Despite the apparent change and development in his thought, Troeltsch was certainly always consistent and persistent in his Christian theistic faith in "the conceptually inexhaustible, creative vitality of the divine will."/36/ It was precisely this "energetic theism" *(ein energischer Theismus)*/37/ that functioned as the hinge of his lifework.

In conclusion, Troeltsch was the systematic theologian of *Historismus* in the fullest sense of the word. But such a designation is actually a self-contradiction. *Historismus* dissolves everything in the flow of historical becoming, while the systematic theologian presupposes a normative truth to explicate. Only by creative act and venture can such a contradiction be brought into a union *(coincidentia oppositorum)*. In view of the existential moments involved here, it is not far from the truth to designate Troeltsch's standpoint, as Eduard Spranger did, as an "existentialist *Historismus*."/38/ But such a *coincidentia oppositorum* also implies Troeltsch's strenuous efforts to give the Absolute the *Gestalt* possible for it in a particular historical situation by shaping the historical stream of life into a system of values. In consideration of this constructive aspect of his thought, it would be more appropriate to designate Troeltsch's standpoint, as Kondo did, as a "constructive *Historismus*" or a "shaping *Historismus*" *(der gestaltende Historismus)*./39/ We should like therefore to characterize it as a creative constructive *Historismus*. In any case, the constructive aspect of Troeltsch's seemingly dominantly critical thought cannot be emphasized too much. Given the leitmotif of *Gestaltung*, it is obviously wrong to conclude that "the critical dominated the constructive in the theology of Troeltsch."/40/ Rather, "criticism and creation," in Troeltsch's opinion, "are substantially interconnected."/41/ Troeltsch's theological achievement must therefore be evaluated not only by its critical aspect but also by its constructive side. In any event, his theology cannot be adequately understood without reference to the central role of *Gestaltung*.

The Legitimacy of a Troeltschian Conception of Theology

In the preceding, we demonstrated that Troeltsch's claim that a systematic unified thought underlies his work as a whole is justifiable. We also showed that the systematic unified thought of his lifework was at bottom deeply Christian and religious in character. The initial theological concern broadened so that it eventually culminated in a cosmic theology of history or "a mystic philosophy of cosmic fulness and extent"/42/ with a strong ethical drive and impulse. There can be no doubt, therefore, that the most comprehensive frame of reference by which Troeltsch's lifework is most adequately evaluated is theology, not just a philosophy of religion, ethics, or a philosophy of history. The moment we assert this, however, we are confronted by serious questions. Once Troeltsch's entire work is considered in terms of theology, is it theologically adequate? Was not Troeltsch's theological development rather "the story of a collaspe"/43/? Did not Troeltsch lead theology into "a blind alley where we were strolling in realtive comfort but could not advance any further"/44/? Even if Troeltsch should have significance for the future of theology, is he not at most "the negative presupposition for every future construction"/45/? These are typical questions raised against Troeltsch for the last six decades. In my opinion, two different questions are involved here. The one is the *de facto* question of whether Troeltsch's theology really collapsed as critics have unanimously declared. An important question related to this *quid facti* is whether Troeltsch really deemed himself a failure. The other is the *de jure* question concerning the sufficiency of Troeltsch's theology as a Christian theology. The question here is: Is Troeltsch's "distracted" or "diffused" theology/46/ theologically adequate?

With the reference to the first question, Gertrud von le Fort, the most devoted disciple of Troeltsch,/47/ seems to endorse the alleged failure or collapse of Troeltsch with the following testimony:

> In general, it is correct . . . that Troeltsch himself characterized himself as a failure *(einen Gescheiterten)*. In the last conversation which I had with him a few months before his death, he was deeply imbued with a sense of having failed./48/

But did Troeltsch really consider himself a failure? There is no doubt that toward the end of his life Troeltsch was in profound depression and in a melancholy mood. His letters to Friedrich von Hügel reveal how depressed and disturbed he was. For example, according to a letter to his British friend on 25 July 1922, the assassination of his friend Rathenau, the threat of a disintegration of the empire, orgies of the ignorant masses, the further aggravation of his own financial situation, worries about the coming winter (due to the shortage of heating fuel)—all these, coupled with overwork and concern for his wife's health (she was always in a state of ill health), brought Troeltsch into "a gloomy and depressed mental condition." He characterized such a "condition of depression" as "much like a mountain which I can hardly climb." "A deep sorrow," he writes, "will no longer leave me, as long as I live."/49/ In his next letter of 24 August from Lake Starnberg where he was recuperating for a short time, Troeltsch wrote that he had been "utterly exhausted and worn out." He was afraid of returning from a short repose in the wilderness to the actual world of the struggle for existence./50/ Nevertheless he had been elected, meanwhile, to the dean of the philosophical faculty which embraced 80 professors and 5000 students, and that as "a kind of sign of reconciliation" between the nationalist faculty members and the more democratically oriented ones. There is no doubt that this deanship was "a terrible burden" for him./51/

In view of the circumstances in which Troeltsch found himself toward the end of his life, it is too rash to use the fact of Troeltsch's depression and melancholy to draw the conclusion that Troeltsch deemed himself a failure. Besides, Troeltsch's statement in the Foreword to *Der Historismus* which is dated 19 September 1922, thus evidently after le Fort's last encounter with her teacher, would be unintelligible, if he had already adjudged himself to be bankrupt as a philosopher and a religious thinker. There he states:

> I hope that I will be able to explicate at least my philosophy of religion . . . For that matter, however, the thought consoles me that the philosophical study of today is everywhere freshly in motion and that I believe I notice a similar basic tendency . . . among many colleagues, especially among the younger generation. Only cooperative study can solve . . . problems . . ./52/

In any case, as far as the question is that of Troeltsch's own assessment of his work, critics have to demonstrate the "weakness or disintegration of ethical vigor or despair over a religious faith that guarantees a unified goal of things" in him before they list him among the "bankrupt theologians" *(bankerotte Theologen)*. For such an ethical vigor and a religious faith are, in Troeltsch's opinion, the hallmark of living theology./53/ Judged by this criterion, Troeltsch was certainly not a bankrupt theologian.

Precisely at this point, however, the second question must be raised. Is such a Troeltschian conception of theology theologically adequate? We have seen that Theodor Kaftan raised the same question and answered it entirely negatively./54/ By the year 1913, when he published the second volume of his collected writings, Troeltsch was confronted with the charge "that I have been basically more interested in the general analysis of culture and religion than in specifically Christian theological issues." Troeltsch countered this charge with a significant question: "the question of course is what one takes theology and its task to be." What, then, did Troeltsch take theology and its task to be? He never considered systematic theology to be "a simple task of handing down tradition and apologetics." Its proper task, in his opinion, was rather "the task of orienting the tradition in view of the intellectual and religious life of the present day," a task which "will someday necessarily result in a new shaping *(Neugestaltung)* of religious thought and its institutions."/55/

The fundamental question concerning Troeltsch's theology is entirely involved in this definition of theology and its task. If one accepts such a Troeltschian definition, then theologians must assume "a dual responsibility: to the tradition and to the intellectual climate of their own day."/56/ To use Ritschl's famous metaphor,/57/ theology must then be "an ellipse with two foci" instead of "a circle with one center." Theology thus stands under two different stars: the eternal truth of the Christian message and the scientific, cultural, social, and political expression of human self-understanding at a particular moment. The task of theology, then, is naturally thought to consist in a constantly new synthesis of these two poles. All the scientific theologians since Schleiermacher more or less took the task of theology to be such. Troeltsch only represented the most critical edge of this specifically modern trend. But is "orientation in view of the intellectual and religious life of the present" *(Orientierung im geistigen und religiösen Leben der Gegenwart)* really the proper or primary task of theology, as Troeltsch thought? In his review of Troeltsch's first work, Julius Kaftan had already put this fundamental question to his one-time student: "Is it really correct to declare the correlation of Christian knowledge with the total spiritual and intellectual life *(die Inbeziehungsetzung der christlichen Erkenntniss zum geistigen Gesammtleben)* the task of dogmatics?"/58/ As regards this question, theologians like Barth would certainly argue that the primary task of theology is by no means such an orientation in view of the *human* situation, whether it be religious or spiritual. They would insist that the primary task of theology—and this is solely the proper task of theolgoy—is the critical examination of the content of the Christian Church's distinctive talk about God according to the criterion of the Church's own principle. Whenever the primary task of theology is taken to be a synthesis of the two poles mentioned above, the final result is without exception a transformation of the initial ellipse with two foci into a circle with one center, an overriding of the human pole over the divine pole. No one discerned this process of "religious anthropocentrism"/59/ in the theological development of the past century more discriminatingly than Karl Barth. It is not an overstatement to say that his life long efforts were exclusively focused on the regaining of the subject of theology through the thorough demolition of any kind of double-hearted theology. According to Barth, the fatal errors of nineteenth century theology arose from "the conviction that the guiding principle of theology must be confrontation with the contemporary age and its various conception." The theologians of the nineteenth century "had their eyes fixed on the world" and "wrestled with the challenging issue of their times."/60/ Their "openness to the world" meant (1) that with all their energies captivated by the world, they accomplished surprisingly little in terms of a new and profound understanding of Christian truth itself; (2) that they ascribed normative character to the ideas of the surrounding world or the spirit of the age; (3) that they even identified the latter with the Christian ideal, thus feeling quite at home in the modern bourgeois society./61/ Hence Barth pejoratively characterized the modern development of evangelical theology from Schleiermacher through Ritschl up to Troeltsch as "Culture-Protestantism." In frank opposition to this Neo-Protestantism, he persistently emphasized "the absolute primacy of the positive tasks of theology in and for the Church over against the secondary tasks of relating to the various philosophies of the times."/62/ For "modernity, up-to-dateness," in his opinion, "has nothing whatever to do with the question of the truth of the Church."/63/

Barth's assertion, to be sure, involved more than one moment of truth. Though there are very few witnesses of his direct confrontation with Troeltsch,/64/ Barth's theology itself represents the sharpest antithesis to Troeltsch, who embodied, in his own life and thought, the unambiguous consequence of the Neo-Protestantism of which Barth was the most formidable opponent. A critical comparison of these greatest antipodes of contemporary theology, however, reveals simultaneously both strengths and weak points on both sides./65/ Furthermore, it shows that the one is strongest precisely at the point where the other is weakest. Troeltsch as a constructive theologian is most vulnerable to criticism of his Christology, while Barth is strongest at this point. "The principle difficulty with Barth's orientation," in contrast, "is that it does not pay sufficient attention to the impact of modern historical thinking on man's understanding,"/66/ whereas Troeltsch's achievements are most prominent at this point. Although the main chapters of the fifty years of Protestant theology following the death of Troeltsch have been written monochromatically in Barthian "ivory," instead of polychromatically by the mixture of Troeltschian "blue," such a monochromatic picture of theology and its task is no longer permissible in a pluralistic context of contemporary theology. If Troeltsch and Barth "climax," as Hans Frei suggests, "respectively the historical and systematic *Problematik* of the academic tradition of Protestant theology,"/67/ Troeltsch must be taken much more seriously as a viable theological force than Barth and his epigones have deemed him to be. In any case, the present situation of theology unmistakably suggests that a Barthian revelational-monistic theology needs revision from a historically and culturally oriented theology. In this sense, the combination of Troeltsch and Barth, as H. Richard Niebuhr once attempted, remains "work that needs to be done."/68/

However, such a demand involves fundamental acknowledgment of the dual task of theology which was espoused by the pre-Barthian theologians. To quote Horst Stephan, "evangelical theology as scientific self-reflection and representation of Christian faith stands under two different stars." In his view, theology is the function of the Christian *community* on the one hand and a *scientific* examination of the content of Christian faith on the other. Only a theology that "really follows both stars" is "a legitimate theology." Theology denies its essential nature if it sacrifices either its faith-character or its scientific character. Thus theology stands "in a constant battle on the two fronts" *(in beständigem Zweifron-tenkampf)*./69/ Given this twofold character of theology, there must be, however, room for both "intensive" and "extensive" types of faith and theology, and these two must be kept in balance./70/ As Robert Morgan rightly observes, "however permanent the need of the Church for an 'intensive' confessional theology in the service of its evangelical task, it will always be necessary, too, for Christian intel-lectuals to develop the 'extensive' type of theology represented by Troeltsch."/71/ The question is therefore not that of making an either/or choice between "intensive" and "extensive" types of the-ology but rather that of establishing a fruitful relationship of mutual cooperation between both. Among contemporary theologies, Paul Tillich's apologetic theology founded on the method of correlation and H. Richard Niebuhr's conversionist theology based on theo-centric relativism, in my judgment, most successfully exemplify such a possibility./72/

Troeltsch's "extensive" theology itself too, however, consisted of a tense combination of "intensive" and "extensive" movements of faith and therefore involved a possibility of synthesizing both "inten-sive" and "extensive" types of theology within his own conceptual framework. As we have seen, Troeltsch's own religious position was a spiritualism of the Christian stamp and therefore had basically an "intensive" orientation. But he sought "to make room for the histor-ical element and for the cultic and sociological factor bound up with it"—thus for the "extensive" orientation of theology—for the very reason that an intensively oriented theology is culturally and socially impotent./73/ Karl Bornhausen once said that "it seemed both nec-essary and impossible to unite"/74/ Wilhelm Herrmann's "intensive" theological position and Troeltsch's "extensive" one. But the impos-sibility lay on the side of Herrmann, not on Troeltsch's side./75/ Troeltsch on his part perceived his "practical community" with Herrmann and remarked, "I can practically accept the peculiar conception of Christian faith in God and salvation, as Herrmann represents it with such a great simplifying power, completely in my framework of thought." Furthermore, he clearly stated, "I can only wish that anyone who learns from me supplement and reinforce what has been learned [from me] through Herrmann."/76/ Thus,

Troeltsch was not only quite capable of accepting a Herrmannian "intensive" theology into his own "extensive" theological framework but also felt the need for his theology to be supplemented by such a confessional, ecclesiastically oriented theology. In any event, Troeltsch's openness and his sense of balance are a striking contrast to the parochialism and exclusive onesidedness of Herrmann and his student Barth.

In view of these considerations, we can conclude that Troeltsch's conception of theology itself is by no means theologically irrelevant. The task of orienting Christian tradition in view of the intellectual and religious situation of the present must be, in my opinion, the most important theological task. True, theology, defined thus, involves a danger of becoming the so-called "Culture-Protestantism." But it is not always the case that theology is transformed into religious anthropology whenever its primary task is taken to be reorientation of Christian tradition in view of the intellectual and religious situation of the present. H. R. Niebuhr discriminatingly showed that there are at least five dominant types as far as the relation between Christ and culture is concerned. "Culture-Protestantism" is merely one possibility that theology might take in relation to culture. Furthermore, Troeltsch was not "the cultural Christian." He transcended liberal Protestantism by deepening and rendering critical its central agenda and heritage./77/ In any case, theology cannot evade a *dual* responsibility: to the tradition and to the intellectual climate of the present. The question is therefore not whether a Troeltschian conception of theology is legitimate as a Christian theology, but rather how successfully and effectively he performed the enormously difficult task of reshaping theology in response to the cultural crisis of his time.

Troeltsch's Significance for the Future of Theology

Throughout this study we have been trying to understand Troeltsch's rich thought as precisely as possible through immersion in the ocean of his original writings. We have consciously tried to avoid squeezing the immense variety of perspectives and dimensions in his thought into a strait jacket, be it one made by critics or by sympathizers. We have chosen instead to trace empathically the zigzag path which Troeltsch trod in the intellectual, social, and cultural context of his time. Now that the main profile of his lifework and its underlying systematic unified thought have been clarified, Troeltsch's significance for us and for the future of theology must finally be discussed.

Like all other thinkers, Troeltsch's thought is strongly conditioned by the spirit of his age. Historical and contextual conditionality is evident to a high degree with this thinker, who always said that "one must accept one's destiny, love it, and transform it into something better."/78/ Apart from the historical and contextual limitations, his entire work was permeated by his highly personal (ethical, religious, and metaphysical) concerns. The historical and existential concern with the fate of Christianity in the modern world, as we have seen, penetrated his entire scientific endeavor. Accordingly, Troeltsch's thought, despite his constant emphasis on scientific objectivity, broadness of scope, and impartiality of judgment, is in the last analysis burdened considerably with predetermined values.

Troeltsch was often attacked by critics for his antisupernaturalism (T. Kaftan), dissolution of dogmatics (K. Barth, H. Diem, G. Müller), loss of the subject matter of theology (Barth, R. Bultmann, F. Gogarten), Culture-Protestantism (Barth, T. Ogletree), anthropocentrism (Barth, E. Brunner, W. Pannenberg), religionism (Barth), psychologism (Brunner), modernism (Barth, Brunner), speculative view of history (Gogarten), metaphysical bent (H. Herring), flight from history (I. Escribano Alberce), inability to reach a standpoint beyond history (P. Tillich, H. -H. Schrey), conflation of historical scholarship and ethical tasks (B. Schmeidler, F. Meinecke), value-loadedness (H. S. Hughes), radical religious individualism (B. A. Reist, F. v. Hügel), and so forth. Some of them are justifiable to some extent, some are based on misconstruction, and others are rather reflections of the critics' own biases and prejudices. Evaluation or refutation of the validity of each of these charges is not necessary here, for the discussion in this study may serve directly or indirectly as such. Hence only the question that seems to be the major cause of Troeltsch's difficulties should be discussed. This is the question which strikes the heart of Troeltsch's thought. Is it possible at all to overcome history by history? Can history be the source of norms or values as Troeltsch claims? Is it not rather only what transcends history and not history itself, that really overcomes historical relativism?

With regard to this fundamental question, I am basically of the same opinion as Paul Tillich, who once asserted the following: In the case of Troeltsch "it is a historical standpoint from which history is judged, and not *the* transhistorical standpoint. However, it is only from this transhistorical standpoint that history can be interpreted."/79/ Although I do not endorse Tillich's other judgment that "the standpoint from which he [Troeltsch] viewed religion was culture, not religion,"/80/ Troeltsch's way of viewing things was certainly too contextual and too bound up with history to take a critical and prophetic attitude toward history, culture, and religion. As Tillich observes, "the immanent view, which is a self-evident presupposition for Troeltsch, is broken through at no point, and for this reason no standpoint is reached from which *Historismus* is really overcome."/81/ Heinz-Horst Schrey makes the same point:

> In one phase of his thought Troeltsch strives for the depths of history and in the other for the widths of history. In no case, however, does he arrive at *the point beyond history (Jenseits der Geschichte)* from which alone the overcoming of *Historismus* is possible./82/
>
> Troeltsch, in view of the empirical concreteness of the historical process and owing to a justifiable skepticism toward false absolutes, precludes this possibility [of an interpretation of history which goes beyond the limits of relative understanding]. He is therefore also not in the position to overcome *Historismus* in a decided way. This point at which the relation of the unconditional to the conditional manifests itself, and from which alone history receives its meaning, is however revelation. Historicalness *(Geschichtlichkeit)* and revelation demand each other . . ./83/

I take these criticisms of Troeltsch by Tillich and Schrey as largely relevant and justifiable. Troeltsch's idea of an overcoming of history sounds indeed very attractive and is even much preferable to the easy solution of the problem of history by simple appeal to the absolute. But is it really possible to overcome history with history without a metaphysics and theology of history based on a definite idea of God? True, Troeltsch himself presupposed and even felt a necessity for evolving such a metaphysics of history. He suggested a historically modified Leibnizian-Malebranchean monadology, a doctrine of finite minds' identify with and participation in the infinite mind, as his own metaphysical position. For him, however, metaphysics was "not a prerequisite of history but a result of the judgment made on history out of inner necessity."/84/ Metaphysics was therefore not the foundation of his reflection upon history but an "extra allowance" *(Zuschuß)*/85/ for it. Again, Tillich is right when he contends that "the metaphysical element should never be an 'extra allowance,'" and that "it is either the foundation or it is nothing."/86/ Unless one makes the metaphysical or theological element the foundation and starting point of one's reflection, all that one can do is, as Troeltsch rightly observed, merely to "sense and feel" the unity and meaning of the whole. However, historical reflection, in my opinion, is *theologically* insufficient unless it proceeds from the All or the idea of God. Accordingly, Troeltsch's attitude toward history must be reversed. Not "from the establishment of an individual moment can we sense the All," as Troeltsch thought, but "from the All can we establish the individual moment" as a meaningful entity./87/ Otherwise one can never come to a conclusion and completion. The "unfinished" character of Troeltsch's entire work is therefore not only due to his openness to the reality of history but also due to his misconception of the role of the metaphysical or theological element in the interpretation of history. It is no wonder that Troeltsch was "condemned to the labor of a Sisyphus."/88/ One may also attribute Troeltsch's incapability to complete his own system to his "Romantic" background, as Barth did. This great opponent of Troeltsch writes the following as he is talking about the great Romantic poet Novalis:

> It is pure Romanticism only insofar as it draws up its program, and not by carrying it out. It is surely no mere accident that the lifework of the last great Romantic in theology, Ernst Troeltsch, consisted chiefly in the proclamation and ever-renewed proclamation of programs. Pure Romanticism must not wish to extend itself in such a way as to become a science or action, or—the science and action of which it is capable will signify its disloyalty to itself. Romanticism is pure as yearning, and only as yearning./89/

Be that as it may, theology cannot and must not begin with history but with what is beyond history, namely, with the idea of God, as long as it is theology. Troeltsch's idea of overcoming history with history, however, need not be reliquished if God and history are taken as *co-constitutive.* God is not simply beyond history but works within history. In this sense, God is within history, and history is within God. It is true that history cannot be overcome *by* history itself, but history can be overcome only from *within* history. That which transcends history must transcend from within it rather than from beyond it. All that is required of Troeltsch is therefore a more definite idea of God.

With this assertion one may feel compelled to endorse the legitimacy of a Barthian reaction to Troeltsch's radical historicization of theology in principle. However, Barth's theological method, procedure, and results are not the best alternative to Troeltsch's *historical theology*/90/ because Barth hardly seems to have paid sufficient attention to the impact of modern historical thinking on human understanding and because he rejected any kind of scientific corroboration of his theological statements./91/ His decidedly kerygmatic and revelational theology pays a large price for his grand neglect of Troeltsch and the problem of historical relativism which the latter tackled with all his energy and strength. In any case, the future of theology lies, in my opinion, neither in the direction of Barth's positivist revelational theology nor in that of Bultmann's existentialist theology which dissolves history into the historicalness of human existence, but rather in a synthesis of a Troeltschian historical theology and a Barthian revelational theology. This is to say, not only theology must be thoroughly historicized, but also history must be interpreted in a theological light. Historicization of theology is inevitable in a fully historically conscious age. It is also necessary lest theology should absolutize itself dogmatically and thus become false absolutes. This claim for the historicization of theology, however, should not be absolutized. (Such would result in yet another false absolute of history.) History must therefore be viewed in the light of the Ultimate or the Unconditional. Only in this way can a false absolutization of history be avoided. Thus, a theology of the future which combines Troeltsch's moment of truth (historical theology or theology as history) and Barth's moment of truth (theological history or history as theology) must be a sort of 'theology of history' *(Geschichtstheologie)*. Such a theology not only examines the relevance of Christian dogmatic assertions in view of empirical historical knowledge about the actual course of world-history but also interprets the actual course of world-history in the light of the Christian idea of God and Christian symbols. As theologians who offer hints on such a theology of history, Paul Tillich, Reinhold Niebuhr, H. Richard Niebuhr, and Wolfhart Pannenberg are worthy of note. Tillich's kairotic and theonomous view of history in Christian symbols and his theory of the Protestant principle, R. Niebuhr's Christian realism and applied theology of history, H. R.

Niebuhr's theocentric relativism and conversionism, and Pannenberg's theology of universal history and his Christology *von unten*
are all great *theological* steps beyond Troeltsch's predicament. There
is hardly any doubt that the success of these theologians is attributable to a considerable extent to their serious struggle with Troeltsch
and his difficulties. True, it is undeniable that they have moderated
the sharpness and radicalism of Troeltsch's historical questioning in
order to accommodate it to theology. Yet such an accommodation is
necessary for theology, lest it should lose its subject matter in the
ceaseless stream of history. It is also required so that Troeltsch,
instead of remaining the *enfant terrible* of Protestant theology, may
become the creative and constructive power for the future of theology. Troeltsch himself would not have opposed accommodation in
itself, as long as it is performed in a permissible and creative fashion.
For not an impracticable "radicalism of an either/or choice"/92/ but
rather a considered compromise or a "balancing" is "the legacy of
Ernst Troeltsch."/93/

When all is said, Troeltsch's significance for the future of theology consists, in my opinion, in the following six points.

First of all, Troeltsch's openness to the realities of history and
the *world-historical* orientation of his thought are the greatest
legacy that he has bequeathed to contemporary theology, which is
best characterized as a theology of a global age. As Trutz Rendtorff
rightly observes, "the entrance of Christianity upon its world-historical age *(weltgeschichtliches Zeitalter)* determines the situation in
which contemporary theology must solve problems."/94/ Today theology cannot evade the task of coping with the problems of world-
history, such as the political and ideological antagonisms between
East and West, the cultural and economic gaps between North and
South, the real threat of nuclear wars, and so forth, even if the
solutions of these problems do not belong to the specific business of
theology. Indeed, contemporary theology is already deeply involved
in the realities of world-history. The successive emergence of hybrid
theologies, e.g., political theology, economic theology, liberation
theology, black theology, feminist theology, urban theology, etc.,
witnesses to this fact. It is undeniable, however, that these secular
or contextual theologies involve serious problems and dangers.
Therefore, it is important to direct our eyes to a theologian in whose
work the present situation of theology had already been perceived
and its mastery had become the central theme. Though it is an open

question whether it is appropriate to designate Troeltsch the fore-runner of "a theology of involvement," as Reist did, there is no question that Troeltsch most discriminatingly discerned the radical change in the social and cultural context of the modern world and tackled the difficult contextual and situational problems of theology in greater seriousness than anyone else. Accordingly, Troeltsch's significance is immense for the future of theology in this respect.

Second, the *interdisciplinary* character of Troeltsch's thought has exemplary value for the future of theology. If the idea of God signifies, by definition, "the reality which determines every-thing,"/95/ and if "theology can be adequately understood only as the science of God,"/96/ as Pannenberg asserts, then theology can-not limit itself to a particular field of investigation which can be separated or isolated from others. Theology as the science of God must be concerned with all fields of investigation, for God as the all-determining reality works in all reality. Consequently, the interdis-ciplinary concern is not extraneous but rather intrinsic to theology. This being the case, one cannot accuse Troeltsch's great variety of concerns of being "distraction."/97/ Rather, one must agree with Hans-Georg Drescher when he writes the following:

> Troeltsch's ability to relate his work to other disciplines is once again becoming most relevant, and it is his perma-nent contribution to have demonstrated that theology is an open discipline which lives by cooperation with other sorts of intellectual endeavour. The problem of the open and historical character of the basic criteria of theology, a re-sponsibility which must be accepted in all theological work, found in his writings an exemplary expression which will continue to have significance for the future of theology./98/

Third, the *ecumenical* quality of Troeltsch's theology is of no small significance for the future of theology. Decidedly Protestant though he was, Troeltsch's sympathetic understanding of Catholi-cism as illustrated in his treatment of Thomism in *Die Soziallehren* shows his openness to Catholicism. This is also exemplified by his close friendship with the British Catholic thinker Friedrich von Hügel. It is no accident that excellent exponents of Troeltsch's thought, such as Emil Spieß and Karl-Ernst Apfelbacher, are Catho-lic. Though he himself was Lutheran, Troeltsch's higher appreciation of Calvinism in its world-transforming potency also exemplifies his freedom from a denominational bias. Towards the end of his life Troeltsch confessed:

> All that is certain is that Christianity is at a critical moment
> of its further developments, and that very bold and far-
> reaching changes are necessary, transcending anything that
> has yet been achieved by any denomination. I have, in this
> respect, become more and more radical and super-denomi-
> national . . ./99/

Nothing more needs to be said to document the fact that Troeltsch's
position was not only super-denominational but also from the outset
inter-religious.

Fourth, the *activist* and *future* orientation of Troeltsch's thought
arouses theologians to the moral consciousness that they are responsible not only to the dogmatic tradition of the Church but also to the
world of today and tomorrow. Theology must not be aesthetic indulgence in the transmitted Word of God and the ecclesiastical
doctrines. Theologians should not fix the living God within the
Scriptures and the tradition of the Church, as if God had spoken and
worked only in Jesus Christ two millenia ago and thereafter spoke
and worked only through the medium of the scriptural words which
were once spoken. The object of theology must be the living God
who is always working actively and creatively in the realities of
history rather than the Word of God, whether it means the scriptural words, the ecclesiastical doctrines, or even the incarnated
Logos. Theology must be open toward the future and attentive to
God's present act in history. With this openness toward the future
and attentiveness to God's present action, theology must try to give
the Unconditional and Absolute a form *(Gestalt)* possible for it at a
particular moment in a peculiar situation.

Fifth, Troeltsch's *sense of balance* is also a valuable legacy for
the future of theology. "To wish to possess the absolute in an
absolute way at a particular point in history is delusion."/100/ It runs
the risk of false absolutes. "All radicalism," in the long run, "breaks
down in practice, and can only end in disaster."/101/ On the other
hand, however, "any fundamental abandonment of the ideal" and
"all precipitate capitulation to the course which presents itself as
momentarily expedient, or as the easiest way out of a difficulty, but
which may be thus expedient and easy only for the moment"/102/
are fatal mistakes to theology. Accordingly, what is important for
theology is to keep its balance between the radical idealism of the
Gospel and a realistic insight into the conditions of actual human
life. "History within itself cannot be transcended . . . In history
itself there are only relative victories."/103/ Far from "a confession of

failure,"/104/ this judgment by Troeltsch is a sober theological insight. It liberates theology from all the vain attempts to make a pretense of possessing the final truth and solution in its hands. Finally, the full seriousness and earnestness of Troeltsch's scientific pursuit is exemplary for any theologian. With regard to Troeltsch's personality, Harnack attests:

> At all times he [Troeltsch] was upright and honest, frank and free; there was nothing contrived and nothing small about him. But—and this was his most attractive and deepest trait—in this powerful naturalness of his, there breathed a quiet, noble, pure soul./105/

Such a personality is also reflected in his scientific attitude. Tillich remarks:

> The openness and the frankness of his utterance had purifying and liberating effects [on theology]. They brought about a radical elimination of false absolutes in the system of fundamentally conditioned ideas, in which theology too had long placed itself. His honesty was his theological greatness./106/

Thus the "deadly earnest" *(todernst)* of *Ernst* Troeltsch/107/ represents the highest point of scientific conscience that Christian theology has attained in modern times. Therefore—this is our conclusion—, it is the duty of contemporary theology to develop Troeltsch's theological legacy both critically and constructively for the future of Christianity and theology. I do sincerely hope that this study will prove a steady step toward the accomplishment of this immense task of contemporary theology.

NOTES

/1/   H.-H. Schrey, "Ernst Troeltsch und sein Werk," *Theologische Rundschau* 12 (1940):135.

/2/   Troeltsch, *Christian Thought*, p. 4; cf. *Überwindung*, p. 63.

/3/   Id., *Überwindung*, p. 64 cf. *Christian Thought*, p. 6. The English version is too paraphrastic to convey Troeltsch's subtle expressions. It has translated, for example, the phrase "meine ganze wissenshaftliche Fragestellung" as "my entire theoretical standpoint."

/4/   Ibid. cf. *Christian Thought*, p. 6.

/5/   Köhler, *Ernst Troeltsch*, p. 1.

/6/   Meinecke, *Friedrich Meinecke Werke*, vol. 4, p. 269: "It is even
possible to designate it [Troeltsch's *Der Historismus*] in two short catch-
words. As I told him [Troeltsch] after reading the book, one could sum-
marize it in six Greek words, namely, the words of Heraclitus and of
Archimedes: *panta rei, dos moi pou stō* (everything is in flux, but give me a
place to stand), he nodded energetically and said, 'Exactly that's it.'"

/7/   Ibid., p. 98.

/8/   E. Troeltsch, "Zur theologischen Lage," *CW* 12 (1898):629.

/9/   This conviction is best epitomized by his dictum "History can be
overcome by history" (Troeltsch, G.S. III, p. 772).

/10/ Id., "Metaphysik," p. 69.

/11/ Ibid.

/12/ Troeltsch asserted that "the dangers of the situation [caused by *Historismus*] can be overcome only by a metaphysics of history," which, in his
view, "can discern, on the basis of a fundamental investigation of human
spirit and human history, the Christian truth as the heart and goal of
history" (ibid.). He also maintained that "relativism issues from the historical method only for those who use it with atheistic or religiously skeptical
presuppositions, and relativism is overcome by a conception of history as an
unfolding of the divine reason" ("Über historische und dogmatische Methode der Theologie," p. 103; cf. G.S. II, p. 747).

/13/ Id., "Moderne Geschichtsphilosophie," pp. 115–116.

/14/ Id., "Was heißt 'Wesen des Christentums'?," *CW* 17 (1903):653, 179;
Psychologie und Erkenntnistheorie in der Religionswissenschaft, p. 40;
Glaubenslehre, p. 343; G.S. III, p. 771; *Überwindung*, p. 40; cf. "eine
individuelle Tat" ("Moderne Geschichtsphilosophie," pp. 71–72), "eine Tat
des Kompromisses" (*Überwindung*, p. 21); "eine persönliche Lebenstat"
(ibid., p. 40).

/15/ Id., *Absolutheit*, p. xv; cf. *Absolutheit* 2d ed., p. xix.

/16/ Id., *Absolutheit* 2d ed., p. 58 (an interpolation from 1912).

/17/ Id., *Absolutheit*, p. iv; cf. *Absolutheit* 2d ed., p. viii.

/18/ Id., *Absolutheit* 2d ed., p. viii. Though now found in "the Foreword
to the First Edition," this paragraph turns out to be an interpolation from
the year 1912. Accordingly, it is missing in the original "Foreword" in the
first edition.

/19/ Cf. id., G.S. IV, p. 14; *Die Sozialphilosophie des Christentums*, p. 25
n. 1.

/20/ Trutz Rendtorff holds that Troeltsch's "richness in topics as well as
consistency in the formulation of the question *(die Konsequenz der Fra-*

gestellung) have an exemplary character for theology." T. Rendtorff, Introduction to *Die Absolutheit des Christentums und die Religionsgeschichte und zwei Schriften zur Theologie,* by Ernst Troeltsch, ed. T. Rendtorff, Siebenstern-Taschenbuch 138 (Munich and Hamburg: Siebenstern Taschenbuch Verlag, 1973), p. 7.

/21/ Niebuhr, "Ernst Troeltsch's Philosophy of Religion," pp. 87–88.

/22/ Troeltsch, *Psychologie und Erkenntnistheorie in der Religionswissenschaft,* p. 31.

/23/ Id., G.S. IV, p. 3.

/24/ Id., G.S. III, p. viii.

/25/ Id., *Psychologie und Erkenntnistheorie in der Religionswissenschaft,* p. 31.

/26/ Id., G.S. IV, p. 15.

/27/ Troeltsch considered himself a "systematic theologian" *(Systematiker)* (see id., *Absolutheit,* p. vi; G.S. II, p. 500). But he was well aware that the combination of various interests in him made him very different from ordinary systematic thinkers. According to him, the essential feature of his work lay, as with the case of Dilthey, in "the balance of historical and systematic interests." He wanted, however, to "achieve a more solid position than Dilthey did" (G.S. II, p. 754).

/28/ Troeltsch, G.S. III, p. 102.

/29/ Though it is in the second edition of *The Absoluteness of Christianity* (1912) that we first meet that expression, the idea as such was unmistakably already latent in the first edition (1902), which, according to him, "forms the conclusion of a series of earlier studies and the beginning of new investigations of a more comprehensive kind in the philosophy of history" (i.d., *Christian Thought,* p. 4; cf. *Überwindung,* p. 62). In any case, in the two essays which immediately succeeded this classic work, "Modern Philosophy of History" and "What Does 'Essence of Christianity' Mean?" (both 1903), Troeltsch elaborated his original theory of *Gestaltung*.

/30/ See id., G.S. II, pp. 428–435, 712, 726–727, 760–761.

/31/ Id., G.S. II, p. 764.

/32/ Id., *Glaubenslehre,* pp. 139, 148, 167.

/33/ Id., G.S. III, p. 212.

/34/ Id., *Ünberwindung,* p. 40; G.S. I, p. 979.

/31/ Id., G.S. III, p. 212.

/36/ Ibid., p. 184.

/37/   Id., G.S. II, p. 764.

/38/   E. Spranger, "Das Historismusproblem an der Universität Berlin seit
1900," in Eduard Spranger, *Gesammelte Schriften*, vol. 5:
Kulturphilosophie und Kulturkritik, ed. Hans Wenke (Tübingen: Max
Niemeyer Verlag, 1969), p. 438.

/39/   Kondo, "Theologie der Gestaltung bei Ernst Troeltsch," p. 313 n. 66.
B. A. Gerrish has coined the term "constitutive historicism" to characterize
Troeltsch's theological position. But in view of the pivotal importance of the
theme of *Gestaltung*, "constructive *Historismus*" or "shaping *Historismus*"
seems to be a better characterization of Troeltsch's entire position. See B. A.
Gerrish, "The Possibility of a Historical Theology," in *Ernst Troeltsch and
the Future of Theology*, p. 123.

/40/   Reist, *Toward a Theology of Involvement*, p. 155.

/41/   Troeltsch, G.S. III, p. 169. Concerning this point, see Trutz Rendtorff's instructive essay, "Theologie als Kritik und Konstruktion," in *Theorie
des Christentums* (Gütersloh: Gütersloher Verlagshaus Gerd Mohn, 1972),
pp. 182–200.

/42/   H.-G. Drescher, "Troeltsch's Intellectual Development," p. 29.

/43/   Reist, *Toward a Theology of Involvement*, p. 153; cf. ibid., ch. VI.
Bodenstein has passed similar judgment on Troeltsch: "Troeltsch is a
wrecked theologian *(ein gescheiterter Theologe)!*" Bodenstein, *Neige des
Historismus*, p. 207.

/44/   K. Barth, *Die Theologie und die Kirche. Gesammelte Vorträge*, vol. 2
(Zollikon/Zurich: Evangelischer Verlag, 1951), p. 8.

/45/   Tillich, *Gesammelte Werke*, vol. 12, pp. 168, 175. Paul Tillich, who
considered himself a special student of Troeltsch, refers to "the deep
tragedy of Troeltsch's lifework" as follows:
> It is the deep tragedy of Troeltsch's lifework that he finally
> failed also in the last, most energetic effort to find the
> unconditioned in the conditioned. . . . It is the tragedy of
> the greatest [theologian] of his generation. In any case, his
> struggle and his final defeat is more important for us and for
> the future by far than the work of all those who enjoyed
> themselves in false, shattered absolutes or in the lukewarm
> water of relativity. The absolute tension of life and thought
> in which he stood, the tension of the unconditional and the
> conditional, exalts him much higher than those, and his
> failure too is greater and more fruitful than their success
> (ibid., p. 173).

/46/   Cf. Barth, *Die protestantische Theologie im 19. Jahrhundert*, p. 384;
id., *Die kirchliche Dogmatik*, IV/1, p. 425.

/47/   Le Fort was converted from Protestantism to Roman Catholicism immediately after she completed the posthumous editing and publication of Troeltsch's *Glaubenslehre*. Barth construes her conversion to Catholicism as the result of the wreckage of her teacher's ship. Cf. Barth, *Die kirchliche Dogmatik*, IV/1, p. 427.

/48/   Le Fort, *Hälfte des Lebens*, p. 88. Wilhelm F. Kasch recorded his personal interview with le Fort as follows:
">. . . when I visited Miss Gertrud von le Fort in Oberstdorf in the fall of 1961, she reported to me the following: She met Troeltsch the last time in the late summer of 1922, therefore a half year before his death, at Lake Vierwaldstätt. On this encounter Troeltsch bewailed that the whole of his work had gotten to nowhere. He was therefore discouraged and spiritless. Her reference to the earlier answers and solutions which he had offered appeared to be no help to him. So the farewell was one of complete sadness" (W. F. Kasch, *Die Sozialphilosophie von Ernst Troeltsch* [Tübingen: J. C. B. Mohr, 1963], p. 279).

/49/   Troeltsch, *Briefe*, p. 131. Troeltsch continues to write:
"Insofar as I have lived for earthly things, I have lived for my homeland. And yet I see its hopeless ruin now. I am at variance with a great part of the people of my class and profession because I do not believe in the restoration and also do not want it. Completely new paths must be taken, and yet no one wants to see them" (ibid., pp. 131–132).

/50/   Ibid., pp. 134–135.

/51/   Ibid., p. 143; cf. ibid., pp. 135–136.

/52/   Id., G.S. III, viii.

/53/   Id., *Absolutheit*, p. 53. Here Troeltsch characterizes people like Renan as "bankrupt theologians" because they lost such an ethical vigor and a religious faith.

/54/   See Kaftan, *Ernst Tröltsch*, esp. pp. 55–85.

/55/   Troeltsch, G.S. II, p. 227 n. 11.

/56/   Morgan, "Troeltsch and the Dialectical Theology," p. 71.

/57/   Both Troeltsch and Barth often use this metaphor respectively for different purposes and in different senses. Troeltsch uses it to express a characteristic polarity or a fundamental dualism intrinsic to Christianity, whereas Barth employs it mainly for the polemic purpose of characterizing Neo-Protestantism and thus repudiating this liberal theology with two foci. See Troeltsch, G.S. II, pp. 421–423; Barth, *Die protestantische Theologie im 19. Jahrhundert*, esp. chaps. on Schleiermacher and Ritschl.

/58/   J. Kaftan, review of *Vernunft und Offenbarung bei Johann Gerhard und Melanchthon*, by Ernst Troeltsch, in *ThLZ* 17 (1892):210.

/59/   Barth, "Evangelical Theology in the 19th Century," p. 27.

/60/   Ibid., p. 18.

/61/   Ibid., p. 19.

/62/   Ibid., pp. 19–20.

/63/   Id., *Die kirchliche Dogmatik*, IV/1, p. 787.

/64/   See W. Groll, *Ernst Troeltsch und Karl Barth—Kontinuität im Widerspruch*.

/65/   Thomas W. Ogletree's comparative study of Troeltsch and Barth is an excellent example of such a critical comparison. His treatment of Troeltsch, however, is conspicuously limited in scope, so that his comparison is from the beginning favorable to Barth. Consequently, Ogletree's study gives the impression that he is using Troeltsch mainly for the purpose of revision of Barth's standpoint, which he basically accepts. Yet he personally told me that he is now more appreciative of Troeltsch than he was twenty years ago. See T. W. Ogletree, *Christian Faith and History: A Critical Comparison of Ernst Troeltsch and Karl Barth* (New York and Nashville: Abingdon Press, 1965).

/66/   Ibid., p. 220.

/67/   H. Frei, "Niebuhr's Theological Background," in *Faith and Ethics: The Theology of H. Richard Niebuhr*, ed. Paul Ramsey (New York: Harper & Brothers, 1957), p. 64.

/68/   H. R. Niebuhr, *The Meaning of Revelation* (New York: Macmillan, 1941; paperback ed., New York: Macmillan Publishing Co. and London: Collier Macmillan Publishers, 1974), p. xi.

/69/   H. Stephan and M. Schmidt, *Geschichte der evangelischen Theologie in Deutschland seit dem Idealismus*, rev. 3d ed. (Berlin and New York: Walter de Gruyter, 1973), p. 1.

/70/   The categories "intensive" and "extensive" were coined by Horst Stephan. According to Stephan, the "intensive" type of theology "fights for the purity, earnestness, and integrity of an inherited faith," while the "extensive" type of theology is more concerned with "the totality of its nexus of life and its strength for the world mission" (ibid., p. 5).

/71/   R. Morgan, "Troeltsch and Christian Theology," in *Ernst Troeltsch: Writings on Theology and Religion*, tr. and eds. Robert Morgan and Michael Pye (London: Duckworth, 1977), pp. 211–212.

/72/   It is no accident that these two German-American theologians most successfully combined both types of theology (Niebuhr was the second generation of German immigrant parents, and Tillich was an exile from Nazi Germany of the 1930s). For German Christianity and theology are eminently intensively oriented, while American counterparts are basically extensive in character. The same is true of Richard's brother, Reinhold Niebuhr. His ethically oriented applied theology too represents a no less successful combination of both types.

/73/   Troeltsch, G.S. I, p. 926 n. 504a.

/74/   K. Bornhausen, "Ernst Troeltsch und das Problem der wissenschaftlichen Theologie," ZThK n.s. 4 (1923):196.

/75/   In 1908 Hermann Diel referred to the opposition between Herrmann and Troeltsch as follows:

> "In the present situation of systematic theology, Herrmann and Troeltsch undoubtedly play a central role. And yet their mutual relationship usually appears in the light of an opposition. Especially from Herrmann's side was it on occasion made quite unmistakable what a great gulf he saw between his own work and the methods and scientific aims of Troeltsch" (H. Diel, "Thesen und Antithesen," ZThK 18 [1908]:473).

/76/   Troeltsch, G.S. II, pp. 767–768. In a letter to Herrmann on 10 March 1918, Troeltsch wrote the following:

> "Of course I heard through [my] students that you often and sharply polemicized against me in lectures and seminars. I have never retaliated because I am of a completely different nature. To the contrary, I have called people's attention to your works and have recommended people to study them as a supplement to my lectures. I hope that people profit from your warmth and energy. I hope this especially because I am afraid that my study has had to bring such a religious warmth and energy too strongly into complications and purely scientific interests. . . . I myself have been . . . well aware of the difference but have never emphasized it. There is none of the disputatiousness characteristic of professors and theologians on my side. Perhaps I am too indifferent and worldly-minded on this point. In the long run, however, what do such differences matter to the larger world?" (Ernst Troeltsch to Wilhelm Herrmann, 10 March 1918, cited in Apfelbacher, Frömmigkeit und Wissenschaft, p. 35 n. 35).

/77/   Niebuhr grouped Troeltsch into the "dualists" ("Christ and Culture in Paradox" type). In view of the leitmotif of Gestaltung in his thought, however, he could be regarded as a "conversionist" ("Christ the Transformer of Culture" type). Sie Niebuhr, Christ and Culture, pp. 181–183.

/78/   A. v. Harnack, "Rede am Sarge Ernst Troeltschs" CW 37 (1923):104; cf. Troeltsch, G.S. III, p. 710.

/79/ Tillich, *Gesammelte Werke,* vol. 12, p. 178.

/80/ Ibid., p. 176. True, Troeltsch persistently emphasized the close ties between religion and culture, and the final phase of his thought, as we have seen, clearly represented a dangerous cultural captivity of Christianity. Nevertheless, he was also always very emphatic in his assertion that religion must be distinguished from culture. Accordingly, it is not right to say that Troeltsch viewed religion from the standpoint of culture. The fact is rather that his view of religion was too contextual to assert its simple transcendence over culture and history. On this point, H. R. Niebuhr is rather right in listing Troeltsch among the dualists who hold "Christ and culture in paradox" instead of among those who assert "a fundamental *agreement* between Christ and culture" ("the Christ-of-Culture" type). However, given the leitmotif of *Gestaltung,* Troeltsch could be even regarded as a "conversionist" ("Christ the Transformer of Culture" type). Niebuhr failed to discern this aspect of Troeltsch's thought.

/81/ Tillich, review of *Der Historismus und seine Überwindung,* by Ernst Troeltsch, in *ThLZ* 49 (1924):234.

/82/ Schrey, "Ernst Troeltsch und sein Werk," p. 158.

/83/ Ibid., pp. 159–160.

/84/ Troeltsch, G.S. II, p. 727.

/85/ Id., G.S. III, p. 692.

/86/ Tillich, *Gesammelte Werke,* vol. 12, p. 209.

/87/ Troeltsch, G.S. III, p. 183.

/88/ Kaftan, *Ernst Tröltsch,* p. 71.

/89/ Barth, *Die protestantische Theologie im 19. Jahrhundert,* p. 308.

/90/ Here I am using the term "historical theology" in the same sense as Gerrish uses it. See Gerrish, "Ernst Troeltsch and the Possibility of a Historical Theology."

/91/ To my knowledge, the best argument on this point is found in Pannenberg's discussion of "the positivity of revelation in Karl Barth." See W. Pannenberg, *Wissenschaftstheorie und Theologie* (Frankfurt am Main: Suhrkamp Verlag, 1977), pp. 266–277. See also the Conclusion of T. Ogletree's pioneering work, *Christian Faith and History,* pp. 220–231. W. Groll's argument is hardly persuasive for me at least on this point. See Groll, *Ernst Troeltsch und Karl Barth—Kontinuität im Widerspruch.*

/92/ Troeltsch, *Überwindung,* p. 104; cf. ibid., pp. 60–61, 105.

/93/ Köhler, *Ernst Troeltsch,* p. 414.

/94/ Rendtorff, Introduction to *Die Absolutheit des Christentums,* by Ernst Troeltsch, p. 7.

/95/   This is Pannenberg's definition of God. The German words are "eine alles bestimmende Wirklichkeit."

/96/   Pannenberg, *Wissenschaftstheorie und Theologie*, p. 299.

/97/   This is Barth's criticism of Troeltsch. See Barth, *Die protestantische Theologie im 19. Jahrhundert*, p. 384; cf. id., *Die kirchliche Dogmatik*, IV/1, p. 425.

/98/   Drescher, "Ernst Troeltsch's Intellectual Development," pp. 31–32.

/99/   Troeltsch, *Überwindung*, p. 81; cf. *Christian Thought*, p. 31.

/100/ Id., *Absolutheit*, p. 86.

/101/ Id., *Überwindung*, p. 104; cf. *Christian Thought*, pp. 164–165.

/102/ Id., *Christian Thought*, pp. 166–167 (missing in the German original).

/103/ Ibid., pp. 128–129; cf. *Überwindung*, p. 60.

/104/ Hughes, *Consciousness and Society*, p. 241; cf. Reist, *Toward a Theology of Involvement*, pp. 197–201.

/105/ Harnack, "Rede am Sarge Ernst Troeltschs," col. 104.

/106/ Tillich, *Gesammelte Werke*, vol. 12, p. 168.

/107/ Le Fort, *Hälfte des Lebens*, p. 91.

SELECTED BIBLIOGRAPHY

Following is a list of the primary and secondary sources on which this study is based, though they are not necessarily referred to in this study. For the full information about Troeltsch's writings, see Friedrich Wilhelm Graf and Hartmut Ruddies, eds., *Ernst Troeltsch Bibliographie* (Tübingen: J. C. B. Mohr, 1982). A more extensive bibliography of the secondary sources on Troeltsch is contained in John Powell Clayton, ed., *Ernst Troeltsch and the Future of Theology* (Cambridge: Cambridge University Press, 1976), pp. 200–214.

Works by Ernst Troeltsch

Collected Works

Gesammelte Schriften. Vol. I: *Die Soziallehren der christlichen Kirchen und Gruppen*. Tübingen: J. C. B. Mohr (Paul Siebeck), 1912; reprint ed., Aalen: Scientia Verlag, 1977.

Gesammelte Schriften. Vol. II: *Zur religiösen Lage, Religionsphilosophie und Ethik*. Tübingen: J. C. B. Mohr (Paul Siebeck), 1913; reprint ed., Aalen: Scientia Verlag, 1962.

Gesammelte Schriften. Vol. III: *Der Historismus und seine Probleme. Erstes Buch: Das logische Problem der Geschichtsphilosophie*. Tübingen: J. C. B. Mohr (Paul Siebeck), 1922; reprint ed., Aalen: Scientia Verlag, 1961.

Gesammelte Schriften. Vol. IV: *Aufsätze zur Geistesgeschichte und Religionssoziologie*. Edited by Friedrich von Hügel [Hans Baron]. Tübingen: J. C. B. Mohr (Paul Siebeck), 1925; reprint ed., Aalen: Scientia Verlag, 1966.

Other Published Writings
(Listed in chronological order)

"Thesen welche mit Genehmigung der Theologischen Fakultät zur Erlangung der Theologischen Licentiatenwürde an der Georg-Augusts-Universität zu Göttingen Sonnabend den 4. Februar 1891 11 Uhr öffentlich vertheidigt wird Ernst Troeltsch Predigtamtskandidat." In *Troeltsch-Studien. Untersuchungen zur Biographie und*

Werkgeschichte. Mit den unveröffentlichten Promotionsthesen der "Kleinen Göttinger Fakultät" 1888–1893, pp. 299–300. Edited by Horst Renz and Friedrich Wilhelm Graf. Gütersloh: Gütersloher Verlagshaus Gerd Mohn, 1982.

Vernunft und Offenbarung bei Johann Gerhard und Melanchthon. Untersuchung zur Geschichte der altprotestantischen Theologie. Göttingen: Vandenhoeck & Ruprecht, 1891.

"Die christliche Weltanschauung und die wissenschaftlichen Gegenströmungen." *Zeitschrift für Theologie und Kirche* 3 (November/December 1893):493–528; 4 (May/June 1894):167–231.

"Religion und Kirche." *Preußische Jahrbücher* 81 (August 1895):215–249.

"Die Selbständigkeit der Religion." *Zeitschrift für Theologie und Kirche* 5 (September/October 1895):361–436; 6 (January/February 1896):71–110; 6 (March/April 1896):167–218.

"Atheistische Ethik." *Preußische Jahrbücher* 82 (November 1895):193–217.

Die historischen Grundlagen der Theologie unseres Jahrhunderts. Vortrag auf der Versammlung des Wissenschaftlichen Predigervereins zu Karlsruhe am 2. Juli 1895. Karlsruhe: Druck von Friedrich Gutsch, 1895.

Review of *Der Kampf um einen geistigen Lebensinhalt. Neue Grundlegung einer Weltanschauung,* by Rudolf Eucken. *Theologische Literaturzeitung* 21 (July 1896):405–409.

"Religionsphilosophie und theologische Principienlehre." *Theologischer Jahresbericht* 15 (1896):376–425.

"Neue Triebe der Spekulation." *Die Christliche Welt* 10 (December 1896):1163–1165.

Review of *Untersuchungen zur Phänomenologie und Ontologie des menschlichen Geistes,* by Gustav Class. *Theologische Literaturezeitung* 22 (January 1897):51–57.

"Christentum und Religionsgeschichte." *Preußische Jahrbücher* 87 (March 1897):415–447.

"Religionsphilosophie und theologische Principienlehre." *Theologischer Jahresbericht* 16 (1897):498–557.

"Geschichte und Metaphysik." *Zeitschrift für Theologie und Kirche* 8 (January/February 1898):1–69.

Review of *Die wissenschaftliche und die kirchliche Methode in der Theologie,* by C. A. Bernoulli. *Göttinger gelehrte Anzeigen* 160 (June 1898):425–435.

"Zur theologischen Lage." *Die Christliche Welt* 12 (June 1898):627–631;
12 (July 1898):650–657.

Review of *Die Philosophie der Geschichte als Sociologie.* I. Teil:
Einleitung und kritische Übersicht, by Paul Barth. *Theologische
Literaturzeitung* 23 (July 1898):398–401.

"Religionsphilosophie und prinzipielle Theologie." *Theologische Jahresbericht* 17 (1898):531–603.

"Richard Rothe." *Die Christliche Welt* 13 (January 1899):77–81.

Richard Rothe. Gedächtnisrede. Freiburg, Leipzig, and Tübingen: J. C.
B. Mohr (Paul Siebeck), 1899.

Review of *Die neue historische Methode,* by Georg von Below; *Kulturwissenschaft und Naturwissenschaft,* by Heinrich Rickert. *Theologische Literaturzeitung* 24 (June 1899):375–377.

"Religionsphilosophie und prinzipielle Theologie." *Theologische Jahresbericht* 18 (1899):485–536.

Die wissenschaftliche Lage und ihre Anforderungen an die Theologie.
Tübingen, Freiburg, and Leipzig: J. C. B. Mohr (Paul Siebeck),
1900.

"Über historische und dogmatische Methode der Theologie." *Theologische Arbeiten aus dem rheinischen wissenschaftlichen Predigerverein,* New Series 4 (1900):87–108.

"Thesen zu dem am 3. Oktober in der Versammlung der Freunde der
Christlichen Welt in Mühlacker zu haltenden Vortrage über die
Absolutheit des Christentums und die Religionsgeschichte." *Die
Christliche Welt* 15 (September 1901):923–925.

"Voraussetzungslose Wissenschaft." *Die Christliche Welt* 15 (December
1901):1177–1182.

Die Absolutheit des Christentums und die Religionsgeschichte.
Tübingen and Leipzig: J. C. B. Mohr (Paul Siebeck), 1902; 2d ed.,
Tübingen: J. C. B. Mohr (Paul Siebeck), 1912; 3d ed., 1929; reprint
ed., Edited and with an Introduction by Trutz Rendtorff. Munich
and Hamburg: Siebenstern Taschenbuch Verlag, 1969.

"Grundprobleme der Ethik. Erörtert aus Anlaß von Herrmanns Ethik."
Zeitschrift für Theologie und Kirche 12 (January/February
1902):44–94; 12 (March/April 1902):125–178.

"Theologie und Religionswissenschaft des 19. Jahrhunderts." *Jahrbuch
des Freien Deutschen Hochstifts 1902,* pp. 91–120. Frankfurt am
Main: Druck von Gebrüder Knauer, 1902.

"Moderne Geschichtsphilosophie." *Theologische Rundschau* 6 (January
1903):3–28; 6 (February 1903):57–72; 6 (March 1903):103–117.

"Was heißt 'Wesen des Christentums'?." *Die Christliche Welt* 17 (May–July 1903):443–446, 483–488, 532–536, 578–584, 650–654, 678–683.

"Die theologische Lage der Gegenwart." *Deutsche Monatsschrift für das gesamte Leben der Gegenwart* 4 (June 1903):385–398.

"Religionswissenschaft und Theologie des 18. Jahrhunderts." *Preußische Jahrbücher* 114 (December 1903):30–56.

Das Historische in Kants Religionsphilosophie. Zugleich ein Beitrag zu den Untersuchungen über Kants Philosophie der Geschichte. Berlin: Verlag von Reuther & Reichard, 1904.

Politische Ethik und Christentum. Göttingen: Vandenhoeck & Ruprecht, 1904.

"Religionsphilosophie." In *Die Philosophie im Beginn des zwanzigsten Jahrhunderts.* Festschrift für Kuno Fischer, pp. 104–162. Edited by Wilhelm Windelband. Heidelberg: Carl Winter's Universitätsbuchhandlung, 1904; 2d ed., rev. and enl., pp. 423–486, 1907.

Psychologie und Erkenntnistheorie in der Religionswissenschaft. Eine Untersuchung über die Bedeutung der Kantischen Religionslehre für die heutige Religionswissenschaft. Tübingen: J. C. B. Mohr (Paul Siebeck), 1905.

"Die Mission in der modernen Welt." *Die Christliche Welt* 20 (January 1906):8–12, 26–28, 56–59.

"Protestantisches Christentum und Kirche in der Neuzeit." In *Die Kultur der Gegenwart, I/IV: Die christliche Religion mit Einschluss der israelitisch-jüdischen Religion,* 1st Half: *Geschichte der christlichen Religion,* pp. 253–458. Edited by Paul Hinneberg. Berlin and Leipzig: Druck und Verlag von B. G. Teubner, 1906; 2d ed., rev. and enl., in *Die Kultur der Gegenwart, I/IV,* Vol. 1: *Geschichte der christlichen Religion. Mit Einleitung: Die israelitisch-jüdischen Religion,* pp. 431–755. Edited by Paul Hinneberg. Berlin and Leipzig: Druck und Verlag von B. G. Teubner, 1909.

"Wesen der Religion und der Religionswissenschaft." In *Die Kultur der Gegenwart, I/IV: Die christliche Religion mit Einschluss der israelitisch-jüdischen Religion,* 2d Half: *Systematische christliche Theologie,* pp. 461–491. Edited by Paul Hinneberg. Berlin and Leipzig: Druck und Verlag von B. G. Teubner, 1906; 2d ed., rev. and enl., in *Die Kultur der Gegenwart, I/IV,* Vol. 2: *Systematische christliche Religion,* pp. 1–36. Edited by Paul Hinneberg. Berlin and Leipzig: Druck und Verlag von B. G. Teubner, 1909.

"Die Bedeutung des Protestantismus für die Entstehung der modernen Welt." *Historische Zeitschrift* 97 (July/August 1906):1–66.

Die Trennung von Staat und Kirche, der staatliche Religionsunterricht und die theologischen Fakultäten. Tübingen: J. C. B. Mohr (Paul Siebeck), 1907.

"Autonomie und Rationalismus in der modernen Welt." *Internationale Wochenschrift für Wissenschaft, Kunst und Technik* 1 (May 1907):199–210.

"Missionsmotiv, Missionsaufgabe und neuzeitliches Humanitätschristentum." *Zeitschrift für Missionskunde und Religionswissenschaft* 22 (May 1907):129–139; 22 (June 1907):161–166.

"Die letzten Dinge." *Die Christliche Welt* 22 (January 1908):74–78, 97–101.

"Glaube und Geschichte." *Religion und Geisteskultur* 2 (January-March 1908):29–39.

"Modernismus." *Die neue Rundschau* 20 (April 1909):456–481.

"Rückblick auf ein halbes Jahrhundert der theologischen Wissenschaft." *Zeitschrift für wissenschaftliche Theologie* 51 (1909):97–135.

"Zur Frage des religiösen apriori. Eine Erwiderung auf die Bemerkungen von Paul Spieß." *Religion und Geisteskultur* 3 (October-December 1909):263–273.

"Schleiermacher und die Kirche." In *Schleiermacher der Philosoph des Glaubens,* pp. 9–35. Edited by Friedrich Naumann. Berlin-Schöneberg: Buchverlag der "Hilfe," 1910.

"Aus der religiösen Bewegung der Gegenwart." *Die neue Rundschau* 21 (September 1910):1169–1185.

"Die Bedeutung des Begriffs der Kontingenz." *Zeitschrift für Theologie und Kirche* 20 (November/December 1910):421–430.

"Die Zukunftsmöglichkeiten des Christentums." *Logos* 1 *(1910/1911):165–185.*

"Gewissensfreiheit." *Die Christliche Welt* 25 (July 1911):677–682.

Die Bedeutung des Protestantismus für die Entstehung der modernen Welt. Historische Bibliothek, no. 24. Munich and Berlin: Druck und Verlag von R. Oldenbourg, 1911; 6th ed., Aalen: Otto Zeller Verlagsbuchhandlung, 1963.

Die Bedeutung der Geschichtlichkeit Jesu für den Glauben. Bern: Verlag von A. Francke, 1911; variant ed., Tübingen: J. C. B. Mohr (Paul Siebeck), 1911; reprint ed., In Ernst Troeltsch. *Die Absolutheit des Christentums und die Religionsgeschichte,* pp. 132–162. Edited and with an Introduction by Trutz Rendtorff. Munich and Hamburg: Siebenstern Taschenbuch Verlag, 1969.

"Die Kirche im Leben der Gegenwart." In *Weltanschauung, Philosophie und Religion*, pp. 438–454. Edited by Max Frischeisen-Köhler. Berlin: Verlag Reichl & Co., 1911; reprint ed., In Ernst Troeltsch, *Die Absolutheit des Christentums und die Religionsgeschichte*, pp. 163–180. Edited and with an Introduction by Truz Rendtorff. Munich and Hamburg: Siebenstern Taschenbuch Verlag, 1969.

"Empiricism and Platonism in the Philosophy of Religion. To the Memory of William James." *The Harvard Theological Review* 5 (October 1912):401–422.

Review of *Ernst Tröltsch. Eine kritische Zeitstudie*, by Theodor Kaftan. *Theologische Literaturzeitung* 37 (November 1912):724–728.

Review of *Christentum und Geschichte bei Schleiermacher. Die geschichtsphilosophische Grundlagen der Schleiermacherschen Theologie, untersucht. I. Teil: Die Absolutheit des Christentums und die Religionsgeschichte*, by Hermann Süskind. *Theologische Literaturzeitung* 38 (January 1913):21–24.

"The Dogmatics of the 'Religionsgeschichtliche Schule.'" *The American Journal of Theology* 17 (January 1913):1–21.

"Logos und Mythos in Theologie und Religionsphilosophie." *Logos* 4 (January–April 1913):8–35.

"Religion." In *Das Jahr 1913. Ein Gesamtbild der Kulturentwicklung*, pp. 533–549. Edited by David Sarason. Leipzig and Berlin: Druck und Verlag von B. G. Teubner, 1913.

Nach Erklärung der Mobilmachung. Heidelberg: Carl Winters Universitätsbuchhandlung, 1914.

Deutscher Glaube und Deutsche Sitte in unserem großen Kriege. Berlin: Verlag Kameradschaft, Wohlfahrtsges. m.b.H., 1914.

Das Wesen des Deutschen. Heidelberg: Carl Winters Universitätsbuchhandlung, 1915.

Augustin, die christliche Antike und das Mittelalter. Historische Bibliothek, no. 36. Munich and Berlin: Druck und Verlag von R. Oldenbourg, 1915; reprint ed., Aalen: Scientia Verlag, 1963.

"Der Völkerkrieg und das Christentum." *Die Christliche Welt* 29 (April 1915):294–303.

Der Kulturkrieg. Berlin: Carl Heymanns Verlag, 1915.

"Zum Gedächtnis Otto Lempps und Hermann Süskinds." *Die Christliche Welt* 29 (August 1915):653–657.

"Konservativ und Liberal." *Die Christliche Welt* 30 (August 1916):647–651, 659–666, 678–683.

Review of *Die Grundlagen der Religionsphilosophie Troeltsch'*, by Walter Günther. *Theologische Literaturzeitung* 41 (October 1916):448–450.

Review of *Wilhelm Windelband*, by Heinrich Rickert. *Theologische Literaturzeitung* 41 (November 1916):469–471.

Humanismus und Nationalismus in unserem Bildungswesen. Berlin: Weidmannsche Buchhandlung, 1917.

"Die ethische Neuorientierung als christlich-soziales Programm." *Die Christliche Welt* 31 (February 1917): 146–152.

"Die Anstrum der westlichen Demokratie." In *Die deutsche Freiheit.* Fünf Vorträge von Adolf von Harnack, Friedrich Meinecke, Max Sering, Ernst Troeltsch, und Otto Hintze, pp. 79–113. Gotha: Verlag Friedrich Andreas Perthes A.-G., 1917.

[Troeltsch, Ernst] "Briefe über religiöses Leben und Denken im gegenwärtigen Deutschland." *Schweizerische Theologische Zeitschrift* 34 (October 1917):259–264; 35 (February 1918):24–31; 35 (June 1918):57–66; 36 (April 1919):86–95; 36 (June 1919):140–148.

"Ostern." *Deutsche Wille. Des Kunstwarts* 31 (April–June 1918):2–7.

"Zur Religionsphilosophie. Aus Anlaß des Buches von Rudolf Otto über 'das Heilige' (Breslau 1917)." *Kant-Studien* 23 (1918):65–76.

"Die 'kleine Göttinger Fakultät' von 1890." *Die Christliche Welt,* 34 (April 1920):281–283.

"Luthers Kirchenbegriff und die kirchliche Krisis von heute II. Erwiderung." *Zeitschrift für Theologie und Kirche* New Series 1 (March/April 1920):117–123.

"Adolf v. Harnach und Ferd. Christ. v. Baur." In *Festgabe von Fachgenossen und Fruenden A. von Harnack zum siebzigsten Geburtstag dargebracht,* pp. 282–291. Edited by Karl Holl. Tübingen: J. C. B. Mohr (Paul Siebeck), 1921.

Der Berg der Läuterung. Berlin: Verlag von E. S. Mittler & Sohn, 1921.

"Zum Dante-Jubiläum." *Kunstwart und Kulturwart* 34 (September 1921):321–327.

"Die Krisis des Historismus." *Die neue Rundschau* 33 (March 1922):572–590.

"Die Geisteswissenschaften und der Streit um Rickert. Aus Anlaß von Erich Becher, Geisteswissenschaften und Naturwissenschaften. Untersuchungen zur Theorie und Einteilung der Realwissenschaften." In *Schmollers Jahrbuch für Gesetzgebung, Ver-*

waltung und Volkswirtschaft im Deutschen Reich. Vol. 46, pp. 35–64. Munich and Leipzig: Verlag von Duncker & Humblot, 1922.

"Erwiderung." In *Schmollers Jahrbuch für Gesetzgebung, Verwaltung und Volkswirtschaft im Deutschen Reich*. Vol. 46, p. 570. Munich and Leipzig: Verlag von Duncker & Humblot, 1922.

Die Sozialphilosophie des Christentums. Gotha/Stuttgart: Verlag Friedrich Andreas Perthes A.-G., 1922.

Der Historismus und seine Überwindung. Fünf Vorträge. Introduction by Friedrich von Hügel. Berlin: Pan Verlag Rolf Heise, 1924; reprint ed., Aalen: Scientia Verlag, 1966.

Spektator-Briefe. *Aufsätze über die deutsche Revolution und die Weltpolitik 1918/1922*. Introduction by Friedrich Meinecke. Edited by Friedrich von Hügel [Hans Baron]. Tübingen: J. C. B. Mohr (Paul Siebeck), 1924; reprint ed., Aalen: Scientia Verlag, 1966.

Deutscher Geist und Westeuropa. *Gesammelte kulturphilosophische Aufsätze und Reden*. Edited by Friedrich von Hügel [Hans Baron]. Tübingen: J. C. B. Mohr (Paul Siebeck), 1925; reprint ed., Aalen: Scientia Verlag, 1966.

Glaubenslehre. *Nach Heidelberger Vorlesungen aus den Jahren 1911 und 1912*. Foreword by Marta Troeltsch. Edited by Gertrud von le Fort. Munich and Leipzig. Verlag von Duncker & Humblot, 1925; reprint ed., with an Introduction by Jacob Klapwijk. Aalen: Scientia Verlag, 1981.

Ernst Troeltsch. Briefe an Friedrich von Hügel 1901–1923. Edited and with an Introduction by Karl-Ernst Apfelbacher and Peter Neuner. Paderborn: Verlag Bonifacius-Druckerei, 1974.

"Ernst Troeltsch. Briefe aus der Heidelberger Zeit an Wilhelm Bousset 1894–1914." Edited by Erika Dinkler-von Schubert. In *Heidelberger Jahrbücher* Vol. 20, pp. 19–52. Berlin, Heidelberg, and New York: Springer Verlag, 1976.

Articles in Encyclopedias

S.v. "Aufklärung," "Deismus," "Idealismus, deutscher," "Moralisten, englisch." In *Realencyklopädie für protestantische Theologie und Kirche*. Edited by Albert Hauck, 24 vols. Leipzig: J. C. Hinrichs'sche Buchhandlung, 1896–1913.

S.v. "Aemter Christi," "Akkommodation Christi," "Berufung," "Concurus Divinus," "Dogma," "Dogmatik," "Erlösung," "Eschatologie," "Gericht Gottes," "Gesetz," "Glaube," "Glaube und Geschichte," "Glaubensartikel," "Gnade Gottes," "Gnadenmittel," "Heilstatsachen," "Kirche," "Naturrecht, christliches," "Offenbarung," "Prädestination," "Prinzip, religiöses," "Protestantismus im Verhältnis zur Kultur," "Theodizee," "Weiterentwicklung der christlichen Religion." In *Die Religion in Geschichte und Gegenwart*. Edited by F. M. Schiele and L. Zscharnack. 5 vols. Tübingen: J. C. B. Mohr (Paul Siebeck), 1909–1914.

Correspondence
(Listed in alphabetical order)

Letters of Ernst Troeltsch to:

Karl Barth, 26 April 1912. Quoted in Wilfried Groll, *Ernst Troeltsch und Karl Barth—Kontinuität im Widerspruch*. Beiträge zur evangelischen Theologie. Theologische Abhandlungen, no. 72, p. 32. Munich: Chr. Kaiser Verlag, 1976; also quoted in Karl-Ernst Apfelbacher, *Frömmigkeit und Wissenschaft: Ernst Troeltsch und sein theologisches Programm*. Beiträge zur ökumenischen Theologie, no. 18, p. 134 n. 11. Munich-Paderborn-Vienna: Verlag Ferdinand Schöningh, 1978.

Wilhelm Bousset. See Troeltsch, Ernst. "Briefe aus der Heidelberger Zeit an Wilhelm Bousset 1894–1914."

Konrad Burdach, 19 December 1918. Quoted in Konrad Burdach, "Die seelischen und geistigen Quellen der Renaissancebewegung." *Historische Zeitschrift* 149 (1934):486–488.

Albert Einstein, 4 February 1918 and 1 May 1918. Quoted in Felix Gilbert, "Einstein und das Europa seiner Zeit." *Historische Zeitschrift* 233 (August 1981):17–19.

Gertrud von le Fort, 24 October 1918. Quoted in Hans-Jürgen Gabriel, *Christlichkeit der Gesellschaft? Eine kritische Darstellung der Kulturphilosophie von Ernst Troeltsch*, p. 25. Berlin: Union Verlag Berlin, 1975.

————, 2 December 1918. Quoted in Gerhold Becker, *Neuzeitliche Subjektivität und Religiosität. Die religionsphilosophische Bedeutung von Heraufkunft und Wesen der Neuzeit im Denken von Ernst Troeltsch*, p. 291 n. 13. Regensburg: Verlag Friedrich Pustet, 1982.

Hugo Greßmann, 4 July 1913. Quoted in Werner Klatt, *Hermann Gunkel. Zu seiner Theologie der Religionsgeschichte und zur Entstehung der formgeschichtlichen Methode*. Forschungen zur Religion und Literatur des Alten und Neuen Testament, no. 100, pp. 22–23. Göttingen: Vandenhoeck & Ruprecht, 1969.

Adolf von Harnack, 23 March 1900. Quoted in Karl-Ernst Apfelbacher, *Frömmigkeit und Wissenschaft*, pp. 69, 119.

———, 19 May 1907. Quoted in Agnes von Zahn-Harnack, *Adolf von Harnack*, pp. 413–414. Berlin-Tempelhof: Hans Bott Verlag, 1936; also quoted in Karl-Ernst Apfelbacher, *Frömmigkeit und Wissenschaft*, p. 249.

Wilhelm Herrmann, 27 October 1898. Quoted in Karl-Ernst Apfelbacher, *Frömmigkeit und Wissenschaft*, pp. 235, n. 52.

———, 10 March 1918. Quoted in Karl-Ernst Apfelbacher, *Frömmigkeit und Wissenschaft*, pp. 35, 121, 138, 151 n. 35, 157 n. 46.

Paul Honigsheim, 12 June 1917. Quoted in Eduard Baumgarten, *Max Weber: Werk und Person*, p. 489. Tübingen: J. C. B. Mohr (Paul Siebeck), 1964.

Friedrich von Hügel. See Troeltsch, Ernst. *Briefe an Friedrich von Hügel 1901–1923*.

Adolf Jülicher, 17 April 1897. Quoted in Karl-Ernst Apfelbacher, *Frömmigkeit und Wissenschaft*, p. 171 n. 29.

———, 4 November 1901. Quoted in Karl-Ernst Apfelbacher, *Frömmigkeit und Wissenschaft*, p. 211.

Theodor Kaftan, n.d. [1911]. Quoted in Theodor Kaftan, *Ernst Tröltsch: Eine kritische Zeitstudie*, p. 2. Schleswig: Druck und Verlag von Julius Bergas, 1912.

Carl Neumann, June 1908. Quoted in Carl Neumann, "Zum Tode von Ernst Troeltsch." *Deutsche Vierteljahrsschrift für Literaturwissenschaft und Geistesgeschichte* 1 (April–June 1923):165.

Rudolf Otto, 17 November 1904. Quoted in Karl-Ernst Apfelbacher, *Frömmigkeit und Wissenschaft*, pp. 59–60.

———, n.d. [perhaps 1905]. Quoted in Karl-Ernst Apfelbacher, *Frömmigkeit und Wissenschaft*, p. 48 n. 19.

Martin Rade, December 1917 or January 1918. Quoted in Günter Brakelmann, *Der deutsche Protestantismus in Epochenjahr 1917*, pp. 295–297. Witten: Luther-Verlag, 1974.

Works in English Translation
(Listed in alphabetical order)

The Absoluteness of Christianity and the History of Religions. Translated by David Reid. London: SCM Press, 1972.

"Adolf von Harnack and Ferdinand Christian von Baur." In Wilhelm

Pauck, *Harnack and Troeltsch: Two Historical Theologians*, pp. 97–115. New York: Oxford University Press, 1968.

"Calvin and Calvinism." *Hibbert Journal* 8 (1909):102–121.

Christian Thought: Its History and Application. Translated by various hands. Edited and with an Introduction and Index by Friedrich von Hügel. London: University of London Press, 1923.

S.v. "Contingency," "Free-Thought," "Historiography," "Idealism," "Kant." In *Encyclopedia of Religion and Ethics*. Edited by James Hastings. 13 vols. New York: Charles Scribner's Sons, 1908–1926.

Ernst Troeltsch: Writings on Theology and Religion. Translated and edited by Robert Morgan and Michael Pye. London: Gerald Duckworth & Co., 1977.

"The Ethics of Jesus." *The Unitarian Universalist Christian* 29 (Spring–Summer 1974):38–45.

"The Formal Autonomous Ethics of Conviction and the Objective Teleological Ethics of Value." In *The Shaping of Modern Christian Thought*, pp. 226–244. Translated and edited by Warren F. Groff and Donald E. Miller. Cleveland and New York: World Publishing, 1968.

"On the Historical and Dogmatic Methods in Theology." Translated by Jack Forstman. Unpublished manuscript.

"The Ideas of Natural Law and Humanity in World Politics." Compiled as an Appendix to Otto Gierke, *Natural Law and the Theory of Society, 1500–1800*, pp. 201–222. Translated with an Introduction by Ernest Barker. Cambridge: Cambridge University Press, 1934.

S.v. "Deism," "Enlightenment," "Idealism, German," "Moralists, British." In *New Schaff-Herzog Encyclopedia of Religious Knowledge*. Edited by S. M. Jackson with the assistance of C. C. Sherman and G. W. Gilmore. New York and London: Funk and Wagnalls Company, 1908–1914.

"On the Possibility of a Free Christianity." *The Unitarian Universalist Christian* 29 (Spring–Summer 1974):27–45.

Protestantism and Progress. Translated by W. Montgomery. London: William & Norgate and New York: G. P. Putnam's Sons, 1912.

"Religion, Economics, and Society." In *Society and Religion*, pp. 197–204. Edited by Norman Birnbaum and Gertrud Lenzer. Englewood Cliffs, New Jersey: Prentice Hall, 1969.

"The Religious Principle." In *Twentieth Century Theology in the Making*. Vol. 2, pp. 334–341. Edited by Jaroslav Pelikan. New York: Harper and London: Fontana, 1970.

The Social Teaching of the Christian Churches. Translated by Olive Wyon. London: George Allen & Unwin and New York: Macmillan Co., 1931; reprint ed., with an Introduction by H. Richard Niebuhr, Chicago: University of Chicago Press, 1976.

Unpublished Manuscripts

Heidelberg, University Library, Manuscript Collection. Gertrud von le Fort, typescripts of lectures by Ernst Troeltsch on praktische christliche Ethik, 1911–1912; allgemeine Ethik, 1911–1912; Religionsphilosophie, 1912; Einleitung in die Philosophie, 1911–1912.

Troeltsch: Secondary Sources

Adams, James Luther. "Ernst Troeltsch as Analyst of Religion." *Journal for the Scientific Study of Religion* 1 (1961): 98–109.

———. Introduction to *The Absoluteness of Christianity and the History of Religions*, by Ernst Troeltsch. Translated by David Reid. London: SCM Press, 1972.

———. "Why the Troeltsch Revival?" *The Unitarian Universalist Christian* 29 (Spring–Summer 1974):4–15.

———. Foreword to *Crisis in Consciousness: The Thought of Ernst Troeltsch*, by Robert J. Rubanowice. Tallahassee: University Press of Florida, 1982.

Althaus, Paul. Review of *Glaubenslehre*, by Ernst Troeltsch. *Theologische Literaturzeitung* 52 (December 1927):593–595.

Apfelbacher, Karl-Ernst. *Frömmigkeit und Wissenschaft: Ernst Troeltsch und sein theologisches Programm.* Beiträge zur ökumenischen Theologie, no. 18. Munich-Paderborn-Vienna: Verlag Ferdinand Schöningh, 1978.

———. Review of *Neuzeitliche Subjektivität und Religiosität*, by Gerhold Becker. In *Mitteilungen der Ernst-Troeltsch-Gesellschaft* I, pp. 53–58. Augsburg: Ernst-Troeltsch-Gesellschaft, 1982.

Antoni, Carlo. *Vom Historismus zur Soziologie.* Translated by Walter Goetz. Stuttgard: K. F. Koehler Verlag, 1940.

Bainton, Roland. "Ernst Troeltsch—Thirty Years Later." *Theology Today* 8 (April 1951):70–96.

Becker, Gerhold. *Neuzeitliche Subjektivität und Religiosität: Die religionsphilosophische Bedeutung von Heraufkunft und Wesen der Neuzeit im Denken von Ernst Troeltsch.* Regensburg: Verlag Friedrich Pustet, 1982.

Beer, Rainer. *Selbstkritik der Geschichtsphilosophie bei Ernst Troeltsch*. Munich: UNI-Druck, 1957.

Benckert, Heinrich. "Der Begriff der Entscheidung bei Ernst Troeltsch: Ein Beitrag zum Verständnis seines Denkens." *Zeitschrift für Theologie und Kirche* n.s. 12 (1931):422–442.

————. *Ernnst Troeltsch und das ethische Problem*. Göttingen: Vandenhoeck & Ruprecht, 1932.

————. S.v. "Troeltsch, Ernst." In *Die Religion in Geschichte und Gegenwart*. 3d ed. Vol. 6. Tübingen: J. C. B. Mohr (Paul Siebeck), 1962.

Bodenstein, Walter. *Neige des Historismus: Ernst Troeltschs Entwicklungsgang*. Gütersloh: Gütersloher Verlagshaus Gerd Mohn, 1959.

Bornhausen, Karl. "Ernst Troeltsch und das Problem der wissenschaftlichen Theologie." *Zeitschrift für Theologie und Kirche* n.s. 4 (1923):196–223.

————. S.v. "Troeltsch, Ernst." In *Die Religion in Geschichte und Gegenwart*. 2d ed. Vol. 5. Tübingen: J. C. B. Mohr (Paul Siebeck), 1931.

Bosse, Hans. *Marx-Weber-Troeltsch: Religionssoziologie und marxistische Ideologiekritik*. Munich: Chr. Kaiser and Mainz: Grünewald, 1970.

Brandenburg, Albert. "Es wackelt alles—Ernst Troeltsch." *Catholica* 28 (1974):334–336.

Brüning, Walter. "Naturalismus-Historismus-Apriorismus (Das Werk Ernst Troeltschs)." *Studia Philosophica* 15 (1955):35–52.

Clayton, John Powell, ed. *Ernst Troeltsch and the Future of Theology*. Cambridge. Cambridge University Press, 1976.

Diel, Hermann. "Thesen und Antithesen: Herrmann und Troeltsch." *Zeitschrift für Theologie und Kirche* 18 (1908):473–478.

Dietrich, Albert. "Troeltsch, Ernst Peter Wilhelm." *Deutsche Biographisches Jahrbuch*, vol. 5: *Das Jahr 1923*. Berlin and Leipzig: Deutsche Verlags-Anstalt, 1930.

Drescher, Hans-Georg. *Glaube und Vernunft bei Ernst Troeltsch: Eine kritische Deutung seiner religionsphilosophischen Grundlegung*. N.p., 1957.

————. "Das Problem der Geschichte bei Ernst Troeltsch." *Zeitschrift für Theologie und Kirche* n.s. 57 (1960):186–230.

————. "Ernst Troeltsch's Intellectual Development." In *Ernst

Troeltsch and the Future of Theology, pp. 3–32. Edited by John Powell Clayton. Cambridge: Cambridge University Press, 1976.

————. "Entwicklungsdenken und Glaubensentscheidung: Troeltschs Kierkegaardverständnis und die Kontroverse Troeltsch-Gogarten." *Zeitschrift für Theologie und Kirche* n.s. 79 (1982):80–106.

Dyson, A. O. "History in the Philosophy and Theology of Ernst Troeltsch." Ph.D. dissertation, Oxford University, 1968.

————. "Ernst Troeltsch and the Possibility of a Systematic Theology." In *Ernst Troeltsch and the Future of Theology*, pp. 81–99. Edited by John Powell Clayton. Cambridge: Cambridge University Press, 1976.

Eschbach, Victor. "Ernst Troeltsch im französischen Urteil." *Die Christliche Welt* 37 (1923):315–316.

Escribano Alberca, Ignatio. *Die Gewinnung theologischer Normen aus der Geschichte der Religion bei E. Troeltsch: Eine methodologische Studie*. Münchener theologische Studien, II. Systematic Division, no. 21. Munich: Max Hueber, 1961.

Fischer, Hermann. "Luther und seine Reformation in der Sicht Ernst Troeltschs." *Neue Zeitschrift für systematische Theologie und Religionsphilosophie* 5 (1963):132–172.

————. *Christliche Glaube und Geschichte: Voraussetzungen und Folgen der Theologie Friedrich Gogartens*. Gütersloh: Gütersloher Verlagshaus Gerd Mohn, 1967.

Frei, Hans W. "The Relation of Faith and History in the Thought of Ernst Troeltsch." In *Faith and Ethics: The Theology of H. Richard Niebuhr*, pp. 53–64. Edited by Paul Ramsey. New York: Harper & Brothers, 1957; reprint ed., Gloucester, Mass.: Peter Smith, 1977.

Fülling, Erich. *Geschichte als Offenbarung: Studien zur Frage Historismus und Glaube von Herder bis Troeltsch*. Berlin: Verlag Alfred Töpelmann, 1956.

Gabriel, Hans-Jürgen. *Christlichkeit der Gesellschaft? Eine kritische Darstellung der Kulturphilosophie von Ernst Troeltsch*. Berlin (East): Union Verlag Berlin, 1975.

Gerrish, Brian Albert. "Jesus, Myth, and History: Troeltsch's Stand in the 'Christ-Myth' Debate." *The Journal of Religion* 55 (January 1975):13–35.

————. "Ernst Troeltsch and the Possibility of a Historical Theology. In *Ernst Troeltsch and the Future of Theology*, pp. 100–135. Edited by John Powell Clayton. Cambridge: Cambridge University Press, 1976.

Getzeny, Heinrich. "Ernst Troeltsch als Theologe und Soziologe." *Hochland* 25 (1927/28):582–597.

Gogarten, Friedrich. *Ich glaube an den dreieinigen Gott: Eine Untersuchung über Glauben und Geschichte.* Jena: Eugen Diederichs, 1926.

———. "Against Romantic Theology: A Chapter on Faith." In *The Beginning of Dialectical Theology.* Vol. 1, pp. 317–327. Edited by James M. Robinson. Richmond: John Knox Press, 1968.

———. "Historicism. " In *The Beginning of Dialectical Theology.* Vol. 1, pp. 343–358. Edited by James M. Robinson. Richmond: John Knox Press, 1968.

Graf, Friedrich Wilhelm, and Ruddies, Hartmut., eds. *Ernst Troeltsch Bibliographie.* Tübingen: J. C. B. Mohr (Paul Siebeck), 1982.

———. See Renz, Horst, and Graf, Friedrich Wilhelm.

Groll, Wilfried. *Ernst Troeltsch und Karl Barth—Kontinuität in Widerspruch.* Beiträge zur evangelischen Theologie, no. 72. Munich: Chr. Kaiser Verlag, 1976.

Günther, Walter. *Die Grundlagen der Religionsphilosophie Ernst Troeltsch'.* Leipzig: Quelle & Meyer, 1914.

Hanson, John R. "Ernst Troeltsth's Concept of Compromise." *The Lutheran Quarterly* 18 (1966):351–361.

Harnack, Adolf von. "Ernst Troeltsch." In Adolf von Harnack, *Erforschtes und Erlebtes*, pp. 360–367. Giessen: Verlag von Alfred Töpelmann, 1956.

———. "Ernst Troeltsch. Rede am Sarge Troeltschs." *Die Christliche Welt* 37 (1923):101–105.

Harvey, Van A. *The Historian and the Believer: The Morality of Historical Knowledge and Christian Belief.* Philadelphia: Westminster Press, 1981.

Hashagen, Justus. "Troeltsch und Ranke." *Philosophische Anzeiger* 4 (1929/30):1–12.

Herberger, Kurt. *Historismus und Kairos: Die Überwindung des Historismus bei Ernst Troeltsch und Paul Tillich.* Marburg am Lahn: Buchdruckerei Hermann Bauer, 1935.

Herring, H. "Max Weber und Ernst Troeltsch als Geschichtsdenker." *Kant-Studien* 59 (1968):410–434.

Herrmann, Wilhelm. Review of *Die Absolutheit des Christentums und die Religionsgeschichte*, by Ernst Troeltsch. *Theologische Literaturzeitung* 27 (May 1902):330–334.

————. Review of *Die Bedeutung der Geschichtlichkeit Jesu für den Glauben*, by Ernst Troeltsch. *Theologische Literaturzeitung* 37 (1912):245–249; reprinted in "Wilhelm Herrmann über Ernst Troeltsch." *Zeitschrift für Theologie und Kirche* n.s. 57 (1960):231–237.

Hintze, Otto. "Troeltsch und die Problem des Historismus." In Otto Hintze, *Gesammelte Abhandlungen*. 3 vols. 1962–1967. Edited by Gerhard Östreich. Vol. 2: *Soziologie und Geschichte. Gesammelte Abhandlungen zur Soziologie, Politik und Theorie der Geschichte*, pp. 323–373. Göttingen: Vandenhoeck & Ruprecht, 1964.

Hoffmann, Heinrich. "Ernst Trosltsch zum Gedächtnis." *Theologische Blätter* 2 (1923):77–83.

Hügel, Friedrich von. *Essays and Addresses on the Philosophy of Religion*. London: J. M. Dent & Sons and New York: E. P. Dutton & Co., 1921.

————. "Ernst Troeltsch: To the Editor of the Times." *The Times Literary Supplement*, 29. 3. 1923, p. 216.

————. "Ein Brief Friedrich von Hügel über Ernst Troeltsch." *Die Christliche Welt* 37 (1923):311–315.

————. Introduction to *Christian Thought: Its History and Application*, by Ernst Troeltsch. Translated by various hands and edited by Friendrich von Hügel, pp. xi–xxxi. London: University of London Press, 1923.

————. Introduction to *Der Historismus und seine Überwindung*, by Ernst Troeltsch, pp. v–xii. Berlin: Pan Verlag Rolf Heise, 1924; reprint ed., Aalen: Scientia Verlag, 1966.

Hughes, H. Stuart. *Consciousness and Society: The Reorientation of European Social Thought 1890–1930*. Revised edition. New York: Vintage Books, 1977.

Iggers, Georg G. *The German Conception of History: The National Tradition of Historical Thought from Herder to the Present*. Revised edition. Middletown, Connecticut: Wesleyan University Press, 1983.

Ittel, Gerhard Wolfgang. "Die Hauptgedanken der 're-ligionsgeschichtlichen Schule.'" *Zeitschrift für Religions- und Geistesgeschichte* 10 (1958):61–78.

Jaeger, Paul. "Ist das Christentum unüberbietbar?" *Die Christliche Welt* 16 (September 1902):914–921; 16 (October 1902):938–942.

Johnson, Roger A. "Troeltsch on Christianity and Relativism." *The Journal for the Scientific Study of Religion* 1 (1961):220–223.

Kaftan, Julius. Review of *Vernunft und Offenbarung bei Johann Gerhard und Melanchthon*, by Ernst Troeltsch. *Theologische Literaturzeitung* 17 (April 1892):208–212.

———. "Die Selbständigkeit des Christentums." *Zeitschrift für Theologie und Kirche* 6 (1896):373–394.

———. "Erwiederung. 1) Die Methode; 2) der Supranaturalismus." *Zeitschrift für Theologie und Kirche* 8 (1898):70–96.

Kaftan, Theodor. *Ernst Tröltsch: Eine kritische Zeitstudie*. Schleswig: Julius Bergas, 1912.

Kasch, Wilhelm F. *Die Sozialphilosophie von Ernst Troeltsch*. Beiträge zur Historischen Theologie, no. 34. Tübingen: J. C. B. Mohr (Paul Siebeck), 1963.

Klapwijk, Jacob. *Tussen Historisme en Relativisme: Een studie over de dynamiek van het historisme en de wijsgerige ontwikkelingsgang van Ernst Troeltsch*. Assen: Van Gorcum & Co., 1970.

———. Introduction to *Glaubenslehre*, by Ernst Troeltsch, pp. v–xxvi. Reprint ed. Aalen: Scientia Verlag, 1981.

Klemm, Harald. "Die Identifizierung des christlichen Glaubens in Ernst Troeltschs Vorlesung über Glaubenslehre." *Neue Zeitschrift für systematische Theologie und Religionsphilosophie* 16 (1974):187–198.

Köhler, Walther. *Ernst Troeltsch*. Tübingen: J. C. B. Mohr (Paul Siebeck), 1941.

———. "Ernst Troeltsch." *Zeitschrift für deutsche Kulturphilosophie* 9 (1943):1–21.

Kollman, Eric C. "Eine Diagnose der Weimarer Republik." *Historische Zeitschrift* 182 (1956):291–318.

Kondo, Katsuhiko. "Theologie der Gestaltung bei Ernst Troeltsch." Inaugural-Dissertation, University of Tübingen, 1977.

Lessing, Eckhard. *Die Geschichtsphilosophie Ernst Troeltschs*. Theologische Forschung, no. 39. Hamburg-Bergstedt: Herbert Reich, 1965.

Liebert, Arthur. "Ernst Troeltschs letztes Werk." *Kant-Studien* 29 (1924):359–364.

Little, David. "Religion and Social Analysis in the Thought of Ernst Troeltsch." *Journal for the Scientific Study of Religion* 1 (1961):114–117.

Little, H. Ganse, Jr. "Ernst Troeltsch and the Scope of Historicism." *The Journal of Religion* 46 (1966):343–364.

————. "Ernst Troeltsch on History, Decision, and Responsibility." *The Journal of Religion* 48 (1968):205–234.

Loofs, Friedrich. "Troeltschs 'Soziallehren der christlichen Kirchen und Gruppen.'" *Deutsche Literaturzeitung* 34 (1913):2885–2893.

Macintosh, Douglas Clyde. "Troeltsch's Theory of Religious Knowledge." *American Journal of Theology* 23 (July 1919):274–289.

Mackintosh, Hugh Ross. *Types of Modern Theology: Schleiermacher to Barth*. London: Nisbet and Co., 1937.

Mannheim, Karl. *Wissenssoziologie. Auswahl aus dem Werk*. Edited and with an Introduction by Kurt H. Wolff. Berlin and Neuwied: Hermann Luchterhand Verlag, 1964.

Meinecke, Friedrich. *Friedrich Meinecke Werke*. 9 vols. Edited by Hans Herzfeld, Carl Hinrichs, Walther Hofer, Eberhard Kessel, and Georg Kotowski. Vol. 4: *Zur Theorie und Philosophie der Geschichte*. Edited and with an Introduction by Eberhard Kessel. 2d ed. Stuttgart: K. F. Koehler Verlag, 1965.

Meyer, Arnold. "Ernst Troeltsch nach persönlicher Erinnerung." *Neue Züricher Zeitung*, 15. 2. 1923, pp. 1–2.

Miller, Donald E. "Troeltsch's Critique of Karl Marx." *Journal for the Scientific Study of Religion* 1 (1961):117–121.

Müller, Gotthold. "Die Selbstauflösung der Dogmatik bei Ernst Troeltsch." *Theologische Zeitschrift* 22 (September/October 1966):334–346.

Morgan, Robert. "Ernst Troeltsch and the Dialectical Theology." In *Ernst Troeltsch and the Future of Theology*, pp. 33–77. Edited by John Powell Clayton. Cambridge: Cambridge University Press, 1976.

————. "Ernst Troeltsch on Theology and Religion." Introduction to *Ernst Troeltsch: Writings on Theology and Religion*, pp. 1–51. Edited by Robert Morgan and Michael Pye. London: Gerald Duckworth & Co., 1977.

————. "Troeltsch and Christian Theology." In *Ernst Troeltsch: Writings on Theology and Religion*, pp. 208–233. Edited by Robert Morgan and Michael Pye. London: Gerald Duckworth & Co., 1977.

Neumann, Carl. "Zum Tode von Ernst Troeltsch." *Deutsche Vierteljahrsschrift für Literaturwissenschaft und Geistesgeschichte* 1 (1923):161–171.

Niebuhr, Helmut Richard. "Ernst Troeltsch's Philosophy of Religion." Ph.D. dissertation, Yale University, 1924; microfilm reproduction, . Ann Arbor, Michigan: University Microfilms, Inc., 1965.

————. Introduction to *The Social Teaching of the Christian Churches*. 2 vols., by Ernst Troeltsch. Translated by Olive Wyon, pp. 7–12. New York: Harper & Brothers, 1960; reprint ed., Chicago: University of Chicago Press, 1976.

Obayashi, Hiroshi. "Pannenberg and Troeltsch: History and Religion." *Journal of the American Academy of Religion* 38 (1970):401–419.

————. *Toreruchi to Gendai Shingaku* [Troeltsch and Contemporary Theology]. Tokyo: Shinkyo Shuppan, 1972.

Ogletree, Thomas W. *Christian Faith and History: A Critical Comparison of Ernst Troeltsch and Karl Barth*. New York and Nashville: Abingdon Press, 1965.

Pannenberg, Wolfhart. *Wissenschaftstheorie und Theologie*. Frankfurt am Main: Suhrkamp Verlag, 1977.

————. *Ethik und Ekklesiologie*. Göttingen: Vandenhoeck & Ruprecht, 1977.

Pauck, Wilhelm. *Harnack and Troeltsch: Two Historical Theologians*. New York: Oxford University Press, 1968.

Perkins, Darrell Davis, Jr. "Explicating Christian Faith in a Historically Conscious Age: The Method of Ernst Troeltsch's Glaubenslehre." Ph.D. dissertation, Vanderbilt University, 1981.

Pretzel, Ulrich. "Ernst Troeltschs Berufung an die Berliner Universität." In *Studium Berolinense: Aufsätze und Beiträge zu Problemen der Wissenschaft und zur Geschichte der Friedrich-Wilhelms-Universität zu Berlin*, pp. 507–514. Edited by H. Leussink, E. Neumann, and E. Kotowsky. Berlin: Walter de Gruyter & C., 1960.

Przywara, Erich. "Ernst Troeltsch." *Stimmen der Zeit* 53 (February 1923):75–79.

Pye, Michael. "Ernst Troeltsch and the End of the Problem about 'Other' Religions." In *Ernst Troeltsch and the Future of Theology*, pp. 171–195. Edited by John Powell Clayton. Cambridge: Cambridge University Press, 1976.

————. "Troeltsch and the Science of Religion." In *Ernst Troeltsch: Writings on Theology and Religion*, pp. 234–252. Edited by Robert Morgan and Michael Pye. London: Gerald Duckworth & Co., 1977.

Quarberg, David. "Historical Reason, Faith and the Study of Religion." *Journal for the Scientific Study of Religion* 1 (1961):122–124.

Rachfahl, Felix. "Kalvinismus und Kapitalismus." *Internationale Wochenschrift für Wissenschaft, Kunst und Technik* 3 (1909); now reprinted in *Max Weber: Die protestantische Ethik*. Vol. 2: *Kritiken und Antikritiken*, pp. 57–148. Edited by Johannes Winckelmann. Gütersloh: Gütersloher Verlagshaus Gerd Mohn, 1982.

Rand, Calvin G. "Two Meanings of Historicism in the Writings of Dilthey, Troeltsch, and Meinecke." *Journal of History of Ideas* 25 (1964):503–518.

Reist, Benjamin A. *Toward a Theology of Involvement: The Thought of Ernst Troeltsch*. Philadelphia: Westminster Press, 1966.

Reitsema, Gaathe Willem. "Einheit und Zusammenhang in Denken von Ernst Troeltsch." *Neue Zeitschrift für systematische Theologie und Religionsphilosophie* 17 (1975):1–8.

Rendtorff, Trutz. *Theorie des Christentums*. Gütersloh: Gütersloher Verlagshaus Gerd Mohn, 1972.

————. Introduction to *Die Absolutheit des Christentums und die Religionsgeschichte*, by Ernst Troeltsch. Munich and Hamburg: Siebenstern Taschenbuch Verlag, 1969.

————. "Europäismus als geschichtlicher Kontext der Theologie. Bemerkungen zur heutigen Kritik an 'europäischer' Theologie im Licht von Ernst Troeltsch." In *Europäische Theologie: Versuche einer Ortsbestimmung*, pp. 165–179. Edited by Trutz Rendtorff. Gütersloh: Gütersloher Verlagshaus Gerd Mohn, 1980.

————. "17. 2. 1865–17. 2. 1981. Warum Ernst-Troeltsch-Gesellschaft." Pamphlet. Augsburg: Ernst-Troeltsch-Gesellschaft, 1981.

Renz, Horst, und Graf, Friendrich Wilhelm, eds. *Troeltsch-Studien. Untersuchungen zur Biographie und Werkgeschichte*. Gütersloh: Gütersloher Verlagshaus Gerd Mohn, 1982.

Rinteln, Fritz-Joachim von. "Der Versuch einer Überwindung des Historismus bei Ernst Troeltsch." *Deutsche Vierteljahrsschrift für Literaturwissenschaft und Geistesgeschichte* 8 (1930):324–372.

Röhricht, Rainer. "Zwischen Historismus und Existenzdenken: Die Geschichtsphilosophie Ernst Troeltschs." Inaugural-Dissertation, University of Tübingen, 1954.

Rollmann, Hans. "Troeltsch, von Hügel and Modernism." *The Downside Review* 96 (1978):35–60.

Rubanowice, Robert J. *Crisis in Consciousness: The Thought of Ernst Troeltsch*. Foreword by James Luther Adams. Tallahassee: University Press of Florida, 1982.

Rupp, George. *Culture-Protestantism: German Liberal Theology at the Turn of the Twentieth Century*. AAR Studies in Religion 15. Missoula, Montana: Scholars Press, 1977.

Scheler, Max. "Ernst Troeltsch als Soziologe." *Kölner Vierteljahreshefte für Soziologie* 3 (1923/24):7–21.

Schlippe, Gunnar von. *Die Absolutheit des Christentums bei Ernst Troeltsch auf dem Hintergrund der Denkfelder des 19. Jahrhunderts.* Neustadt an der Aisch: Verlag Degener & Co., 1966.

Schmeidler, B. "Zur Psychologie des Historikers und zur Lage der Historie in der Gegenwart." *Preußische Jahrbücher* 202 (1925):219–239, 304–327.

Schmidt, Gustav. *Deutscher Historismus und der Übergang zur parlamentarischen Demokratie: Untersuchungen zu den politischen Gedanken von Meinecke-Troeltsch-Max Weber.* Lübeck and Hamburg: Matthiesen Verlag, 1964.

———. "Ernst Troeltsch." In *Deutsche Historiker.* Vol. 2, pp. 91–108. Edited by Hans-Ulrich Wehler. Göttingen: Vandenhoeck & Ruprecht, 1972.

Schmidt, Martin. "Züge eines theologischen Geschichtsbegriffs bei Ernst Troeltsch." In *Reformatio und Confessio: Festschrift für D. Wilhelm Maurer zum 65. Geburtstag am 7. Mai 1965,* pp. 244–258. Edited by Wilhelm Kantzenbach and Gerhard Müller. Berlin and Hamburg: Lutherisches Verlagshaus, 1965.

Schrey, Heinz-Horst. "Ernst Troeltsch und sein Werk." *Theologische Rundschau* 12 (1940):130–162.

Schüler, Alfred. "Christlicher Personalismus: Gedanken zu Ernst Troeltschs Werk." In *Der Mensch vor Gott. Beiträge zum Verständnis der menschlichen Gottesbegegnung (Th. Steinbüchel zum 60. Geburtstag),* pp. 264–277. Edited by P. Weindel and R. Hofmann. Düsseldorf: Patmos Verlag, 1948.

Seeberg, Erich. "Zu Troeltschs Glaubenslehre." In Erich Seeberg, *Menschwerdung und Geschichte: Aufsätze,* pp. 149–155. Stuttgart: Kohlhammer, 1938.

Sleigh, R. S. *The Sufficiency of Christianity. An Enquiry concerning the Nature and the Modern Possibilities of the Christian Religion, with Special Reference to the Religious Philosophy of Dr. Ernst Troeltsch.* Introduction by William Fulton. London: James Clarke & Co., 1923.

Spieß, Emil. *Die Religionstheorie von Ernst Troeltsch.* Paderborn: Verlag Ferdinand Schöningh, 1927.

Spranger, Eduard. "Das Historismusproblem an der Universität Berlin seit 1900." In Eduard Spranger, *Gesammelte Schriften.* 10 vols. Vol. 5: *Kulturphilosophie und Kulturkritik,* pp. 430–446. Edited by Hans Wenke. Tübingen: Max Niemeyer Verlag, 1969.

Süskind, Hermann. "Zur Theologie Troeltschs." *Theologische Rundschau* 17 (January/February 1914):1–13, 53–62.

Swatos, William H., Jr. "Weber or Troeltsch?: Methodology, Syndrome, and the Development of Church-Sect Theory." *Journal for the Scientific Study of Religion* 15 (1976):129–144.

Thielicke, Helmut. *Glauben und Denken in der Neuzeit. Die großen Systeme der Theologie und Religionsphilosophie.* Tübingen: J. C. B. Mohr (Paul Siebeck), 1983.

Tillich, Paul. *Gesammelte Werke.* 12 vols. Edited by Renate Albrecht. Vol. 12: *Begegnungen: Paul Tillich über sich selbst und andere.* Stuttgart: Evangelisches Verlagswerk, 1971.

————. Review of *Der Historismus und seine Überwindung*, by Ernst Troeltsch. *Theologische Literaturzeitung* 49 (May 1924):234–235.

Tödt, Heinz Eduard. "Ernst Troeltsch." In *Tendenzen der Theologie im 20. Jahrhundert. Eine Geschichte in Porträts*, pp. 93–98. Edited by Hans Jürgen Schultz. Stuttgart: Kreuz-Verlag, 1966.

————. "Ernst Troeltschs Bedeutung für die evangelische Sozialethik." *Zeitschrift für evangelische Ethik* 10 (1966):227–236.

Tönnies, Ferdinand. Review of *Die Soziallehren der christlichen Kirchen und Gruppen*, by Ernst Troeltsch. *Theologische Literaturzeitung* 39 (January 1914):8–12.

————. "Troeltsch und die Philosophie der Geschichte." In *Schmollers Jahrbuch für Gesetzgebung, Verwaltung und Volkswirtschaft im Deutschen Reich.* Vol. 49, pp. 147–193. Munich and Leipzig: Verlag von Duncker & Humblot, 1925.

Wendland, Johannes. "Philosophie und Christentum bei Ernst Troeltsch im Zusammenhang mit der Philosophie und Theologie des letzten Jahrhunderts." *Zeitschrift für Theologie und Kirche* 24 (1914):129–165.

Wichelhaus, Manfred. *Kirchengeschichtsschreibung und Soziologie im neunzehnten Jahrhundert und bei Ernst Troeltsch.* Heidelberg: Carl Winter Universitätsverlag, 1965.

Wünsch, Georg. "Ernst Troeltsch zum Gedächtnis." *Die Christliche Welt* 37 (1923):105–108.

————. "Ernst Troeltsch." In *Lebensbilder aus dem Bayerischen Schwaben.* Vol. 9, pp. 384–425. Edited by Wolfgang Zorn. Munich: Verlag Max Heuber, 1966.

Wyman, Walter E., Jr. *The Concept of Glaubenslehre. Ernst Troeltsch and the Theological Heritage of Schleiermacher.* AAR Academy Series 44. Chico, California: Scholars Press, 1983.

Yasukata, Toshimasa. "The Concept of 'Kompromiß' in Ernst Troeltsch." *Journal of Christian Studies* 2 (December 1979):104–118.

———. "Theology as History in Ernst Troeltsch." *Journal of Christian Studies* 5 (December 1982):76–89.

Other Works

Barth, Karl. *Die kirchliche Dogmatik*. Vols. I–IV. Zurich: Theologischer Verlag Zürich, 1932–1967.

———. *Die protestantische Theologie im 19. Jahrhundert. Ihre Vorgeschichte und Geschichte*. Zurich: Theologischer Verlag Zürich, 1946.

———. *Die Theologie und die Kirche. Gesammelte Vorträge*. Vol. 2. Zollikon/Zurich: Evangelischer Verlag, 1951.

———. *Karl Barth Gesamtausgabe*. Vol. 5/1: *Karl Barth-Rudolf Bultmann Briefwechsel 1922–1966*. Edited by Bernd Jaspert. Zurich: Theologischer Verlag Zürich, 1971.

———. *The Humanity of God*. Translated by John Newton Thomas and Thomas Wieser. Atlanta: John Knox Press, 1982.

Bornkamm, Heinrich. "Die Heidelberger Theologische Fakultät." *Ruperto-Carola*. Special volume: *Aus der Geschichte der Universität Heidelberg und ihrer Fakultäten* (1961):135–161.

Baumgarten, Eduard. *Max Weber: Werk und Person*. Tübingen: J. C. B. Mohr (Paul Siebeck), 1964.

Diem, Hermann. *Dogmatics*. Translated by Harold Knight. Edinburgh and London: Oliver and Boyd, 1959.

Ermarth, Michael. *Wilhelm Dilthey: The Critique of Historical Reason*. Chicago: University of Chicago Press, 1978.

Ecke, G. *Die theologische Schule Albrecht Ritschls*. Berlin: Reuther & Reichard, 1897.

Heussi, Karl. *Die Krisis des Historismus*. Tübingen: J. C. B. Mohr (Paul Siebeck), 1932.

Hodges, H. A. *Wilhelm Dilthey: An Introduction*. London: Kegan Paul, Trench, Trubner & Co., 1944.

Kantzenbach, Friedrich Wilhelm. "Briefe und Karten Adolf von Harnacks." *Theologische Zeitschrift* 33 (May/June 1977): 159–167.

Kattenbusch, Ferdinand. "In Sache der Ritschlschen Theologie." *Die Christliche Welt* 12 (January 1898):59–62, 75–81.

———. *Die deutsche evangelische Theologie seit Schleiermacher*. 6th ed. Gießen: Verlag von Alfred Töpelmann, 1934.

Kranz, Gisbert. *Gertrud von le Fort: Leben und Werk in Daten, Bildern und Zeugnissen*. Frankfurt am Main: Insel Verlag, 1976.

Le Fort, Gertrud von. *Hälfte des Lebens: Erinnerungen*. Munich: Ehrenwirth Verlag, 1965.

———. *Der Kranz der Engel: Roman*. 10th ed. Munich: Ehrenwirth Verlag, 1968.

Niebuhr, Helmut Richard. *The Meaning of Revelation*. New York: Macmillan, 1941; paperback ed., New York: Macmillan Publishing Co. and London: Collier Macmillan Publishers, 1974.

———. *Christ and Culture*. New York: Harper & Row, 1951.

———. *Radical Monotheism and Western Culture*. New York: Harper & Row, 1960.

Niebuhr, Reinhold. *The Nature and Destiny of Man*. 2 vols. New York: Charles Scribner's Sons, 1941–1943.

Niebuhr, Richard Reinhold. *Schleiermacher on Christ and Religion*. New York: Charles Scribner's Sons, 1964.

Pannenberg, Wolfhart. *Basic Questions in Theology*. 2 vols. Translated by George H. Kehm. Philadelphia: Fortress Press, 1971; reprint ed., Philadelphia: Westminster Press, 1983.

Pauck, Wilhelm. "Schleiermacher's Conception of History and Church History." In *Schleiermacher as Contemporary*, pp. 41–56. Edited by Robert W. Funk. New York: Herder & Herder, 1970.

Popper, Karl. *The Poverty of Historicism*. Boston: Beacon Press, 1957.

Rathje, Johannes. *Die Welt des freien Protestantismus: Ein Beitrag zur deutsch-evangelischen Geistesgeschichte. Dargestellt an Leben und Werk von Martin Rade*. Stuttgart: Ehrenfried Klotz Verlag, 1952.

Robinson, James M., and Cobb, John B., Jr., eds. *Theology as History*. New York: Harper & Row, 1967.

Robinson, James M., ed. *The Beginning of Dialectical Theology*. 2 vols. Translated by Keith R. Crim and Louis DeGrazia. Richmond: John Knox Press, 1968.

Schleiermacher, Friedrich D. E. *Der christliche Glaube nach den Grundsätzen der evangelischen Kirchen im Zusammenhang dargestellt*. 7th ed. Edited by Martin Redecker. 2 vols. Berlin: Walter de Gruyter, 1960.

———. *Kurze Darstellung des theologischen Studiums zum Behuf einleitender Vorlesungen*. Edited by Heinrich Scholz. Leipzig: A. Deichert, 1910; reprint ed., Darmstadt: Wissenschaftliche Buchgesellschaft, 1973.

————. *Brief Outline on the Study of Theology.* Translated by Terrence N. Tice. Atlanta: John Knox Press, 1977.

Stephan, Horst, and Schmidt, Martin. *Geschichte der evangelischen Theologie in Deutschland seit dem Idealismus.* 3d ed., rev. Berlin and New York: Walter de Gruyter, 1973.

Schweitzer, Albert. *Geschichte der Leben-Jesu-Forschung.* Tübingen: J. C. B. Mohr (Paul Siebeck), 1913.

"A Theological Conversation with Wolfhart Pannenberg." *Dialog* 11 (1972):286–295.

Tillich, Paul. *Systematic Theology.* 3 vols. Chicago: University of Chicago Press, 1951–1963.

Weisert, Hermann. "Verfassung der Universität Heidelberg im 19. Jahrhundert/Teil VI." *Ruperto-Carola* 54 (1975):17–33.